German National Identity after the Holocaust

German National Identity after the Holocaust

Mary Fulbrook

Polity Press

First published in 1999 by Polity Press in association with Blackwell Publishers Ltd.

Editorial office:
Polity Press
65 Bridge Street
Cambridge CB2 1UR, UK

Marketing and production:
Blackwell Publishers Ltd
108 Cowley Road
Oxford OX4 1JF, UK

Published in the USA by
Blackwell Publishers Inc.
Commerce Place
350 Main Street
Malden, MA 02148, USA

ISBN 0-7456-1044-7
ISBN 0-7456-1045-5 (pbk)

A catalogue record for this book is available from the British Library.

Typeset in 10.5 on 12 pt Palatino
by Puretech India Ltd, Pondicherry
http://www.puretech.com
Printed in Great Britain by MPG Books, Bodmin, Cornwall

This book is printed on acid-free paper.

Contents

Preface

This book tackles a complex, highly sensitive and often inchoate subject. Some of the complexities and sensitivities are inherent in the subject matter: to analyse ways of representing and interpreting the Holocaust, for example, is to approach agonizing questions which are not only intrinsically difficult but are also of acute personal relevance to many of those about whom one is writing. The difficulty with form is also in part inherent in the subject matter: to interpret the nation as a social, political and cultural construct, with multiple overlaps and interrelations between different aspects, does not allow any easy and simple organization of contents (such as a conventional chronological framework, however much this, too, implicitly imposes themes on periods). An exploration of fractures and dissonances seems to entail a somewhat fractured organization of topics. It also entails crossing innumerable disciplinary boundaries, and often treading on the toes (though I hope also sometimes standing on the shoulders) of specialists who are far more knowledgeable, far better placed to comment, on individual topics; but doing this in the interests of seeking to place these pieces in a wider whole.

Much has already been written from a very wide variety of perspectives on the question of history and identity in Germany after Hitler. As we shall see, processes of 'confronting the past' and 'defining national identity' have attained almost obsessive dimensions in Germany at different times: both during the period of political division into opposing states, and with renewed intensity after the formal unification of two very different societies in 1990. What I seek to do here is to set these debates into a broader perspective, locating the uniquely tortured case of the fracturing of German identities within the wider context of general theoretical interpretations of national identity construction. I seek also to analyse and illustrate a range of facets of this problematic in Germany, including some quite lengthy quotations from a variety of sources, for the purposes of informed debate among English-speaking readers to whom all the original German sources may not be entirely accessible. I do this too, I hope, from the vantage point of a relatively disinterested outsider. Although I hold quite strong views on the topics explored below, I do not believe I have the kind of personal emotional investment (in seeking either to construct or to denounce an 'acceptable' German identity) which is characteristic of so much writing on this theme.

This book could have been organized and written in many different ways; it could have discussed quite different examples, taken notice of a variety of other bodies of literature and discussion. But it is my hope that, for all its emphases and omissions, it helps at least to clarify ways of approaching intrinsically complex issues. In what follows, I have simply attempted to do an honest job, in a restricted compass, with an inherently difficult problem which could be expanded in an almost infinite variety of directions.

I would particularly like to thank John Breuilly for his characteristically perceptive comments on a full first draft of this book, and my colleague Judith Beniston for her very helpful comments on many of the chapters concerned with cultural representation. Needless to say, they bear no responsibility for shortcomings which remain. I am also grateful to friends, colleagues and students at UCL and elsewhere who have helped my processes of thinking aloud in seminars and informal discussions.

My greatest debts are, as always, to my family: to my father, whose sudden death in 1995 brought home to me in the most painful way possible the difficulties of grieving, remembering and reconstructing; to my mother, the progressive loss of whose memory again made me more personally engaged with the topic than I would have wanted to be; and most of all to Julian and our children, who again and again convince me of the importance of the present, and of identities based in moral and political choices rather than the alleged collective legacies of the past.

Mary Fulbrook
London, July 1998

Abbreviations

CDU	Christian Democratic Union
CSU	Christian Social Union
EKD	German League of Evangelical Churches
FDGB	League of Free German Trade Unions
FDP	(liberal) Free Democratic Party
FDJ	Free German Youth
GDR	German Democratic Republic
HJ	Hitler Youth
JP	Young Pioneers
KPD	German Communist Party
NDPD	National Democratic Party of Germany
NSDAP	National Socialist German Workers Party (Nazis)
NVA	National People's Army
OMGUS	Office of Military Government for Germany (U.S.)
PDS	Party of Democratic Socialism (successor to the SED)
Pg	Party member (of the NSDAP)
RSHA	Reich Security Main Office
SD	Security Service (*Sicherheitsdienst*)
SED	Socialist Unity Party of Germany
SPD	Social Democratic Party of Germany
SS	*Schutzstaffel* (lit. Protection Squad; elite troops)
Stasi	State Security Service
VVN	Association of those Persecuted by the Nazi Regime

1

National Identity and
German History

As I was going up the stair
I met a man who wasn't there
He wasn't there again today
I wish, I wish he'd stay away.[1]

National identity does not exist, as an essence to be sought for, found and defined. It is a human construct, evident only when sufficient people believe in some version of collective identity for it to be a social reality, embodied in and transmitted through institutions, laws, customs, beliefs and practices.

So why write a book about something which does not exist? How, as a historian, does one write a history of something which was never there (and 'isn't there again today')? The answer is, because the belief in a collective national identity, and the desire to define one, is in many quarters remarkably strong. The political power of such beliefs, and the widespread faith in the capacity of a collective belief to resolve all manner of social conflicts and anxieties, to mobilize and weld together people from all manner of backgrounds, is quite extraordinary.

This is particularly the case with respect to Germany.[2] The near obsession with defining a German national identity is not a new

[1] Hughes Mearns, Lines written for an amateur play. *The Psycho-ed*, Philadelphia, 1910.
[2] See esp. John Breuilly, *The State of Germany* (London: Longman, 1992), for discussions of the 'national idea' in German history. See also Michael Hughes, *Nationalism and Society: Germany 1800–1945* (London: Arnold, 1988); Harold James, *A German Identity 1770–1990* (London: Weidenfeld and Nicolson, rev.

pastime: two centuries ago, before the formation of any unified German 'nation state', a variety of German literati were deeply engaged with the task of identifying what 'being German' consisted in. A relatively wide range of answers were given to this question through the nineteenth century, prior to the imposition and institutionalization of new answers in Bismarck's 'small Germany' of 1871. Culturalist variants were submerged under more stridently ethnic overtones in the first half of the twentieth century, reaching their most appalling and extreme expression in Hitler's conception of a 'racially pure' ethnic community, or *Volksgemeinschaft*. And it is primarily this – and the genocidal consequences of the Nazi version of German identity – which provoked intensely problematic questions about German identity after the Holocaust.

The definition of German national identity has been central to much of German politics and public debate over the best part of the last half-century. A divided nation after 1945 was almost continuously preoccupied, on occasion convulsed, with vitriolic debates over its own identity and history, in a way which scarcely has parallels elsewhere. For one thing, an unthinking national pride or taken-for-granted patriotism was no longer possible after Auschwitz. For another, there were now two mutually hostile states on German soil, pawns in the Cold War battle of the superpowers. Their official political definitions of each other were in black-and-white terms of friend and foe, good and evil; and yet, at the same time, they had to tread a delicate line of emphasizing a residual sense of some common national identity, a belonging together.

In a complex game of mutual antagonism and self-definition, history came to play a key political role in both Germanies. Both, in different ways, claimed to be the 'better' Germany: the one that had more completely, decisively, made a break with the immediate Nazi past. Both sought to define and to anchor new partial identities – West and East German identities – in differing reinterpretations of selected aspects of a common past. Both came to use history for political ends – most obviously and directly in the East, more subtly, indirectly and subject to greater public debate and pluralist diversity of approach in the West. The interpretation and presentation of the past became an integral and often hotly contested element of the present.

After the unexpected collapse of the German Democratic Republic (GDR) and the dramatically rapid political unification of the two states in 1990, the unprecedented experiment of combining a former

edn, 1989); Mary Fulbrook (ed.), *German History since 1800* (London: Arnold, 1997).

communist dictatorship with a successful capitalist democracy on the basis of a fragile bond of constitutional commitment and residual sense of former brotherhood posed new problems of identity construction.[3] While economic and social strains stretched belief in the nation to the limits, debates over de-stasification and restructuring in the former GDR lent new meaning and significance to older debates over denazification and allegedly missed opportunities in the western past. On the extremist fringes, in the first couple of years after unification a resurgent right-wing racism was expressed in acts of violence against immigrants, asylum-seekers, long-term resident 'guest-workers' and other apparently ethnic 'others'. Even some moderate liberals who had previously raised their voices in praise of a 'post-nationalist' German identity in the context of European integration suddenly appeared to find a vindication of the reality of the nation. The perennial game of the German political classes, 'What does it mean to be German?', entered a new round.

It is not only in Germany that the problem of German identity has been addressed with an interest bordering on obsession. Older, essentially racist conceptions of 'national character' may have been discredited; but the belief in some long-term hereditary disposition or national identity – and belief in the need to define one – remains remarkably powerful, in all manner of quarters, both expected and unexpected. Many neighbours and observers from across continental borders, the Channel, or the Atlantic, have had a long-standing problem with seeking to define a German national identity.

To take one by now notorious example: after the fall of the Berlin Wall, the then British Prime Minister Mrs Thatcher was so worried by the prospect of German unification that in 1990 she took expert advice on the German 'national character'. This, she was informed, was characterized by '*angst*, aggressiveness, assertiveness, bullying, egotism, inferiority complex, sentimentality... a capacity for excess, to overdo things, to kick over the traces.'[4] Even after the united Germany revealed itself to be remarkably pacifist and wrapped up in its own domestic problems of unemployment and other economic costs of unification, the image of German jackboots could still be mobilized for the headlines of the British tabloid press

[3] Cf. the essays in *Germany in Transition* (Daedalus, winter 1994), repr. in M. Mertes, S. Muller and H. A. Winkler (eds), *In Search of Germany* (New Brunswick, NJ: Transaction Books, 1996).

[4] Charles Powell, 'What the PM Learnt about the Germans', in Harold James and Marla Stone (eds), *When the Wall Came Down* (London: Routledge, 1992), p. 234.

on the occasion of an innocent international football match; and a fear of future German dominance in some centralized European super-state hovered behind many conservative Eurosceptic pronouncements in the run-up to the British 1997 General Election. West Germans, having spent half a century leaning over backwards to prove that they were the least nationalistic, most pacifist, most 'European' of nations, found that every flutter of xenophobia, every racist attack or incident, was magnified a thousandfold in the international press.

One might dismiss such views of a German 'national character' as purely figments of journalists' and politicians' fevered brains, imposed on an unsuspecting public who could not help but be duped. But such views could be found lurking even in the higher reaches of academia. It was a group of largely Oxbridge academics, including such renowned figures as Norman Stone, Timothy Garton Ash, and Lord Dacre (Hugh Trevor-Roper) who served as advisers to Mrs Thatcher at the infamous Chequers meeting quoted above. And one of the best-selling history books published in 1996, *Hitler's Willing Executioners: Ordinary Germans and the Holocaust* – which was effectively an indictment of the whole German people and its alleged anti-semitic traditions over centuries – was written by a Harvard historian.[5] Although the new empirical material in this book was rightly acclaimed in many quarters, the underlying premises are extraordinary: in particular, the socially reductionist notion that, because certain murderers represented a sociological cross-section of the German population as a whole, they similarly reflected and were representative of general attitudes; and the extraordinarily anti-empiricist notion that, even across large tracts of time when no manifest anti-semitism could be discerned, some essentially reified German anti-semitism led a hibernatory life of its own, allegedly dormant, latent beneath the surface of visible events. The public reactions to this book, on both sides of the Atlantic, were equally extraordinary: acclaimed and condemned with remarkable fervour, indicative of a tremendous public interest in the issue of German history and German identity.

To summarize: in Germany itself, debates over the past and national identity have at times reached almost obsessive proportions – whether seeking to construct a new sense of national pride, to become a 'normal nation', or whether arguing that the German

---

[5] Daniel Goldhagen, *Hitler's Willing Executioners: Ordinary Germans and the Holocaust* (New York: Knopf, 1996). See also some of the early reactions in Julius Schoeps (ed.), *Ein Volk von Mördern?* (Hamburg: Hoffmann and Campe, 1996).

past should never be 'normalized' and hence relativized. Germany has a past, which, in the words of one German conservative philosopher, 'refuses to become history'.[6] No bad thing, one might think, in view of what that past actually consisted in. The horrors of the Holocaust should indeed never be forgotten; the dangers of resurgent racism should indeed be guarded against, at all times and everywhere. But to view 'Germans' as essentially and always nasty and implicitly threatening is wrong.

Let me emphasize that I am not seeking in this book to present any new characterization of an alleged German national identity. I do not wish to argue that, contrary to widespread misconceptions, 'the Germans' (or the very diverse sets of residents of political states deemed to constitute 'Germany' at any particular time, who are so often lumped together as an undifferentiated whole) are basically not nasty but nice. Nor do I wish to contribute – on either side – to the characteristically shrill debates about whether 'the Germans' should cease to be 'ashamed to be German' and should instead be 'allowed to be normal' and to construct a positive version of national identity. Rather, the purpose of this book is precisely to examine, to take apart, what is meant by 'national identity'; to explore the peculiarly fractured constructions of national identity which have been developed in different quarters and to different effects within the German states, East and West, since 1945; and, through the example of this particularly contentious case, to propose a theoretical framework which may be of wider application to the analysis of the construction of national identity in other places, among other peoples and at other times.

Theoretical excursus: defining the nation and national identity[7]

What is a 'nation'? Unsuspecting readers might find this question surprising: surely it is quite obvious, at first glance, that someone is French, German, American, Italian – or whatever. But this is an illusion. 'Nations' are social, political and cultural constructions, which may be collectively experienced and reproduced, or challenged, to greater or lesser extents. This book will seek to elucidate some of the conditions which make widespread, unexamined beliefs

[6] The title of Ernst Nolte's notorious brief piece, 'Die Vergangenheit, die nicht vergehen will', repr. in *'Historikerstreit'* (Munich: Piper Verlag, 1987). This played a key role in unleashing the so-called 'historians' controversy' of 1986–7 (discussed further below in ch. 5).

[7] Those readers not interested in theory may wish to skip this section.

in a nation more or less convincing to greater or lesser numbers of people. Moreover, 'nation states', now so taken for granted as either existent or the obvious focus of nationalist aspiration (although numerically, on whatever definition one adopts, probably in a minority of types of political unit worldwide) are historically emergent phenomena, achieving perhaps some form of apogee in nineteenth-century and early twentieth-century Europe.[8] The notion that a body of people in some way identified as a 'nation' should be the primary inhabitants of a particular political territory is a peculiar feature of European history in the last two centuries, displacing early modern notions of *states* as essentially religious or dynastic possessions.[9] Thus the specific combination of the two concepts of state and nation, in the notion of a nation state, is perhaps what is quintessentially modern.

The hitherto unsuspecting reader should pause for a moment to consider what initial definition of 'nation' might spring to mind, given the diversity of obvious empirical candidates for 'nation-hood' readily available as a basis for thought.

It should immediately be apparent that self-professing nations do not have to be homogenous ethnic groups, or claim a common ethnic core. From the French Revolution of 1789, the concept of nation gained populist tones, which carried over into the American concept of 'We, the People'. In the American case there is no attempt to claim common ancestry or ethnic roots: the fundamental feature is, rather, commitment to common ideals and goals. Flying the American flag implies a commitment to the American view of 'freedom and democracy', and carries with it a bundle of associations about individualism, mobility, active citizenship (however imperfectly the ideals may be realized in practice). Given time, virtually any legal immigrant may become American – often in 'hyphenated' form with reference to a dual identity: black American, Irish American, Polish American, Italian American (and not forgetting the non-immigrant, indigenous 'native American'), and so on. The French retain somewhat more of a commitment to the principle of descent, but their definition of citizenship combines the principles of the right of birth (being born on French soil) and the experience of socialization, being

[8] See the brilliant, if at times somewhat idiosyncratic, interpretation of Eric Hobsbawm, *Nations and Nationalism since 1780* (Cambridge: Cambridge University Press, 1990).
[9] Such notions of states as essentially patrimonial (or religious) possessions in early modern Europe could still be combined with a conception of 'nation' (e.g. 'The Holy Roman Empire of the German Nation') as distinct from 'tribe' or other grouping.

educated to become a French person.[10] By contrast, over the last century Germany has tended to prioritize belief in a community of common descent.[11]

Similarly, a brief mental tour of the world of 'nations' will suggest that substantive homogeneity of any sort – linguistic, religious, cultural – is not the key to definition. The 'Swiss', for example, are characterized by considerable religious and linguistic diversity, with German, French, Italian and Romansch alongside a variety of dialects. Yet, however much people from different cantons and localities within Switzerland may feud with one another, they are clear that they are quite distinct, as Swiss, from their neighbours, and are not Germans, French people or Italians, whether or not they share a common language with these external neighbours. The creation myth embodied in the William Tell story, the hallowed ground of the Rütli meadow, a widespread public commitment to certain political structures and values (such as participatory democracy, international neutrality, defence of the mountain redoubts by a citizen militia, affluence and cleanliness) – all combine as elements in the construction of a Swiss national identity, whether or not the ideals are realized in practice.

It may perhaps be objected that 'peculiar' cases have been chosen, in order to play devil's advocate. But even the case of Britain – often taken to be a straightforward instance of a unitary nation state – exemplifies the complexities of the issues involved: the Welsh, Irish and Scottish inhabitants of this realm, as well as the many immigrant communities and descendants of former immigrants, may reject attempts by a dominant (south-eastern) 'English' culture to define an overriding 'national identity' (as in Conservative MP Norman Tebbitt's famous 'cricket test' of patriotic loyalty). Many British citizens may have felt a little uncomfortable, following the sudden death of Princess Diana on 31 August 1997, with the generous use of the word 'nation' in the singular, in such headlines and phrases as 'the nation mourns' or 'dramatic outpourings of the nation's grief'.

This last example, however, begins to indicate some of the parameters of the question. It is easy enough for the word to be used in a very general, vague sense – as in the Queen's 'Address to the

[10] Cf. Patrick Weil, 'Nationalities and Citizenships: The Lessons of the French Experience for Germany and Europe' in D. Cesarani and M. Fulbrook (eds), *Citizenship, Nationality and Migration in Europe* (London: Routledge, 1996).
[11] See esp. Rogers Brubaker, *Citizenship and Nationhood in France and Germany* (Cambridge, Mass.: Harvard University Press, 1992). The issue of citizenship and nationality in Germany is discussed in detail in ch. 7, below.

Nation' on 5 September 1997, the day before Princess Diana's funeral. It is also appropriate enough for a catchy label such as 'the People's Princess' to be applied to a world-famous woman who used the extraordinary press attention which her appearances attracted to bring publicity to the plight of the rejected and suffering across the world, whether victims of Aids or of leprosy or of landmines. It is, however, when the other side of the label – the 'nation' whom the Queen addresses, or the 'people' who mourn the death of 'their' princess – is deemed to be in some way homogenous, with an essence or identity that can be defined, and to which collective attitudes and emotions can be attributed, that the matter becomes more problematic.

Broadly speaking, those who have written on nations and national identity have fallen into several more or less clearly defined camps. We may perhaps very crudely distinguish between the 'essentialists' and the 'constructionists'.

Essentialists

First of all, there are those whom we might call 'essentialists': those who view 'nations' as if they were natural entities, given elements of the real world, fundamentally based on the premise – which to be accepted must remain unexamined – that nations have some lasting 'essence'. A cursory glance, not only at common usage in the media, but also at most history books up until the last couple of decades, will reveal the unthinking use of the word nation as though it were the most natural unit of analysis in the world: the nation is an obvious entity, which has a history, often to be written almost anthropomorphically (infancy, coming to maturity, even decline and fall). On the world stage – in 'inter-national' history – nations interact with each other as though they have volitions of their own ('it was in the interests of the nation', 'the British nation stood resolute to the last' and so on). Similarly, as just indicated, it is common in everyday usage: 'the British nation is not good at openly showing its emotions', and so on.

A seriously essentialist view is based on a number of assumptions. 'Identity' presupposes a continuity of an essence over time, with certain underlying, enduring characteristics, ways of reacting, good and bad attributes, qualities and capacities, irrespective of changing appearances over time and environmental influences on behaviour, performance, and achievement. Aspects or characteristics can of course change, but these are in some way attributed, again, to a persisting singular entity with clearly defined boundaries: 'the British nation is beginning to learn to show its grief openly, to learn the value of expressing its emotions' (and so on).

Even those scholars who are professionally employed to trace, measure, chart in great detail changes in public attitudes and opinions may rest their work on the premise of an underlying, essentially singular identity of a nation. Let us switch from the recent and somewhat exceptional British events, in which the word nation appeared more frequently in a week than it had done in decades, to the long-standing and virtually obsessive concern in some quarters with defining German national identity, often accompanied by the implicit or explicit hope that to reach a definition will in some way 'resolve' the 'German problem'.

For example, a senior doyen of German national identity analysis, Werner Weidenfeld, together with Karl-Rudolf Korte, concludes one of his most recent attempts to define German national identity (which, it should be emphasized, is highly interesting in terms of the empirical material presented), with the following statement:

> Insofar as, with the end of political division, the nation is becoming an everyday reality, normality is resuming... The completion of unity offers Germans the possibility of reconciliation with themselves. The Germans too have a yearning (*Sehnsucht*) for an undamaged identity. At the same time they can now continue, unquestioningly, the success story of several decades of European integration. The pragmatic Germans have thus been given a double chance.[12]

Note the assumptions on which this passage is based: that there is some form of collective identity which had been 'damaged', and that the Germans 'need', or – even more strongly in terms of attributing collective feelings – 'have a yearning' for an 'undamaged identity', for 'reconciliation with themselves';[13] and that political unification of East and West constitutes 'normality'. There is also a fairly typical (typical at least when this work was published in 1991, the year after unification) pious note at the end, perhaps to

---

[12] Werner Weidenfeld and Karl-Rudolf Korte, *Die Deutschen: Profil einer Nation* (Stuttgart: Klett-Cotta, 1991), p. 240.

[13] It might not be entirely misplaced to suggest that it is with their former victims, and with surviving friends and relatives of victims, that some – but only some – Germans might have needed to seek 'reconciliation'. The notion of 'the Germans' as a collective entity seeking 'an undamaged identity' (in the singular) through 'reconciliation with themselves' is almost metaphysical – and can only, incidentally, help to propagate notions of 'collective guilt'.

indicate to any observer who might perhaps fear resurgent German nationalism, that this newly healed identity will continue what is deemed to be the irreproachably good work towards the goal of European integration.

Weidenfeld's assumptions about a continuing identity of 'the Germans' over decades, even generations and centuries, is echoed in the questions put by the other doyenne of German attitude analysis, Elisabeth Noelle-Neumann. There is no doubting the importance of the findings of her surveys, many of which will be drawn upon in the following chapters, but it is at the same time worth noting with at least a little interest the premises on which some of these surveys were carried out. Again, if one takes questions from surveys carried out in 1991, one finds a phraseology which presupposes the existence of a long-term collective identity of a German nation: for example, respondents were invited to decide whether they agreed or disagreed (strongly, moderately and so on) with statements such as the following: 'The Germans are a people (*Volk*) which, despite all wars and defeats, always manages to recover and to get on top of things again within the shortest possible time (*in kürzester Zeit wieder hochkommt*)'; 'The Germans have always been a particularly orderly and clean people (*ordentliches und sauberes Volk*)'; 'We Germans have, because of the crimes of National Socialism, a particular political responsibility'; 'We Germans have certain good characteristics which other peoples (*Völker*) do not have'; 'Precisely we Germans should guarantee asylum to politically persecuted people'; and so on.[14] Questions such as these all presuppose (or at the very least assume that the vast majority of those answering such questions will take the questions as meaningful and worth answering because they believe in the reality of) the existence of a collective entity ('We Germans') which has an identity which persists over time. As with Werner Weidenfeld, these assumptions are presented in the context of very detailed empirical findings showing the range of differences in attitudes and opinions across different social and (particularly) generational groups, which should give the lie to any notion of a perduring identity of a German *Volk*.

The game of 'define German national identity' (based on the assumption that there is one to find, if only one could define it correctly) is played, not only by professional opinion pollsters and attitude analysts, but across the German political spectrum. It was a particular pastime among articulate West Germans in the 1980s,

---

[14] Elisabeth Noelle-Neumann and Renate Köcher (eds), *Allensbacher Jahrbuch der Demoskopie 1984–1992*, vol. 9 (Munich: K. G. Saur, 1993), pp. 377ff.

usually in pursuit of some political cause. These ranged from the conservative desire for a resurrection of national pride, to left-wing arguments against reunification (pre-1990) or for the resurrection of identity on the part of forgotten underdogs. Well to the right, we have authors such as Hellmut Diwald, Caspar von Schrenck-Notzing, Armin Mohler, or the self-professed 'new Right' such as Botho Strauss, Ulrich Schacht and Rainer Zitelmann, arguing for a rejection of the culture of collective shame and a 'normalization' of German national identity.[15] In the liberal middle, we have, for example, the *Friedrich-Naumann Stiftung* bringing together German and Anglo-American scholars, diplomats and policy-makers in Washington for measured and inconclusive deliberations on German identity; or Guido Knopp providing a forum for more heated debates in Germany.[16] On the (social-democratic) left, we have the by now notorious, and perhaps somewhat idiosyncratic, example of the writer Günter Grass fulminating against any thought of German unification because of an overwhelming sense, after Auschwitz, that the national 'disposition' was such that 'the Germans' could and should never be trusted again with power in a unified state.[17] Even among those articulate left-liberals who explicitly opted for Jürgen Habermas's notion of 'constitutional patriotism', there was often, at the same time, a (somewhat self-contradictory) diffuse sense of eternal shame and collective unease at 'being German'.

My discussion so far has implied that such approaches – from whichever end of the political spectrum, and irrespective of my own political sympathies and dislikes – have in common that they have got something wrong. I think that what is wrong is the premise that there is an underlying entity, an essence, which has an

---

[15] See, for an early 1980s example, the essays in Caspar von Schrenck-Notzing and Armin Mohler (eds), *Deutsche Identität* (Krefeld: SINUS-Verlag, 1982). For post-unification continuation of such themes, note the title of the collection and see particularly the essays by Botho Strauss, 'Anschwellender Bocksgesang', Ulrich Schacht, 'Stigma und Sorge. Über deutsche Identität nach Auschwitz', and Rainer Zitelmann, 'Position und Begriff. Über eine neue demokratische Rechte', in Heimo Schwilk and Ulrich Schacht (eds), *Die selbstbewußte Nation* (Berlin: Ullstein, 1995).

[16] Friedrich-Naumann Foundation (ed.), *German Identity – Forty Years after Zero* (Sankt Augustin: Liberal Verlag, 1986), incidentally including a somewhat disappointing essay by Ralf Dahrendorf under the promising, iconoclastic title, 'The Search for German Identity: An Illusory Endeavour'; Guido Knopp (ed.), *Die deutsche Einheit: Hoffnung – Alptraum – Illusion?* (Aschaffenburg: Paul Pattloch Verlag, 1981)

[17] Günter Grass, *Two States – One Nation? The Case against German Reunification* (London: Secker and Warburg, 1990).

identity which persists over time, irrespective of changes in profile, attitudes, appearances, and which can be defined if one tries hard enough.

Constructionists

Not all scholars (or indeed all members of any ethnic group, society or polity which is sometimes held to constitute a nation) accept the essentialist view. As Ernest Renan put it in his classic essay, published over a century ago: 'A nation is a soul, a spiritual principle... [constituted by] a rich legacy of remembrances... [and] the actual consent, the desire to live together, the will to continue to value the heritage which all hold in common... A nation is a grand solidarity constituted by the sentiment of sacrifices which one has made and those that one is disposed to make again.'[18] Even Max Weber, who himself felt a strong sense of empathy with the idea of the nation, could dispassionately survey the wide range of variations in substantive claims to nationhood and argue that the nation was a social construction, in which certain strata acted as bearers of a valued culture, with a sense of 'mission' and prestige, ideally to be protected by a strong state.[19]

To concede that nations are historically emergent constructions rather than eternal givens or natural entities is an important beginning, but does not in itself provide any sort even of generally accepted definition, let alone explanation. In pursuing the issue further, scholars diverge in a variety of directions. As John Breuilly has pointed out in his perceptive and wide-ranging comparative historical analysis of national*ism* (which is more specific than, or slightly different from, national identity) and the state, some scholars focus on ideas of the nation among articulate intellectuals ('the nation as idea'); others focus on collective attitudes and emotions ('the nation as sentiment'); others – particularly those concerned specifically with nationalist movements – with politics and political movements ('the nation as politics').[20] As far as the construction of the nation is concerned, some scholars focus on a particular substantive quality of the group itself which appears to provide the

---

[18] Ernest Renan, 'Qu'est-ce qu'une nation?', extract from John Hutchinson and Anthony Smith (eds), *Nationalism* (Oxford: Oxford University Press, 1994), p. 17.
[19] Max Weber, 'The Nation', in H. H. Gerth and C. Wright Mills (eds), *From Max Weber* (London: Routledge and Kegan Paul, 1948), pp. 171–9.
[20] John Breuilly, *Nationalism and the State* (Manchester: Manchester University Press, 2nd edn, 1993).

basis of a sense of identity; others focus rather on those factors which may explain why a sense of group identity emerges at a particular time. And while 'modernity' is a key thread running through many analyses, different specific aspects of this highly evasive term are singled out as important by different scholars.

Recent contributions on national identity by Ernest Gellner, Benedict Anderson, Eric Hobsbawm, Anthony Smith and others, while sharing some version of a constructionist approach, have nevertheless emphasized very different factors in the explanatory framework.[21] Broadly, one may say that Gellner, Anderson and Hobsbawm each focus on different aspects of changing conditions in 'modernity': the social processes concomitant on industrialization (Gellner); the emergence of 'print capitalism' which allowed a broadening of the 'imagined community' (Anderson); and the state system of modern capitalism (Hobsbawm). Their contribution has been to focus attention on the *substantive conditions* under which, historically, conceptions of the nation could emerge and develop in the last two centuries (although Hobsbawm, in his magisterial historical survey, is less willing to engage in any explicit theorizing than are Gellner and Anderson).

Anthony Smith, by contrast, tends towards a more typological, rather than explanatory approach. He lists a set of elements which together, in varying combinations, appear to him crucial ingredients of national identity. We are told that there are two basic models of the nation: the 'western', on the one hand, and the 'non-western', East European or Asian, on the other. 'Historic territory, legal-political community, legal-political equality of members, and common civic culture and ideology; these are the components of the standard, western model of the nation.'[22] The 'non-western' model, by contrast, supposedly prioritizes 'ethnic' elements: it is 'first and foremost a community of common descent'.[23] (As examples of the latter, supposedly East European and Asian, model, we are given Ireland and Norway.) Then the pretence at geographical distinction is dissolved, as the models are re-presented as ideal types: 'Conceptually, the nation has come to blend two sets of dimensions, the one civic and territorial, the other ethnic and genealogical, in

[21] See e.g. Ernest Gellner, *Nations and Nationalism* (Ithaca, NY: Cornell University Press, 1983); Benedict Anderson, *Imagined Communities* (London: Verso, rev. edn, 1991); E. J. Hobsbawm, *Nations and Nationalism since 1780* (Cambridge: Cambridge University Press, 1990); Anthony Smith, *National Identity* (Harmondsworth: Penguin, 1991).

[22] Smith, *National Identity*, p. 11.

[23] Ibid.

varying proportions in particular cases.'[24] For all his qualifications and self-contradictions along the way, Smith's underlying view is that 'ethnic cores' form the original and essential basis of nations. (Note that this ethnic element is no longer 'non-western', nor an 'ideal-typical' element, but somehow chronologically and possibly also logically 'prior to' the nation.) Despite a wealth of exceptions (which Smith himself lists), '*ethnies*' are held to form the original (if sometimes only the 'dominant') 'core' of nations; and even where 'nations' clearly were not based on any ethnic principle, the ethnic model would be followed and the myth created, since 'without some ethnic lineage the nation-to-be could fall apart'.[25] Smith nowhere produces compelling reasons why a belief in a fabricated myth of common descent should prove more powerful than any other factor in holding together a group which might otherwise 'fall apart'. Nor is it ever very clear whether a particular sub-set or combination or minimum number of the allegedly defining characteristics is sufficient to constitute a nation.

These (and related non-essentialist) contributions have, in different ways, stimulated very fruitful theoretical and empirical work. In particular, they have highlighted the problematic, historically emergent character of that particular form of collective identity we have come to take for granted as self-evident, the nation. They have pointed up some of the complexities of the issues involved; and, in their often exploratory and path-breaking character, have illustrated some of the difficulties in providing a coherent approach. But they leave certain problems.

Where, then, does the present analysis of national identity in Germany stand in relation to these more general approaches?

Legacy and destiny: the nation as process of collective identity construction

This book does not seek to explain the origins of conceptions of the nation or the emergence and creation of 'nation states'; nor does it focus specifically on the issue of nationalism as a political movement. It takes for granted the general historical context of later twentieth-century Europe, in which nation states were seen by many as the 'natural' political form. It seeks rather to explore some of the processes through which national identity construction and reconstruction takes place within these general parameters,

[24] Ibid., pp. 13, 15.
[25] Ibid., p. 42.

looking at the peculiarly revealing example of a case where the processes of national identity construction did not work very well.

It seems to me that to seek to develop an all-encompassing definition of nation or national identity by listing a set of *substantive characteristics* (language, culture/religion, territory, economy, or whatever) is not necessarily the most helpful way in to the question. The question of national identity construction is perhaps better viewed in terms of analysing *processes of formation and reformation of particular forms of collective identity, which are claimed to be national, under particular historical circumstances.*

I start, as indicated, from the premise that there is no such thing as an 'essential' national identity. 'Nations' (as what Durkheim would have called a 'social fact') exist in part because people believe in the importance of certain criteria, and not others, as those which define *their* group as different from (and often superior to) others; in part because one particular set of beliefs is held by people who are in a position to propagate their particular criteria for inclusion and exclusion in such a way that these are politically victorious and can hence be institutionalized in a variety of ways; and in part because particular constructions sufficiently accord with 'experienced social reality' such that these (and not other) versions come to appear part of the 'natural' order of things. All of this is, thus, a matter not only of 'imagined communities', or the existence of a system of 'nation' states, but also of the clashes of domestic politics, the character of legal, political and societal institutions, the nature of social interaction and of everyday experiences. Constructions of identity can only work if they are politically viable, socially reproduced, and strike or echo popular chords.

All those communities which have made claims to be 'nations' have based their claims on some alleged common attributes or criteria; but both the substantive criteria, and the means through which they have been propagated, have varied extraordinarily widely across different nations. The key to successful claims to nationhood lies in the plausibility of the claims to community among large numbers of people, and their capacity to enforce, express or enact these claims; it does not lie in the intrinsic, essential character of the claims themselves.

One of Gauguin's paintings carries the title: 'Who am I? Where do I come from? Where am I going?' Gauguin's title encapsulates much of what is entailed by identity construction. In seeking to answer the question 'who am I?', an individual (or, in more complex ways, a society) must consider certain fundamental themes. What are my values? What do I uphold, believe in, hold sacred? What am I prepared to defend (with my life, if necessary)? To what, and to whom, am I opposed? What negatives determine or define my boundaries – who is like me, who is 'other'? In considering 'where do I come from?' there are questions of belonging, of sense of a group existing through time, of ancestry; a sense of place and home-land; and of heritage, of traditions which one seeks to bring for-ward, to relay to the next generation. And in answering the final question, 'where am I going?', the focus is on what one is seeking to realize in life, on ultimate aims, goals, strengths and potential achievements. Multiple, mutually overlapping identities are of course possible: in different contexts, an individual may define herself or himself primarily as a parent, a resident of a particular state or region, a member of a political party, ethnic group, religious organization; all of these entail certain values, certain heritages and choices, certain relationships and oppositions. An individual identity lies at the complex intersection, at any point in time, of changing sets of roles, relationships, aspirations, views and values, influenced by prior attributes, patterns of socialization and responses to experiences. To transpose these complexities to a whole 'nation' – to search for a *national* identity' – is a problematic enterprise.

While concepts of group belonging may reflect actual perceptions of large numbers of people, they are very often also propagated by more limited groups, from particular quarters, for particular pur-poses. Defining values, boundaries, self and otherness is a key feature of the construction of any collective identity. There are a range of factors which affect patterns of identity formation. Elites claim divergent legitimations for the state, based partly in interpre-tations of the past (overcoming the past, the 'better' Germany, the culmination or fulfilment of historical trends) and partly in a view of the present and programme for the future (economic productiv-ity now, or striving towards utopia tomorrow). Different social and generational groups are exposed to different experiences which affect their views of the world, their modes of orientation and behaviour, in ways not always intended by elites. Actual experi-ences over a period of time also serve to transform what it is that the 'imagined community' of belonging is felt to consist in. And the construction of 'national' identity inevitably faces challenges and has to change in a context of increasing population mobility, the dramatic expansion of communication systems, and the readjust-ment of the functions of regions, states and inter- or transnational organizations in a changing global context.

To develop a strong sense of collective identity as a community, certain very general preconditions are important. In particular,

there has to be *some sense of the continuing existence of that community as a coherent entity over time;* and there has to be *some sense
of the importance of communal identification in the present, with
certain common values, interests, and clearly defined boundaries
between this particular collective identity and others.* This we may
perhaps summarize very briefly (and hence somewhat inadequately) as follows:

A sense of collective identity will be stronger if there is

A. Legacy. or, A shared myth of a common past

A notion of a shared history: common 'collective memory'; common myths, traditions; a common historical picture (*Geschichtsbild*)
and historical consciousness (*Geschichtsbewußtsein*);

B. Destiny: A community of common fate

Shared positive values; shared view of the other, the enemy (*Feind-
bild*); common experiences in the present. A sense of a common fate
or perceived future.

In other words, *if there is a widespread sense of a shared historical
legacy, and a shared fate and destiny, then there is more likely to be a
shared sense of a common collective identity.*
    Whether or not this collective identity develops claims to be a
'national' identity is somewhat contingent. Regional or local identities can be built up in much the same way. If one takes, for
example, the mining communities which sprang up very rapidly
in the later nineteenth century, almost exactly this model can be
applied. In coal-mining communities as far apart as Springhill in
Nova Scotia, or the Rhondda valleys of South Wales, people were
brought together from a wide range of different geographical origins. Men and boys were thrust together into the darkness and
common dangers of the work below the ground, while women
shared their anxieties and bereavements in conditions of cramped
misery above. Communal entertainments and often a strong religious faith reinforced what can only be described as a community
of fate: new forms of collective identity displaced memories of
divergent ancestral origins, and the salient history became that
of these new communities, with their disasters, defeats, and tales
of heroism and bravery. This is not the place to inquire into the
conditions under which certain forms of local or regional collective
identity may become candidates (or not) for 'national' status,
although the character and boundaries of modern states, often the

result more of international power politics than any pre-existing sense of collective identity, have a lot to do with this question.[26] I simply wish to indicate that we are dealing here with a spectrum, and that there are common processes involved across quite a large span of this spectrum.

Fractured identities in Germany since 1945

Let us return, then, more specifically to the German case. If we analyse the tortured history of constructions of national identity in Germany since 1945, we discover key dissonances between different levels and aspects of identity formation. At both 'official' and 'popular' levels, we find disjunctures between, for example, public myths and private memories, between official values and personal prejudices, between taught ideology and everyday experience. It is these dissonances which led to the curiously fractured character of German identity since 1945.

The dissonances work differently in each of the two German states, and the parameters of identity change differently over time. For example, we shall see a curiously symmetrical but opposite development with respect to official and popular conceptions of identity in East and West: while in the West the state formally adhered to the concept of one German nation, this was decreasingly felt as a reality among the people; and in the East, despite the state's official attempt to construct a new notion of GDR citizenship, many of the people still clung to a notion of one German nation (which probably partook somewhat more of the much criticized 'Deutschmark nationalism' than of the notion of a German *Kulturnation*). Similarly, there is a dissonance in the prevalence of the memory of war in the two states: in the East, the Wall was a constant reminder of a common past, even for those who had never lived through it, in a way that it was not in the West. The construction of the enemy, so crucial to the construction of national identities, was easier to swallow in the West (traditional anti-communism) than it was in the East, where the West Germans could never quite be seen as the foe they were made out to be in official propaganda. (The *Klassenfeind* was never a completely plausible description of one's great-aunt in the West.) Nor did the East Germans ever quite internalize the

---

[26] To pursue this question any further would require at least a separate chapter, if not another book, which might not be of direct interest to those readers anxious to get on with pursuing the intrinsically fascinating case of German identity after the Holocaust.

regime's official values. Meanwhile, the experience of life in the two Germanies was in many ways increasingly divergent, such that at the level of shared experience there was less and less in common over time.

To preview, then, the argument of this book: in seeking to define a 'national' identity, there are two major respects in which Germany constitutes a peculiar case. One has to do with its Nazi past; the other has to do with its post-war division into two opposing states. In neither respect is there any exact parallel among other European states. Although debates over resistance and collaboration are certainly shared, in different ways, among a number of other European states (fascism in Italy, the Vichy regime in France), none has to shoulder the main burden of responsibility for the Holocaust; and no other European state was divided into two, with the artificial creation of antagonistic states glaring at each other in mirror-image symmetry across the Iron Curtain which divided Cold War Europe. No other European state had to work so hard, not merely to construct one new viable post-war identity, but two; and that within the wider notion of a tainted, yet still to be sustained, concept of a common German nation.

In the shadow of the Holocaust any notion of German national identity was uniquely problematic, uniquely tortured. It was not only that, after unleashing two world wars and organizing a programme of mass genocide with unparalleled efficiency, any German *nationalism* was clearly utterly unacceptable, totally discredited: Germans, alone among European nations, could not even be 'patriotic' without arousing hackles and fears among their neighbours. It was also more broadly that any attempt to explain this disastrous course of German history must entail examination of a whole range of attributes and qualities of 'German-ness': even the very cultural creativity of the Germans – the archetypal *Land der Dichter und Denker* ('land of poets and thinkers') – was up for critique as an 'apolitical' precondition for the rise of Hitler.

Secondly, the two post-war German states were created by the forcible division of a defeated state, which had not only propagated a very strong version of national identity defined in racist terms, but had divided its own people between those who were accepted in the *Volk* community and those who were outcasts on 'racial' or political grounds. Each of the new states became engaged in a process of defining its own new identity, in opposition not only to the common past, but also to each other. Over four decades of separation, this process had progressed far enough – although often in ways unintended by the respective regimes – that East and West Germans were in many ways developing quite divergent patterns of collective identity, in ways comparable to the divergence between, say, West Germans and Austrians.

In West Germany, despite the self-conscious difficulties with a sense of national identity, there were emerging strands of acceptable forms of West German partial identity, ranging from the much-denigrated popular 'Deutschmark nationalism' to the proposed 'patriotism of the constitution' preferred by left-liberal intellectuals. Nevertheless, the official view remained that, even after *Ostpolitik* and the formal recognition of the GDR, there were 'two German states within one German nation'. What the common 'German-ness' was alleged to consist in was never entirely clear. An essentially ethnic definition of German citizenship (including resettlement rights for ethnic Germans living elsewhere in eastern Europe) remained official West German policy. And a key hallmark of official political culture was that of collective shame for being German.

In East Germany, by contrast, after *Ostpolitik* a new notion of nation defined in *class* terms was propagated: the GDR became, officially, the socialist state of workers and peasants, seeking to develop a specific GDR form of national identity which was premised on there being, not only two German states but also two German nations. Nevertheless, particularly in the 1980s the East German regime began to lay claim to the whole of the German past, including previously neglected or criticized figures such as Martin Luther and Frederick the Great, who were co-opted in support of legitimizing the GDR in the present. In contrast to the West, the GDR officially propagated a sense of pride in being the truly 'anti-fascist state'.

So there were attempts to create and propagate emergent 'sub-national', or even 'national', identities for what were seen as two essentially permanent states. But at the same time, both Germanies in different ways kept alive wider notions of a common German identity. This was of course official policy throughout the period as far as West Germany was concerned, since its constitution (the allegedly only provisional Basic Law) committed it to work for reunification of the German nation. It was also implicit in the East German regime's new resort to history in the 1980s, as well as, more immediately, in the GDR's use of its unique links with West Germany to reach economically beneficial trade and credit agreements. In any event, whatever the official view, it was unavoidable: the presence of another, more affluent and pluralist German state, which extended automatic rights of citizenship to any East German able to leave, meant that the notion of a common German nation simply could not be ignored by even the most determined GDR enthusiasts.

Official attempts to propagate new notions of national identity, whether partial/sub-national or all-encompassing 'German', misfired in a number of respects. On the one hand, official East German views of there being a separate GDR nation were treated with widespread cynicism, while East Germans retained a high degree of interest in West Germany. They watched West German television almost exclusively, received West German visitors and fostered western links with enthusiasm. East Germans retained a very lively sense of being part of a divided nation. On the other hand, despite the official West German commitment to reunification, West Germans of the younger generation by and large had very little interest in their East German brethren, and viewed them as having very little in common. The asymmetry between young East and West Germans in levels of knowledge, interest, and sense of community with each other was very striking. That physical boundary between East and West, the Iron Curtain, ironically succeeded in turning the attentions of West Germans – who could pass through it – westwards, while it signally backfired in failing to provide a symbolic boundary for East Germans, whose sights were set beyond the border they could not cross.

In practice, the two Germanies did, however, grow apart in significant ways, while at the same time both participated in broader western and eastern European currents. The very different international locations and domestic political, economic and social patterns of the two Germanies – capitalist democracy in the West, Soviet-style 'actually existing socialism' in the East – served to render the two Germanies increasingly different in reality.

This book develops, then, a non-essentialist definition of 'nation' as a self-identifying community of common memory and common destiny, which under certain conditions – such as warfare and external threats – can command a remarkable emotional power, political shape, and mass following. It seeks to analyse the social and political character and role of historical consciousness at various levels: national myth-making, history as a 'scientific' discipline and a political endeavour, popular memory as a reinterpretation of personal experiences in a collective conversation about the past. It explores the extent to which and the respects in which the two Germanies developed new, 'sub-national' or 'quasi-national' identities, or retained a broader sense of overriding German nationhood.

There are many ways in which this argument could be presented, the different facets arrayed and explored. Let me briefly introduce the organization of the book, which has had to be highly selective in choice of topic and illustrative material included for discussion.

The first several chapters focus on attempts, in a variety of media and from a variety of quarters, to tell a coherent tale about the common past: to write a 'common memory' for the collective identity of the nation through time. It turns out that the nation in this sense could not be so easily constructed: the candidates for the role of accepted story about a common past were simply too numerous, often mutually contradictory, always sensitive, essentially contested.

Chapter 2 examines the reinterpreted and reconstructed landscapes of the past, reflecting on some of the ways in which sites of significance were variously demolished, disguised, neglected, preserved, re-orientated, re-presented in new ways, as the physical traces of the past became integral parts of the new symbolic politics of the present. Transformations with respect to the human collaborators and perpetrators are explored in chapter 3, which reviews patterns of denazification and practical, legal and political modes of 'overcoming the past' in the first couple of decades after the war. Chapter 4 turns to the issue of the public presentation of the nation through anniversaries and commemorations of a collective past; in neither German state could there be simple, unthinking 'celebrations' of 'national holidays' or 'holy days'. Chapter 5 addresses the equally sensitive issue – with awkward self-reflexive implications for authors of historical works! – of the would-be objective, 'scientific' presentation of the common past by professional historians in the two German states. The differences in the historiographical traditions, under conditions of democratic pluralism in the West and state-ordained Marxism-Leninism in the East, are not quite as simple as might at first blush appear to innocent believers (on either side of the Wall) in 'truth' versus 'ideology'. Chapter 6 then considers broader patterns of historical consciousness among the general population. Experiences are reinterpreted and transmitted across generations, in informal conversations about the past: and it turns out that, very often, the tales presented in public by the state's intellectuals and spokespeople have very little resonance with the memories and emotions embedded in different social, generational and political communities.

If contested presentations of an awkward past could not easily be harnessed to the task of presenting the nation as a community of common memory, then a divided present was little better as a basis for the construction of the nation as a community of common destiny. Here, too, the story is complex and multi-faceted. Chapter 7 analyses the issues of citizenship entitlement and conceptions of nationhood in the two German states, where, once more, there were serious dissonances between official views and popular perceptions of the nation. These were further complicated, however, by divergent experiences of identity in everyday life. Chapter 8 suggests that the very different social, economic and political structures over forty years began to have a crucial impact on prevalent attitudes, expectations, modes of behaviour in East and West. Thus the Wall fell at a time when the Germans were growing apart in practice, but when the government of one side, and a majority of the people on the other, still either proclaimed or believed in the unity of the nation in principle. It was against this background, and in these conditions, that attempts to create a sense of inner unity are taking place today. The final chapter, chapter 9, ruminates more broadly on the implications of these – necessarily brief and selective – analyses of facets of German national identity after the Holocaust.

The aim of this book is neither to provide an exhaustive account of the conceptions developed by articulate Germans of national identity (on which there are innumerable tomes), nor to provide a moralizing indictment of the perceived inadequacies and failures of German attempts at 'overcoming the past' (on which there are again innumerable volumes), but rather to stand back a little from these well-trodden domains and analyse the general parameters of the problem. It is as much about history as an intellectual discipline and human enterprise, and about national identity as a social and historical construct, as it is about the two Germanies and the united Germany of today. The German case, in which national identity is dissected, divided, reconstructed in the most self-conscious and proactive manner, provides a superb example of the elements involved in national identity construction – or rather, of the elements which cumulatively amounted to a failure to construct a stable and generally accepted national identity in divided Germany after the Holocaust. These elements are neither 'naturally given' nor purely imagined: neither intrinsic to the nature of the world, nor merely figments of fevered intellectual brains. To explore the multitude of ways in which different conceptions of identity intersect, collide, overlap, are institutionalized, politicized, downplayed, in a case with its own unique difficulties and distortions, is to illuminate the factors involved in identity construction, transmission and transformation more generally.

Thus, while the subject of the book concerns history and national identity in Germany since Hitler, a complementary aim is to raise wider questions about these issues in principle, with broader relevance for other countries, other nations, other times. Debates over national identity and the political uses (and misuses) of history, while perhaps peculiarly virulent in Germany, are not peculiarly German phenomena.

2
Landscapes of Memory

A recently licensed newspaper based in Munich, the *Süddeutsche Zeitung*, for a while ran a column entitled *In München fällt auf, daß...* (roughly, 'Noteworthy in Munich...'). Issue 11, of 9 November 1945, remarked on a number of remnants of the Nazi regime still scattered around the ruins of the city: advertisements for the Nazi newspaper, the *Völkische Beobachter*; Nazi references on the city maps, including even the appellation *München, Hauptstadt der Bewegung* ('Munich, Headquarters of the [Nazi] Movement'); an eagle over the portal of the former Luftgaukommando building in the Prinzregentenstraße, still sporting a swastika which had escaped earlier removal.[1] A week later, the same column reminded readers to check their beloved traditional green Bavarian hats for incriminating evidence of former civic commitment: 'on many costume hats (*Trachtenhüten*) there are still whole collections of Winter Relief Work badges that betray the former generosity of their wearers'. In the Ludwigstraße, posters still proclaimed the existence of a 'NS-Reichsbund deutscher Schwestern' (Nazi Reich League of German Sisters). Meanwhile, the Bavarian State Office for the Protection of Memorial Monuments (*Bayerische Landesamt für Denkmalpflege*), suitably goaded by the comments in the previous week's issue, had provided assurances that the offending eagle and swastika in the Prinzregentenstraße would be removed within the next few days.[2] On 30 November it was the turn of the Police Station Munich-North, Kurfürstenplatz 5, to be the subject of gentle ridicule and reminder: a swastika was still displayed at first-floor

---

[1] *Süddeutsche Zeitung* [SZ], 11, 9 Nov. 1945, p. 3.
[2] *SZ*, 13, 16 Nov. 1945, p. 3.

level. Meanwhile, a restaurant (*Gaststätte*) at Kaulbachstraße 2 had forgotten to remove its advertisment for the *Völkische Beobachter*, which included praise for its Editor, Adolf Hitler.[3]

It was clearly going to take quite a while to dismantle all physical reminders of the discredited past. When viewed in the long-term perspective, over half a century later, an irony soon appears. Many Germans wished – for both good and bad reasons – to rid their landscape of every reminder of the discredited and diabolical past as soon as possible. And the Allies, on the whole, agreed with them. The Americans, for example, were very unwilling to leave intact former Nazi locations which might become 'shrines', holy places, sites of pilgrimage and foci of attention for former Nazis. The Russians soon began to impose their own landscape of political symbols, and to reinscribe the remnants of the past with new meanings. Moreover, given the impelling immediate needs of the day, many Nazi buildings, including former concentration camps, were taken over by the occupying authorities for new political purposes: the custody of prisoners of war, former SS members and other political suspects pending trial, even – as in Dachau for many years – for the housing of German refugees awaiting resettlement. The protection of memory was nowhere near the top of the list of priorities of the occupying powers.

Yet, in the process, the physical traces, the outward evidence, of the past were being transformed, sometimes beyond recognition. Rightly, contemporaries rarely wish to live in a museum – particularly one which is filled with painful memories, and which bears witness to an era which is utterly repudiated. One need only consider the way in which Berliners tore down the hated Berlin Wall in the aftermath of 1989 to understand the desire to rid the landscape of a hated excrescence, a symbol of a rejected political past. But the process, if radical, removes all traces, and may later be regretted. No reconstruction is quite the same. For those who lived through it, memory fades, and reminders are needed (or avoided, rejected); for those who come after, the effort of historical imagination is all the greater for lack of a topography of experience.

It took a little distance before the full implications in Germany were clear. What we see in both parts of divided Germany is a complex development, in which the physical reminders of the Nazi past were variously reappropriated, neglected, demolished or re-presented; in which the politics of memory, the construction of memorials, the enactment of commemorations, took on changing and often highly controversial significance. The apparent 'presence

[3] *SZ*, 17, 30 Nov. 1945, p. 6.

of the past' in the physical landscape, and its embedding in historical consciousness, is not a matter of arbitrary survival, but rather the result of active political engagement. And on both sides of the inner-German border, the intent was often less to 'educate', in the academic sense of the word, than to warn, to decry, to commemorate, to propagate new values.

Germans continued to inhabit the same soil, but the landscapes became different. Streets and squares were renamed, buildings were put to different purposes, some places were transformed and re-presented, others allowed to tumble into ruin.[4] There was an almost infinite variety of ways in which the landscapes of the past became all but unrecognizable, except to the eyes of those trained to perceive and imagine. And for millions of Germans, of course, the landscapes were actually different: around twelve million people resettled in the decade and a half after the war, some leaving their former homelands in territories which became Russian or Polish, others fleeing the GDR, resettling in what became the Federal Republic of Germany. This was a period of population movement on a scale which had not been witnessed in central Europe for centuries. But even for those who stayed put, the changes were phenomenal. The immediate need after the war was simply to clean up and rebuild: to clear away the rubble and debris, to rebuild or demolish bombed-out shells of buildings, to make the wartime landscape reinhabitable – and to kick over the traces, announce the Zero Hour, and start anew.

What were the implications of this for constructions of national identity? As Anthony Smith has suggested, nations – even those without their own state, such as diaspora Jews – often focus around 'sacred places', sites of particular and heightened, frequently religious, significance for their history and identity.[5] (The struggle for sole political rights over a given territory – a common feature of modern nationalism – is a slightly separate, although clearly related, issue.) The endowment of 'sacred sites' with a simple national significance was never a straightforward matter in either East or West Germany. As James Young has pointed out, nations usually seek to remember their heroes and triumphs, their struggles and their martyrs – and certainly not their great crimes.[6] In Germany, the 'anti-memory' of the Holocaust was a difficult legacy,

---

[4] On the renaming of streets and squares in the GDR, see Maoz Azaryahu, *Von Wilhelmplatz zu Thälmannplatz: Politische Symbole im öffentlichen Leben der DDR* (Gerlingen: Bleicher Verlag, 1991).

[5] A. Smith, *National Identity* (Harmondsworth: Penguin, 1991).

[6] Cf. James Young, *The Texture of Memory: Holocaust Memorials and Meaning* (New Haven and London: Yale University Press, 1993), pp. 21–6, 53.

which had to be transformed: the definition of the Nazi past had to become the baseline for what the new Germany was *not*, for what it had utterly rejected, while at the same time seeking out acceptable strands and traditions which could serve as the foundations or antecedents of the new. While in the Federal Republic historical sites remained distinctly problematic, contested, places of memory, the communist regime adopted an altogether simpler approach to myth construction and its physical symbolization and enactment.

Heroism, resistance and victory in the GDR

The new occupying power, the Soviet Union, and its political allies among the Germans, brought a fairly clear political message which was imposed on the populace, willing or unwilling. The myth of the antifascist liberation of the innocent German workers and peasants was *the* crucial founding myth of the GDR. The pantheon of heroes was to be celebrated in street names, displayed in statues; the villains, and the heroic struggles against them, were to be portrayed in the erstwhile places of terror and torture, which themselves became national shrines and places of pilgrimage.

There were of course twists and turns in this essentially simple story. Some heroes (most notably Stalin) fell from grace, and a hasty renaming of East Berlin's Stalinallee and its provincial counterparts was in order. Some former Nazi buildings, such as Goering's Air Force headquarters in the (then) Wilhelmstraße, were simply too useful to be turned into historic monuments, and were pragmatically reappropriated (as the House of Ministries, in the renamed Otto-Grotewohl-Straße, in this case).[7] Former concentration camps, such as Buchenwald and Sachsenhausen, proved for a few years to be remarkably useful for housing new political prisoners, once the old were out – on which more in a moment. And limited resources simply did not permit the wholesale rehabilitation of bomb-scarred buildings, the razing and rebuilding of city centres, seen in the more affluent West. The effects of the war could still be seen in crumbling, pock-marked facades half a century later, their dilapidation compounded by subsequent decades of decay and neglect.[8]

The significance of all these visible reminders of the recent past was, however, radically reinscribed, even reversed. Let us take as

[7] Cf. Richard Schneider (ed.), *Historische Stätten in Berlin* (Frankurt am Main and Berlin: Ullstein/Nicolai, 1987), pp. 102–4.

[8] As an East German joke had it, subtly adapting a peace movement slogan: *Ruinen schaffen ohne Waffen* ('create ruins without weapons').

a prime example what became almost the national symbolic heart of the GDR, Buchenwald.

The concentration camp of Buchenwald was erected by the Nazis on top of a hill overlooking Weimar. Weimar was more or less itself the symbolic/cultural heart of Germany, with its associations with Germany's greatest poet, Johann Wolfgang von Goethe, and his friend and collaborator Friedrich Schiller.[9] The picturesque town of Weimar boasts the National Theatre, with its memorial statue to Goethe and Schiller safely preserved from war damage; the Hotel Elefant, in which functionaries of the ruling Socialist Unity Party (SED) and foreign visitors were able to sleep and eat in the rooms once enjoyed by Goethe's friends, including Charlotte von Stein; Goethe's own house, and his 'Garden House', in which he wrote some of his most beautiful lyrics (such as the one to the moon, as it 'filled bushes and valley', and Goethe's soul, with its light). Weimar was also the town to which the new, democratically elected government of Germany fled in the stormy months of early 1919, in order to establish a new constitution and new political order in the Republic which henceforth bore Weimar's name.

On top of the Ettersberg hill was an ancient oak tree, under which Goethe allegedly met his friend Charlotte von Stein, surrounded by the beech trees which gave Buchenwald its name; and it was around Goethe's oak tree that Heinrich Himmler, head of the SS, chose to erect a concentration camp. Between 1937 and 1945 about 250,000 people from thirty-five different countries were incarcerated there, of whom more than 60,000 died. On 11 April 1945 an uprising of prisoners dealt the final blow to an already panicking concentration camp guard force, prefacing the liberation by the approaching US army with the basis for a myth of self-liberation. It was this, along with the legends of solidarity and mutual support among communists, that was picked up and amplified a thousand-fold by the SED.[10]

---

[9] I am not given to unadorned value judgements, and had contemplated putting the word 'arguably' before 'greatest'. However, I think in this case the unqualified superlative has to remain.

[10] On Buchenwald, see esp. Manfred Overesch, *Buchenwald und die DDR, oder Die Suche nach Selbstlegitimation* (Göttingen: Vandenhoeck and Ruprecht, 1995); Lutz Niethammer (ed.), *Der 'gesäuberte Antifaschismus'. Die SED und die roten Kapos von Buchenwald. Dokumente* (Berlin: Akademie Verlag, 1994); Peter Reichel, *Politik mit der Erinnerung* (Munich: Carl Hanser Verlag, 1995), pp. 129–35; Young, *Texture of Memory*, pp. 72–9; Claudia Koonz, 'Germany's Buchenwald: Whose Shrine? Whose Memory?' in James E. Young (ed.), *The Art of Memory. Holocaust Memorials in History* (New York and Munich: Prestel Verlag, 1994).

The Americans briefly opened Buchenwald to citizens of Weimar, forced in for guided tours of what had been done in their name. Contemporary diary entries of surviving prisoners recorded the immediate responses of Germans who had lived a bare five miles from the concentration camp: they had known nothing about it, nothing at all.[11] Film footage of these tours shows women turning away from mounds of corpses, covering their mouths and noses with their head scarves, and looking distinctly physically discomfited.

In June 1945 the Americans withdrew from Thuringia and handed over to Soviet occupation, according to previously agreed occupation boundaries. For several years after the Soviets took over from the US, Buchenwald was used as a Soviet internment camp for a variety of political prisoners, including not only undoubted former Nazis, such as SS-officers and others awaiting trial for war crimes, but also others whom the communists deemed to be a political threat, including Social Democrats and Liberals who opposed the construction of a new dictatorship on the ruins of the old. But in the 1950s the decision was taken to form a museum on the grounds of the now emptied camp, under the twin banners of 'honouring the dead' and 'making a personal commitment (*Selbstverpflichtung*) in the name of the dead'.[12] Buchenwald was all the more a hallowed shrine since among its sanctified dead was the heroized former communist leader, Ernst Thälmann; while, with the myth of antifascist struggle and ultimate self-liberation, it provided a key site to embody the creation myth of the GDR.

In 1958 a memorial designed by Fritz Cremer was erected outside the entrance to Buchenwald. It depicted ten men and a child, all in a defiant posture symbolizing resistance and liberation, looking out over the rolling countryside which stretches for miles around and celebrating the triumph of struggle against oppression. The sense of new life rising out of the ashes, to create a better future, was embodied too in the 'Oath of Buchenwald', frequently reproduced in the course of GDR political life as a form of covenant binding the past to the future.[13] In the slightly tendentious translation printed in the 1985 brochure, *Upholding the Antifascist Legacy*, which was targeted at an international audience:

[11] Cf. the extract from Ernst Thape's Diary, and the report by Imre Kertesz, reprinted in Overesch, *Buchenwald*, pp. 106–9.

[12] See Volkhard Knigge, 'Antifaschistischer Widerstand und Holocaust. Zur Geschichte der KZ-Gedenkstätten in der DDR' in Bernhard Moltmann et al. (eds), *Erinnerung. Zur Gegenwart des Holocaust in Deutschland-West und Deutschland-Ost* (Frankfurt am Main: Haag and Herchen, 1993), pp. 67–8.

[13] Cf. Alan Nothnagle, *Building the East German Myth* (Ann Arbor: University of Michigan Press, forthcoming), ch. 4.

We, the inmates of Buchenwald – Russians, French, Poles, Czechs, Slovaks and Germans, Spaniards, Italians and Austrians, Belgians and Dutchmen, Britons and Luxemburgers, Romanians, Yugoslavs and Hungarians – fought jointly against the SS, the Nazi criminals and for our liberation. We were inspired by one and the same idea. Our cause is just – the victory must be ours. We waged a common, hard and sacrificing struggle in many languages, a struggle that has not yet come to an end . . .
From this roll-call square, this site of fascist horror we swear to all the world:
We shall stop our struggle only after the very last culprit has been sentenced by the court of the peoples! The elimination of Nazism root and branch is our slogan! The construction of a world of peace and freedom is our goal!
This we owe to our dead and their families.[14]

This 'oath' epitomized the GDR's approach to the Nazi past: it celebrated international political struggle and self-liberation; it emphasized a continuing community united by commitment to an ongoing cause; it made no mention of victims murdered on 'racial' grounds.[15]

Generations of East German children, in the youth organizations Young Pioneers (JP) or Free German Youth (FDJ) were marched in organized hordes around this camp, with its exhibits reiterating the themes of international struggle against fascist repression. Buchenwald, with its distinctive features (self-liberation, the oath, and the heart-rending proximity to the spiritual heartland of German culture, Weimar) was in some respects unique, and came to serve as a national symbolic centre. But the message was repeated, with slight variations on the main refrain, in other sites of Nazi terror in the GDR: the concentration camps of Ravensbrück (for women) and Sachsenhausen, north of Berlin, or the work camp at Mittelbau-Dora, near Nordhausen.

In each case, there were distinctive silences, or distorted patterns of emphasis. In Ravensbrück, for example, no mention was made of the fact that many women who were sent there were lesbians – a taboo theme in the homophobic GDR, which effectively accepted the Nazi definition of homosexuals and lesbians as 'asocials'.[16]

---

[14] *Upholding the Antifascist Legacy* (Dresden: Verlag Zeit im Bild, 1985), p. 5. For the original German, see Overesch, *Buchenwald,*, p. 119.

[15] As we shall see repeatedly, 'racial' victims of Nazism were demoted as passive objects of terror, taking second place a very long way behind 'active resistance fighters'.

[16] Cf. e.g. Sigrid Jacobeit and Lieselotte Thoms-Henrich (eds), *Kreuzweg Ravensbrück. Lebensbilder antifaschistischer Widerstandskämpferinnen* (Leipzig:

In virtually every site of Nazi terror, the fact that many victims were Jewish was disproportionately underemphasized. Unwilling victims, as such, barely got a look in, compared to active resistance. In virtually every site, the theme of political opposition was predominant, and celebrated as the key legacy of the past, the heritage for the present and future in a continuing fight against oppression and injustice.

The official guide to the 'National place of warning and remembrance Sachsenhausen' (*Nationale Mahn-und Gedenkstätte*), for example, opens with an absolutely characteristic couple of paragraphs:

> In deep veneration we bow at this place before our dear dead, the fighters against war, fascism, and militarism, the victims of the Nazi terror. This place is dedicated to remembrance and admonition: remembrance of the innumerable martyrs and heroes of the antifascist resistance fight, admonition – addressed both to our and to succeeding generations – never again to allow fascist and militarist barbarism to break out over our people and other peoples.
>
> Every footstep of this territory is drenched with the blood and the sweat of death of tens of thousands of martyrs from many nations, tens of thousands of people of the most varied world views. Here they were hunted and tortured to death, tormented and murdered, only because they loved their people, freedom and democracy more than their own lives, because they were socialists, because they detested mass hatred and murder of peoples (*Völkerhaß* and *Völkermord*), because they had dedicated their lives to humanism and friendship among peoples (*Völkerfreundschaft*).[17]

The 'Musuem of the antifascist freedom fight of the European peoples' (*Museum des antifaschistischen Freiheitskampfes der europäischen Völker*) erected in Sachsenhausen portrays the usual mixture: it evokes horror at the gruesome atrocities perpetrated by the SS and their helpers; it evokes sympathy for the sufferings of the inmates, 'people of many nations, old and young'; it evokes admiration for the heroism and resistance of those who struggled against the Nazi terror. It celebrates the heroic battle of the common people, aided by resistance fighters of all countries (and, of course, particularly the Soviet Union), strengthened by their 'humanity and

---

Verlag für die Frau DDR, 1987), p. 11: 'Neben Antifaschistinnen aus politischer Überzeugung saßen hier zahlreiche Bibelforscherinnen, Jüdinnen sowie kriminelle und asoziale Häftlinge.' ('Alongside political anti-fascists, there were numerous Jehovah's witnesses, Jews, and criminal and a-social prisoners here').

[17] *Sachsenhausen*, official guide (no place or date of publication: *c.* mid-1980s, picked up by the author on a visit in 1986).

camaraderie', against the fascists. 'Racial' aspects are distorted and downplayed. The one block in Sachsenhausen devoted to presentation of the fate of Jews contained factual distortions and even the use of inauthentic photographs.[18] There was virtually no serious historical research carried out in the GDR on the history of Sachsenhausen, because Buchenwald took the primary role and the SED were more interested in the fate of the communists, rather than the Sinti, Roma and Jews who perished in Sachsenhausen.[19] The official brochure similarly just manages to mention the Jewish victims of Nazi terror, but the rapid reader may be forgiven for overlooking their single, brief and minimalist reference in the midst of the reiterated message about the patriotic resistance fighters of all nations. And it implies a continuing struggle: we are reminded, crucially, that 'many murderers, both recognized and incognito, now live in West Germany'.[20]

Such presentations in former concentration camps are undoubtedly – and inevitably – moving. Details of the perverse 'medical' experiments carried out on inmates, the sadistic methods of torture and the long, slow death through starvation and disease cannot be anything but moving, if one even pauses for a single moment of empathy. But the empathy aroused by the concentration camp memorials in the GDR was abused, instrumentalized, distorted. It

[18] Thomas Lutz, 'Gedenkstätten für die Opfer des NS-Regimes. Geschichte – Arbeitsweisen – Wirkungsmöglichkeit' in Jürgen Dittberger and Antje von Meer (eds), *Gedenkstätten im vereinten Deutschland* (Berlin: Stiftung Brandenburgische Gedenkstätten, Edition Hentrich, 1994), pp. 30–1.

[19] See Günter Morsch, 'Sachsenhausen: auf dem Weg zur Neugestaltung und Neukonzeption der Gedenkstätte' in Dittberger and von Meer (eds), *Gedenkstätten*, p. 50.

[20] Auschwitz, located in Poland (although part of the Greater German Reich at the time of its operation), presented a problem in this respect for the communist authorities of the post-war period until 1989. The scene of the greatest destruction of Jewish life, Auschwitz-II at Birkenau, with its infamous railway tracks leading in to the watchtower gate, the 'selection ramp', and the path to the gas chambers and crematoria, was demoted as far as later tourism was concerned in favour of greater attention being paid to the camp for political prisoners, Auschwitz-I. Tourist coaches arrived at the latter in droves, and the car park was full up within a short time of opening; but the former was off the beaten tourist track, relatively deserted except for determined loners with their own transport. There was no attempt to cover up the fact that the majority of victims were Jews, but in the eyes of many Jews the forms of representation and commemoration were skewed: piles of shoes and spectacles rendering the victims utterly dead (as the Nazis would have wanted), rather than remembering Jewish life and culture; the neighbouring Carmelite convent overemphasizing Polish Catholic resistance; and the general tendency of the museum and exhibition being to stress *communist* political opposition and active resistance.

was deployed, not to open the way for an illumination of the past in all its fullness and contradiction, but rather to legitimize the present, to instil a sense of political commitment that was to be beyond valid questioning. Its purpose was of course – and legitimately – to commemorate the suffering of the victims; but in the process it downplayed the diversity of the people who were killed, and it actively sought to appropriate the emotions aroused in support of the imposed politics of the present. A false dichotomy was erected: if you are against fascism, then you are for the GDR; if you are critical of the GDR, then you are essentially a fascist. This form of psychological coercion, in combination with the blotting out of certain aspects of the past, and the state-sanctioned amnesia and reinterpretation of genuine memory, was a highly effective mechanism for achieving a constrained loyalty, or at least a powerful taboo against criticism, in the first generation or so after the war. For those born later, the real memories were barely preserved.

To take a final example of the presentation of the past in former Nazi concentration camps in the GDR: the relatively small camp of Lichtenburg, used in the 1930s and then replaced first by Sachsenhausen and Buchenwald for men, and a little later by Ravensbrück for women. The brochure and guide to the museum, which was formally opened on 8 May 1965, to commemorate the twentieth anniversary of 'liberation' – a concept to which we shall return – and substantially reconceived and expanded in 1977–8, presents the Nazi system of terror very simply. The evil forces were the 'right-extremist forces of monopoly and finance capital'; the heroes/victims were 'almost without exception communists, social democrats, and other antifascists'. The growth of the concentration camp system in the later 1930s was in order to 'be able to imprison and destroy (*vernichten*) the continually growing number of political opponents. At the same time, preparations were made for being able to lock up and exterminate future antifascists from the lands which were to be overrun and occupied.'[21]

The message in the GDR was simple, clear and constantly reiterated: the villains were the imperialist monopoly capitalist fascists; the heroes were those who fought in the political resistance, including people of many nations and most notably communists; the message for the present was 'Never Again'. The greatest number of victims, pursued on 'racial grounds', barely got mentioned, and certainly victims of racial and eugenic persecution were

[21] Hans Maur, *Antifaschistische Mahn-und Gedenkstätte Lichtenberg* (Prettin/Elbe: Kreismuseum Jessen, n.d. [but after 1978 and before 1983]), no pagination.

proportionately dramatically under-represented as far as the public presentation was concerned. The hereditarily ill, the homosexuals, Sinti and Roma are virtually nowhere to be seen; the Jews have passing, often relatively perfunctory remarks made about them. An innocent observer (as most subsequent generations of GDR young people, frogmarched through these exhibitions, actually were) would have no grounds for believing anything other than the official picture: that Nazism was part of the great battle between monopoly and finance capital on the one hand, and the political vanguard of the working class, in the form mainly of communists with some antifascist allies, on the other. And the need for constant vigilance, the waging of a continuing battle, a sense of comradeship in adversity – all were to be sustained by the message inscribed on the camps, which were as much about the Cold War present as about the Nazi past.

The GDR sought to present the past in a way that would be of current political benefit. It had a relatively guilt-free approach, at least as far as the communists were concerned. They had genuinely struggled against, been persecuted by, and suffered under, the Nazi system of terror. There could be genuine celebration and commemoration of their achievements and sufferings. And the population of the GDR – including many former Nazi party members and fellow-travellers – was officially invited to empathize with the communists, to identify with the former heroes and victims, and to cut their ties from the villains. This was a simple version of history, which could be highly effective in developing and sustaining an official historical consciousness free of collective shame. Absences in the exhibitions had their counterparts in absences in public debate, absences in historical books – and the apparent absence at least of sensitivities and taboos in popular historical consciousness. The compelling and real records of cruelty, torture, death, were emotive and direct: and once emotions against Nazism (or, more generally, 'fascism') are aroused, then the conclusion should follow – loyalty to the antifascist state, the GDR, which is the living embodiment of 'overcoming the past' and the spearhead of the contemporary and continuing fight against fascism today. Without any kind of genuine 'public sphere' in which these interpretations could be openly challenged, debated, or more nuanced views developed, there was really no case to argue. But what we shall see in the following chapters is a curious combination: the non-internalization of the official story, while accepting the moral of the tale; there was no need to be 'ashamed to be German'.[22]

---

[22] See esp. ch. 6 below.

The institutionalization of ritual shame in the West

The politicization of the past was effected rather differently in the West. For all the twists and turns of a much more complex story, the picture is essentially as follows. Initial partial cover-up was partly combined, partly followed, by public hand-wringing and soul-searching, to some extent provoked by public controversies; this transmogrified slowly into an almost ritualized incorporation of national guilt in the official re-presentation of the past, with continuing, unresolved debates between those who wanted, finally, a *Schlußstrich* (a line drawn under the past, redesignating it as 'history'), and those who sought forever to keep the flame of memory alive. A few examples of battles over topography must suffice to illustrate this rather contorted summarizing sentence – a contortion which reflects the complexities of the trajectory, which (as in other areas considered further below) was not simply one of 'collective amnesia' replaced by belated 'collective guilt'.

By the 1950s the immediacy of the Nazi period was fading, while at the same time some of the immediate post-war exigencies were no longer high priorities of the western Allies. Former concentration camps were no longer needed for post-war political prisoners; the fear of 'werewolves' returning to haunt former shrines was no longer quite so acute; new projects of identity construction in the Cold War had taken precedence over the suppression of Nazism.

What was quite striking to the historically minded traveller in pre-1990 West Germany was the almost startling absence of real – or realistic – physical reminders of, or signposts to, the past. There was certainly not the simplicity of appropriation and re-presentation for contemporary political purposes as in the East – but the greater public *Angst* and controversy of the West has also had the effect of losing some of the most straightforward traces from which a fuller imaginative picture could be created. For the sake of summary, perhaps two different ways in which the topography of the past was present in West Germany may be distinguished. First, there was the very ubiquitous approach of allowing historical locations to fall into disuse and ruin, or removing the traces altogether, in the great wave of rebuilding and reconstituting the landscape which was the concomitant of the West German economic miracle. Secondly, there was frequently a partially pious but always contested, sometimes almost hopelessly contorted attempt to reconstruct, represent, commemorate, with a heavy overlay of emotion, guilt and political bias, and only on very rare occasions a general recognition that the 'right' tone had been achieved. Although to some extent there was a shift in emphasis from the former to the latter, the two approaches were also partially overlapping, coterminous strands in the complex texture of post-Nazi democracy.

The scene of the Nuremberg Nazi Party rallies is an excellent example of the 'neglecting' approach. The contrast between historical significance and contemporary neglect is extraordinary. Leni Riefenstahl's film, and archive footage of the Nuremberg rallies, surely supply some of the most frequently shown shots in historical documentaries, the most overplayed visual presentations of Hitler's charisma, projecting an image of the Führer rising through, representing, and being above the people. Here, in the Nuremberg stadium, Hitler strode through the amassed and carefully orchestrated crowds, then rose up to the high point above the podium with the eagle and swastika to address the by now near-hysterical faithful below him. The sense of adoration, the orchestration of fanatic approval, the torchlight patterns, made this one of the most powerful modes of *Inszenierung*, of staging Hitler's charisma.

And what happened to this *Parteigelände* in the post-war period? Extraordinarily, the answer is: nothing. There was just a disused empty space, not turned into the site of a supermarket or car park, not used as a massive playground or football stadium; just left as it was – without eagle and swastika – empty, deserted, with a few weeds edging through the cracks, a few old men in raincoats drinking coffee out of thermos flasks and no doubt engaging in nostalgic recollection of the heady days of old.

Other places of considerable historical significance simply were reused, left unsignposted. Hitler's 'Brown House' in Munich (the *Hauptstadt der Bewegung*), for example, subsequently used as a music school, gave little outward evidence of its former significance. The *Feldherrnhalle*, also in Munich, where the attempted putsch of November 1923 was aborted, and in front of which Hitler held an annual commemoration ceremony, similarly bore silent witness only to those who already knew its twentieth-century significance. Landsberg am Lech, where he wrote *Mein Kampf* during imprisonment after the Beer Hall putsch, did little or nothing in its tourist literature to remind casual visitors of this fact. Hitler's birthplace, Braunau, on the Bavarian/Austrian border, remained well off the beaten tourist track. Memory in such places as these was to be only for the initiated. One can see the conundrum, as far as both local tourist offices and politicians are concerned; those attempting to attract people to the restorative beauties of the southern Bavarian Alps hardly wish to emphasize these uncomfortable aspects of Bavaria's 'heritage', whatever the attractions of a day trip to Hitler's phenomenal base, high up on the mountains with panoramic views, near Berchtesgaden. Nor do they want, necessarily, to encourage still surviving followers of Hitler to engage in nostalgic reminiscences or foment resentment.

But the past could not be entirely ignored. Nor could it be presented with quite the simplicity of the East German approach. Different political and social groups had different interests and agendas: what finally came to be represented in the western landscapes of memory was very much the result of active pressures from particular quarters. In the 1950s it was politically not only acceptable, but even officially desirable, to enshrine the memories of the 'respectable' resistance to Hitler. Hence the 'Gedenkstätte Deutscher Widerstand' was opened in 1952 in the renamed Stauffenbergstraße (formerly Bendlerstraße) in Berlin, commemorating those associated with the 1944 'July Plot'; similarly unproblematic was the 'Gedenkstätte für die Opfer der Hitlerdiktatur', commemorating the (mainly German) victims of Nazism at Berlin's Plötzensee jail. But it was less clear how, if at all, to remember those Germans who were doing the repressing. A not entirely unfair generalization would suggest that it was only by dint of sustained pressure from groups of victims and their political sympathizers that widely shared local desires to cover up the past and kick over the traces could be effectively challenged. Let us take a few examples of places of former Nazi repression and terror which could hardly be ignored: the concentration camps of Dachau, Bergen-Belsen and Flossenbürg, and the so-called *Gestapo-Gelände* (Gestapo territory) in Berlin.

Dachau was the first Nazi concentration camp, opened with a great deal of publicity (and apparently considerable public acclaim, in the interests of 'restoring law and order') in March 1933. Its building – using prisoners as labourers – was finally completed in 1938. Unlike the death camps in the East, which were opened specifically for purposes of extermination on largely 'racial' grounds, Dachau was used in the main for German political prisoners, including members of the German Communist party (KPD), the SPD and Christians. Around 200,000 were imprisoned here; many thousands – perhaps 30,000 – died as a result of execution, torture, malnutrition, illness, or 'medical' experiments; and a further unknown number died as a result of death marches and mass shootings. Dachau was liberated by the Americans, which is why its name became synonymous for Americans with the Nazi system of terror, in the way that 'Belsen' came to resonate with the British.

Dachau was maintained in active use for two major groups of people after 1945: first, political prisoners (including members of the SS, awaiting trial in the 'Dachau trials') immediately after the war; then, from 1948 to 1960, for refugees and displaced persons.[23] The question of whether the place should be a site of memory – and if so, whose memory – or swept under the carpet by contemporary uses was a political flashpoint throughout the 1950s. Dachau local politicians were backed by the Bavarian *Land* government in supporting the latter view, against the opposition of Americans and victims' groups. There was a brief and unsuccessful attempt in the mid-1950s by the Americans to set up an exhibit with photographs of atrocities, which was closed after vociferous protests from local notables. Attempts by Dachau survivors to stage a tenth anniversary commemoration were similarly met with strenuous local opposition, including the extraordinary charge that it was the Americans who had erected the second crematorium and gas chamber as 'anti-German propaganda'.[24] Local Germans often felt that the prisoners of war who had been interned after 1945 were more worthy of remembrance than their pre-1945 predecessors.

It was only in the 1960s that Dachau was finally designated a place of historical significance and remembrance in the broader context of 'overcoming the [Nazi] past'. In largely Catholic Bavaria, it was of considerable importance that many Catholics had died there for their opposition to Hitler, and the first lasting memorial to be erected at Dachau, in 1960, was the Catholic chapel and 'monument of atonement', with a large cross and crown of thorns, inaugurating a controversial tradition of 'Christianization' of the memorial. On 9 May 1965, twenty years after the end of the war, the Dachau Museum was dedicated, and two years later, on 8 May 1967, a Jewish memorial chapel was consecrated. The pressures of the survivors and those speaking for the less fortunate victims had succeeded in placing Dachau on the tourist map (aided by its proximity and good transport links to Munich) but it had become clear that, without political pressure from interested parties, Dachau would have gone much the same way as the Nazi Party Rally stadium in Nuremberg. It appeared to need the efforts of representatives of erstwhile victims and victors to remind the heirs of the perpetrators of their duty to preserve and present the traces of the past. Where there were no victims, but only the actions of the perpetrators, it was easier to ignore the site, cover over the traces.

In order for Dachau to be opened to the public, much of the disused and often also reused remnants had to be physically rebuilt. New barracks were erected on the sites of the original

---

[23] For fuller accounts, see Young, *Texture of Memory*, pp. 60–72, and Reichel, *Politik mit der Erinnerung*, pp. 149–54.
[24] Young, *Texture of Memory*, pp. 63–4.

barracks which had been torn down.[25] What visitors in the 1970s and 1980s saw was – under the tender care of the Bavarian Office for the Administration of Castles, Gardens and Lakes, which until the 1990s held responsibility for the site – a highly sanitized, orderly and hygienic version of the past: clean, neat, calm and in no way an adequate representation of what had actually taken place on this territory nearly half a century before. Furthermore, the small town of Dachau, in its tourist literature, did its best to dissociate itself from the reason for its economically beneficial but nevertheless somewhat unwelcome fame: it reinforced what had effectively become the West German national myth, that the German people had never really welcomed or actively contributed to the Nazi system of terror, that they really had 'known nothing about it', and that subsequent ritualized professions of horror and shame would both prove their innocence and contribute to some form of national atonement.

If it is hard to imagine the realities of the past in Dachau, it is near to impossible in Bergen-Belsen. This site appears less a former concentration camp than a national memorial dropped in a spot of heathland where there happen to be mass graves of victims. One would not know, from visiting Belsen, any more of what it had really been like than if one read any number of books and looked at photos in other exhibitions without having set foot on the Lüneberg Heath itself.

The British decided already in October 1945 to preserve the area as a site of memory and warning (there is, interestingly, no single word in English equivalent to the German '*Mahnmal*'), and to make appropriate and dignified arrangements for the mass graves of those who had died there. But attempts in 1946 by the Jewish Central Committee in the British zone to ensure that some remnants of the actual camp would remain, and that the administration of the memorial site would not be turned over to German hands, were unsuccessful. The prisoners' barracks had already been burnt down in May 1945 by the British occupation forces, fearful of typhus. The barracks which had housed the SS were used as a refugee camp until 1952, when they too were pulled down. On 30 November 1952 the former camp was officially opened as a memorial site by Federal President Theodor Heuss. In the following decades, great efforts were devoted to the construction of a range of appropriate memorials to the members of a variety of groups who had died here (including, in 1979, a memorial to the Sinti and Roma, usually left out of the articulate culture of memory). The educational aspects of

[25] Cf. Reichel, *Politik mit der Erinnerung*, p. 149.

the site also received a good deal of attention, with a documentation centre and exhibition seeking to inform the public about the realities of the Nazi period. Yet, for all the earnestness and undoubted political will which has gone into this site, it remains controversial. In James Young's view, for example, it epitomizes, not the experience of life in the concentration camps for the inmates, but only death and burial; it is a memory, as Young puts it, not of the inmates' experience, but of the Germans' experience.[26]

Flossenbürg provides a further version of West German difficulties in 'getting it right'. Opened in 1938, this concentration camp on the Bavarian/Bohemian border was primarily for political prisoners, including notable figures such as Pastor Dietrich Bonhoeffer of the Protestant anti-Nazi 'Confessing Church' (*Bekennende Kirche*), Admiral Canaris and General Oster of the conservative/nationalist and military resistance, and the lone would-be assassin Georg Elser. Flossenbürg was also the centre of a network of *Außenlager*. Somewhere in the region of 30,000 people lost their lives as a direct result of killing, cruelty, disease, or on the death marches as the American troops closed in and the Nazis fled the camp. From July 1945 to April 1946 it was used as an internment camp for around 4,000 members of the SS awaiting trial; it was also used, from autumn 1945 until the end of 1947, for displaced persons, mostly Polish workers who had been brought to Germany as forced labourers, as well as former concentration camp inmates and prisoners of war.

Despite the relatively early decision to erect a memorial chapel (for which the foundation stone was laid on 1 September 1946), and to give the victims of the death marches their own burial place in a cemetery in the small town of Flossenbürg (where they were buried *en masse* at a ceremony in which locals were forced somewhat unwillingly to participate), a great deal of energy was spent on removing the visible traces of the camp. From 1948 'resettlers' from lost eastern provinces were moved to make new homes there, and by 1950 residents appeared to be making relatively free use of the area of the camp and the excellent building materials offered by its granite stones.[27] This shocked the then Deputy Minister President and Minister of Justice in Bavaria, Dr Josef Müller, himself a former inmate of the camp, and pressures were increased for a more appropriate mode of dealing with the ruins of history. In 1958 the somewhat unwilling local civic authorities were formally

[26] Young, *Texture of Memory*, pp. 56–9.
[27] On Flossenbürg, see e.g. G. E. Schafft and Gerhard Zeidler, *Die KZ-Mahn-und Gedenkstätten in Deutschland* (Berlin: Dietz Verlag, 1996), pp. 119–42. They speak of the 'wilde "Demontage"' of the camp in the early 1950s; cf. p. 137.

obliged to take over the camp as a memorial site, and to remove those who were living happily on its territory. Nevertheless, from 1960 branches of industry started to make use of some of the buildings, and in 1964 the prison building was almost completely demolished. Only as late as 1979 was an 'information room' opened; and in 1982 a trade union youth group began to pressurize for increased research and more active commemoration. The 'Gedenkstätte', which had been officially under the care of the Bavarian Office for the Administration of Castles, Gardens and Lakes since the 1950s, was finally reconceived and publicized as a place of remembrance in 1984.

To any casual visitor in the mid-1980s, Flossenbürg appeared less a 'former concentration camp' than, as the official leaflet serving as a brochure terms it, a 'KZ-Grab-und Gedenkstätte' (Concentration Camp grave and memorial site). While the foundations of the prison barracks have been 'retained...in order to show the original extent of the building and the courtyard', it was necessary to reconstruct two cells to demonstrate what they must have looked like.[28] These cells are models of whitewashing and stripped pine furniture; to this observer at least, they looked more like advertisements for student residences than reconstructions of concentration camp conditions. Mass graves are arranged in a 'garden of remembrance', with assorted memorials erected by members of different nations. Near to the surviving crematorium there is, as the leaflet laconically puts it, 'a memorial stone with a Hebrew inscription' (no attempt at translation or conveying the meaning of the words). Granite stones from one of the watchtowers were used to construct a '*Sühnekapelle*' (chapel of atonement), with a variety of Christian symbols and memorials. A very small exhibition provides some historical information.[29]

Flossenbürg is in many respects an excellent example of the problems West Germans had with their landscapes of memory. The immediate exigencies of the post-war years took priority at first: the need for internment camps, or for housing displaced persons and refugees, took clear precedence over preserving memory. Rationalizations, such as the desire to eradicate 'unhygienic' conditions in which typhus had been rife, or the financial value and practical importance of good building materials in the time of

---

[28] Guide leaflet to *KZ-Grab-und Gedenkstätte Flossenbürg* (probably 1984: no place of publication, date, or pagination).
[29] Far greater efforts were devoted to extending the scope of the Flossenbürg site in 1995, the year of the fiftieth anniversary of its liberation and the end of the war; see Schafft and Ziedler, *KZ-Mahn-und Gedenkstätten*, pp. 138–9.

'*Wiederaufbau*' (rebuilding), were plausible excuses for erasing the traces. Attempts at memorialization, at providing places for contemplation and commemoration, were instigated by victims' organizations, committees of those who had survived, relatives of the deceased, or – initially – by the Americans in a context when denazification was still a live political issue. Whatever their ostensible, conscious motives for particular acts (such as removal of stones or other materials), most local Germans would on the whole have preferred to consolidate the view that 'they never knew anything about it' by removing the evidence for subsequent generations. It is easier to believe that something was never there, that one never knew, when it is no longer visible.

Let us take, as a final example of the acutely sensitive and politicized character of western landscapes of memory, the by now renowned case of the so-called 'Gestapo-Gelände' in Berlin.[30] The area around the former Wilhelmstraße and Prinz-Albrecht-Straße (now Niederkirchnerstraße) in the centre of Berlin was, in the Nazi era, the centre of the terror apparatus of the Third Reich, home to the Gestapo, the SS, the SD, the criminal police, and from 1939 the all-encompassing RSHA (Reichssicherheitshauptamt or Reich Security Main Office). The individuals most closely associated with the activities of these organizations of repression – Himmler, Heydrich, Eichmann, Kaltenbrunner – all had their offices in this area. Around 7,000 bureaucrats came to work daily in the grandiose buildings in this area, including the former Prinz-Albrecht-Palais, Prinz Albrecht Hotel, and Kunstgewerbeschule: these were the men who only 'sat behind desks', but in whose hands lay many of the strings of the system of terror. Nor was this only a site of decision-making and report-filing far from the locations of actual murder: in the cellars below the Gestapo building at Prinz-Albrecht-Straße 8, prisoners were brought for 'hearings', including shorter or longer periods of imprisonment and torture, ending in many cases in death.

The area was effectively divided by the zonal boundary in Berlin, which divided the Soviet zone in the east from the western zones, and which eventually became the no-man's-land and death strip of the Berlin Wall. On the eastern side, in the GDR, the Wilhelmstraße was renamed and the buildings appropriated for other purposes.

---

[30] See esp. the exhibition volume, produced in connection with Berlin's 750th anniversary, under the direction of Reinhard Rürup, *Topographie des Terrors. Gestapo, SS und Reichssicherheitshauptamt auf dem 'Prinz-Albrecht-Gelände'. Eine Dokumentation* (Berlin: Verlag Willmuth Arenhövel, 1987). See also Reichel, *Politik mit der Erinnerung*, pp. 196–202.

On the western side, West Berlin's front-line location in the Cold War provided an enhanced pretext for an early covering over the traces of the past. As far as the Americans were concerned, the Berlin blockade of 1948–9 transformed the West Berliners from ex-Nazis to be instinctively distrusted into bastions of the last outpost of democracy, to be supported at all costs. This was compounded, as elsewhere, by the Germans' prioritization of material needs – the collection of firewood and building materials in a situation of acute shortages – over preservation of the evidence of past crimes committed in their name. Current survival took clear precedence over commemoration, even for those who had any genuine interest in the latter.

In 1949, the bombed-out ruins of the Prinz-Albrecht-Palais were dynamited. Further ruins, including those of buildings which could potentially have been saved, were destroyed in the following years. By 1963, virtually the entire area had been cleared, leaving only a relatively empty landscape with heaps of rubble, which, in this deserted area hard-up against the Wall, were of little interest to the historically uninitiated. With the American crossing point 'Checkpoint Charlie' and its sensationalist museum documenting dramatic tales of escape from the GDR just around the corner, the tourist trail led into the black-and-white story of democracy versus dictatorship in the contemporary world, with little thought for the murky past of this weed-covered landscape.

It was only in the late 1970s that historical interest was again awakened, partly at the instigation of the architectural historian Dieter Hoffmann-Axthelm. Pressure began to mount against resurrected plans (which had been floated but never acted upon since 1957) to build over the area permanently as part of a rapid-transit road, displacing its interim uses for unofficial driving without a driving licence and as a builders' tip. The area was even more sensitive as far as West Germany's memorial culture was concerned because it was located right in front of the Martin-Gropius Building, which in the 1980s started to be used for occasional historical exhibitions (such as the Prussia exhibition of 1981, *Preußen – Versuch einer Bilanz*) and which was scheduled to house the big 'Berlin-Berlin' 750th anniversary exhibition of 1987. In 1982 the issue was debated by the West Berlin city council, where the Social Democrats urged use of the site for memorial purposes. A competition for appropriate designs for a memorial, promoted by the then ruling mayor of West Berlin (and later Federal President) Richard von Weizsäcker, was announced in 1983. The competition, which specified that the winning design would reconcile the mutually incompatible aims of appropriate historical dignity and enjoyment of current leisure, provoked massive political controversies. On the one hand were those who were furious that attempts at putting a line under the past – a *Schlußstrich* – were yet again being thwarted; on the other were those who felt that the appalling past of this quarter should in some way be marked and remembered. The winners of this competition were informed in 1984 by the new ruling mayor, Eberhard Diepgen, that the Berlin Senate had decided that the winning design should not be realized, and that the Martin-Gropius Building would temporarily take over the area in connection with its own preparations for the 1987 Berlin exhibition.

On 8 May 1985 an unforeseen development occurred, effectively deflecting the controversy over modes of symbolic commemoration. An unofficial dig on the site, by members of the local 'Active Museum', revealed the remains of cellars of the building adjacent to the Gestapo Headquarters: the 'house-prison' of the Gestapo, in which many members of the resistance had been interrogated and tortured. This find of 'real' remains of the past was further confirmed as more official excavations continued during the summer. Under the historian Reinhard Rürup's direction, an exhibition was rapidly mounted and installed in time for the 1987 'celebrations' of Berlin's 750-year history.

The 'topography of terror' was an area which lacked the early input of victims' organizations, and where the post-war interests of the Americans lay more in camouflage than commemoration. It was thus only very late that the memory of repression, of truly *German* history, was brought to the surface, literally, by a belated digging up of what remained after the razing to the ground of the early post-war period. That its re-presentation should be accompanied by so much controversy and heated debate is indicative of the continued sensitivity of the Nazi past even in the 1980s, forty years after the Federal Republic had proved its democratic credentials and its massively successful transformation. In many respects, this site at the heart of Berlin epitomizes the ways in which the past refused to become history.

Political topography and historical consciousness

Millions of people, in both East and West Germany, had their brief encounters – whether through enforced school trips, or youth-group outings, or in a voluntary flight of historical tourism – with the places of Nazi terror. It is hard to ascertain the extent to which, and the ways in which, these physical encounters left traces in popular historical consciousness. At a superficial level, post-war citizens of both West and East Germany could not claim ignorance of the physical brutality and sadism of the Nazis: it is virtually impossible to make even the most superficial visit to a place of Nazi terror without experiencing feelings of sheer revulsion and disbelief, an incapacity to understand how it was possible for such inhumanity, such cruelty, to have been perpetrated on so many people for so long. The evidence suggests that by the time of unification Germans, both East and West, were remarkably well informed about the Nazi concentration camps; basic factual knowledge (for example, recognition of concentration camp names, or correctly naming the yellow star as the symbol Jews were made to wear) was even marginally higher among East Germans than West Germans, while both scored far higher than, say, Americans.[31] But, for several reasons, one has to be cautious about extrapolating further than this about the wider historical picture into which such feelings might be inserted.

A number of other influences have to be taken into account, beyond the manner in which the past was presented through these surviving and reconstructed landscapes. We shall look in the following chapters at some other forms in which the past was variously interpreted and re-presented in public, and at their interactions with private conversations and memories. Quite apart from these other influences on historical consciousness, we have to remember too that people for most of the time inhabited other landscapes: landscapes of the present, which might be infinitely more important in determining feelings of identity and belonging; and other landscapes of the past, which might evoke quite different emotions.

The sites and memorials which have been surveyed, however briefly and selectively, in this chapter may be 'lieux de mémoire', to use the expression popularized by Pierre Nora; but they do not, collectively, amount to the simple construction of a 'collective memory'. They are perhaps better viewed as potential triggers, signposts, or camouflage; a symbolic maze which deflects attention, refracts the light, erects distorted mirrors and glazed windows,

---

[31] See the extensive analysis and comparison of a range of surveys and cross-national data in Hermann Kurthen, 'Antisemitism and Xenophobia in United Germany. How the Burden of the Past Affects the Present', in Hermann Kurthen, Werner Bergmann and Rainer Erb (eds), *Antisemitism and Xenophobia in Germany after Unification* (New York and Oxford: Oxford University Press, 1997); see also, for surveys of West German youth in 1985 and 1990, Renata Barlog-Scholz, *Historisches Wissen über die National-Sozialistischen Konzentrationslager bei deutschen Jugendlichen* (Frankfurt am Main: Peter Lang, 1994), esp. pp. 157–8.

throws unexpected spotlights. And not all participants in the maze progress through all parts, are exposed to all corners; not all look in the mirrors, or notice the shady corners, nor even look closely at what is under the strongest beam of light. These landscapes are the outward parameters of potential memory; they are not its contents.

3

Overcoming the Past in Practice? Trials and Tribulations

In his memoirs, Rudolf Höss, Commandant of Auschwitz from May 1940 to November 1943, and there again in 1944 to oversee the mass murder of the Hungarian Jews in the so-called *Aktion Höss*, describes some of the scenes. His is a sober and relatively dispassionate account:

> Jews selected for gassing were taken as quietly as possible to the crematoria... In the undressing room, prisoners of the special detachment...would tell them in their own language that they were going to be bathed and deloused, that they must leave their clothes neatly together and above all remember where they had put them, so that they would be able to find them again after delousing... After undressing, the Jews went into the gas-chambers, which were furnished with showers and water pipes and gave a realistic impression of a bath house...
> The door would now be quickly screwed up and the gas immediately discharged by the waiting disinfectors [*sic*] through vents in the ceilings of the gas chambers, down a shaft that led to the floor. This ensured the rapid distribution of the gas. It could be observed through the peep-hole in the door that those who were standing nearest to the induction vents were killed at once. It can be said that about one-third died straight away. The remainder staggered about and began to scream and struggle for air. The screaming, however, soon changed to the death rattle and in a few minutes all lay still. After twenty minutes at the latest no movement could be discerned. The time required for the gas to have effect varied according to the weather... It also depended on the quality of the gas... and on the composition of the transports which might contain a high proportion of healthy Jews, or old and sick, or children...

Those who screamed and those who were old or sick or weak, or the small children, died quicker than those who were healthy or young.[1]

Fortunately, this was not a memory shared by too many. But it raises central issues about how, in practice and in public, to 'deal with' a past that not only allowed, but even ordered, this almost unimaginable inhumanity to take place.

When we look at aspects of the public 'overcoming of the past', the story is not simple. On both sides, faltering processes of pursuit of evidence, conduct of trials and attribution of guilt were affected by considerations ranging from the banal and practical through to political interests and prejudices. The public presentation of the past had as much to do with the politics of the present as with any realities of the past.

Even the analyses of the different ways of 'coming to terms with' or 'overcoming' the past were coloured by politics. The GDR repeatedly tried to show not only that the Federal Republic had failed to bring former Nazis to justice, but that many former Nazis held high office in the West German system, and that the Federal Republic was continuing to pursue the ('monopoly capitalist imperialist revanchist' and so on) agenda of the Third Reich under new guises. By contrast, according to the SED, the GDR had truly broken with the past and exorcized all ghosts of Nazism. In the West debates raged, and have continued to rage, over whether there were 'missed opportunities': whether the Federal Republic was dogged from the start by morally dubious compromises, characterized by continuities and restoration rather than seizing the opportunity for a clean break, and whether its belated and inadequate attempts at dealing with the past did not, in effect, amount to a 'second burden of guilt'; or whether, on the contrary, the West did not deal much more effectively and thoroughly with the Nazi past, effectively punishing the offenders, making restitution to the victims, and owning up to its responsibilities, in sharp contrast to the alleged sweeping under the carpet and mendacious self-exoneration of the dictatorial GDR. Since 1990, these debates have continued with the added twist of historical comparison: the 'overcoming of two German dictatorships', 1945 and 1989.[2]

---

[1] Rudolf Höss, *Autobiography of Höss*, in *KL Auschwitz seen by the SS* (Publications of Państwowe Muzeum w Oświęcimiu, 1972), pp. 134–5.

[2] For a selection of recent contributions to these debates, see e.g. Ulrich Brochhagen, *Nach Nürnberg. Vergangenheitsbewältigung und Westintegration in der Ära Adenauer* (Hamburg: Junius Verlag, 1994); Norbert Frei, *Vergangenheitspolitik* (Munich: C. H. Beck, 1996); Jörg Friedrich, *Die kalte Amnestie.*

Whatever else the recent discussions have shown, they have revealed the inadequacy of the stock summary of the 1950s as a period of 'collective amnesia'. In the West there was an incorporation of *collective penance* into public political culture; the counterpart in the East was a form of *official heroism*. Moreover, in different ways in both German states, the identification of criminals and the attribution of guilt did to some extent amount to a *collective amnesty*, in which it was possible for the vast majority of people to profess a degree of innocence and ignorance, and to gain new political credentials by expressions of abhorrence of the past. The politically coloured allotment of the roles of heroes, victims and villains did much to lay the tracks for subsequent public engagement with the past.

Where have all the Nazis gone?

In both the western and eastern zones of occupation, and the two German states after 1949, 'overcoming the past' was in fact an integral feature of politics in the present. The story of early attempts at denazification combines a variety of often mutually contradictory strands: Allied attempts to root out erstwhile enemies, committed Nazis, were to some extent mitigated by considerations of administrative and technical competence; German responses varied dramatically in relation both to former involvement in the Nazi regime and considerations of survival in the present.

It has long been well known that the western Allies, and in particular the Americans, soon abandoned their early views on 'collective guilt' in favour of salvaging administrative and technical expertise.[3] Curiously, the massive public efforts devoted to exposing Nazi crimes in the Nuremberg war-crimes trials assisted a

---

NS-Täter in der Bundesrepublik (Frankfurt am Main: Fischer, 1985); Ralph Giordano, *Die zweite Schuld, oder Von der Last Deutscher zu sein* (Hamburg: Rasch and Röhrig, 1987); Ulrich Herbert and Olaf Groehler, *Zweierlei Bewältigung: Vier Beiträge über den Umgang mit der NS-Vergangenheit in beiden deutschen Staaten* (Hamburg: Ergebnisse Verlag, 1992); Jeffrey Herf, *Divided Memory. The Nazi Past in the Two Germanies* (Cambridge, Mass.: Harvard University Press, 1997); Christa Hoffmann, *Stunden Null? Vergangenheitsbewältigung in Deutschland 1945 und 1989* (Bonn and Berlin: Bouvier, 1992); Manfred Kittel, *Die Legende von der 'zweiten Schuld'. Vergangenheitsbewältigung in der Ära Adenauer* (Berlin: Ullstein, 1993); Klaus Suhl (ed.), *Vergangenheitsbewältigung 1945 – 1989: Ein unmöglicher Vergleich?* (Berlin: Verlag Volk und Welt, 1994).
    [3] The initial American policy directive of April 1945, known as *JCS 1067*, is reprinted in Beate Ruhm von Oppen (ed.), *Documents on Germany under*

complementary process amounting, eventually, almost to a collective amnesty for the rest of the German people.

Where there was no immediate suspicion of being classified as a war criminal, denazification in the western zones rapidly became a matter of issuing 'Persil certificates' (to use the popular term *Persilscheine*), providing assurance of political cleansing so that people could return to their former offices and take up normal life again.[4] Despite a few hiccups along the way, the vast majority of teachers, civil servants, and others regained their former positions, and there was no radical restructuring of the economy.[5] A significant number of scientists and other technical experts were even taken directly into the service of the United States in its Cold War efforts against the by now common enemy, the Soviet Union.

Attitudes among West Germans towards the past and to denazification on the whole divided, not surprisingly, according to previous political fault lines: but soon post-war developments overlaid and complicated prior commitments. The enthusiasm of indigenous German anti-fascist committees was rapidly dampened by Allied suspicion and repression. The very process of going through denazification tribunals helped to shape at least the outlines of a (sometimes overstated) 'community of the oppressed' among those adversely affected by denazification. One of the unintended consequences was quite clearly to dissuade a significant proportion of Germans from taking any active part in politics at all.

The Americans in particular carried out detailed opinion polls during the occupation period which, even if the precise results need to be treated with caution, are quite revealing in their broad

---

Occupation, 1945–1954 (London: OUP/Royal Institute of International Affairs, 1955), pp. 13–27.

[4] The classic study of Bavaria is by Lutz Niethammer, *Die Mitläuferfabrik*, originally published as *Entnazifizierung in Bayern* (Frankfurt am Main: Fischer, 1972). For a local study of Hanover, in the British zone, see Barbara Marshall, *The Origins of Post-War German Politics* (London: Croom Helm, 1988), ch. 2. See also e.g. Edward N. Peterson, *The American Occupation of Germany* (Detroit: Wayne State University Press, 1978), ch. 4, 'Retreat from Forced Denazification', and Raymond Ebsworth, *Restoring Democracy in Germany: The British Contribution* (London: Stevens and Sons, 1960), ch. 1, 'The First Appointments and Denazification'. There are now a variety of local studies which come to much the same conclusions.

[5] See e.g. the overviews and collections of documents in: C. Kleßmann, *Die doppelte Staatsgründung. Deutsche Geschichte 1945–1955* (Göttingen: Vandenhoeck and Ruprecht, 1982); R. Steininger, *Deutsche Geschichte seit 1945*, vol. 1 (1945–47) and vol. 2 (1948–55) (Frankfurt am Main: Fischer, rev. and expanded edn, 1996); Clemens Vollnhals, *Entnazifizierung. Politische Säuberung und Rehabilitierung in den vier Besatzungszonen 1945–1949* (Munich: dtv, 1991).

outlines. Responses to the opinion surveys carried out for the Information Control Division of the Office of Military Government for Germany (U.S.) (OMGUS) varied relatively clearly according to whether one was a former member of the Nazi Party or NSDAP (a so-called Pg), a relative of a former Pg, or a non-affiliated person. There were also significant differences in different social groups: for example, lack of acceptance of responsibility for the war was most prevalent among Bavarians, residents of small towns and medium-sized cities, older people, males, those with less then eight years education, Catholics, and conservatives or non-politicals; conversely, those with more education, living in larger towns and cities, Protestants, and SPD members had significantly different views. But there are some interesting generalizations which can be drawn from these surveys.

The adverse economic consequences of denazification for former Pgs seemed the greatest source of irritation to themselves and to their relatives. They also reveal a combination of a formalistic assent to the rules of democracy as a civic duty, and a general unwillingness to recognize responsibility for the sins of the Nazi past. Others felt that former 'big fish' were getting away with relatively lenient treatment, while 'small fry' were taking the brunt of punishment. In the course of 1946, lack of food, and worries over prisoners of war and missing people, topped the list of 'Cares and Worries', while by April 1947, as far as denazification was concerned, in general 'public sentiment...was firmly behind a "forgive and forget" policy.' The professed satisfaction of Germans with denazification policies appears to have declined steadily; meanwhile, although the numbers fluctuated slightly, the proportions agreeing with the statement that 'National Socialism was a bad idea' declined from 41 per cent in November 1945 to 32 per cent in May 1947, and those agreeing that it was a 'good idea, badly carried out' rose slightly from 53 per cent in November 1945 to 55 per cent in May 1947. The proportions opting for 'National Socialism', when asked which government they would prefer to live under if given the choice between that, communism, or neither, steadily rose.[6] Whatever else denazification in the American zone

---

[6] OMGUS, *Records of United States Occupation Headquarters, World War II Record Group 260*, Munich, Institut für Zeitgeschichte, DK 110.001. Similar patterns of response are evident in other sources for the American zone, e.g. *Functional History of Military Government, Bremen Enclave* (IfZ: Fg 23), and for the British zone, e.g. in the *Monthly Reports of the Control Commission for Germany (British Element)* (IfZ: DK 200.001). See also A. J. Merritt and R. L. Merritt, *Public Opinion in Occupied Germany: The OMGUS Surveys 1945–1949* (Urbana: University of Illinois Press, 1963).

was achieving, it was clearly not achieving any kind of adequate reckoning with the past.

The turnover of personnel in the Soviet zone was, for most occupational groups, far higher. The dramatic socioeconomic revolution carried out very early on in the Soviet zone – land reform in 1945, expropriation of industry and finance in 1946 – ensured an apparent denazification, or at least a major turnover of personnel, in many areas of the economy. Professional groups in education, the civil service and local administration, the judiciary and so on were far more thoroughly purged than in the western zones, largely for directly instrumental political reasons: where the position was politically sensitive, former NSDAP members were replaced with politically reliable although often technically less competent individuals, at least for as long as the latter were prepared to toe the party line.[7]

However, even in the Soviet zone the picture is more complex than previously realized. At issue was less any commitment to denazification in principle than putting through communist policies (in all the twists and turns of the official line) in practice. As Naimark has shown, often it was Germans who wanted to oust particular well-known former Nazis from a particular office or enterprise, while the Russian occupation authorities preferred to retain them on the basis of their expertise. And the Russians were arguably even more energetic than the Americans in their pursuit of Nazi scientists, engaging in wholesale but remarkably polite kidnapping of those they deemed essential to Soviet scientific efforts in the post-war arms race.[8] The medical profession was far less severely denazified than other comparable professions, given the urgent health needs of the population (occupiers and occupied alike) after the war; and the churches were left to 'denazify themselves', in which task they revealed a signal lack of energy despite a greater degree of willingness to confess a sense of moral guilt and responsibility for the past.[9] Even where there was a relatively high degree of initial turnover of personnel, as among schoolteachers,

---

[7] See e.g. the detailed statistical breakdowns in Vollnhals, *Entnazifizierung*, pp. 227–36. It is notable that, for example, by Dec. 1948 only 6.1 per cent of those employed in Thuringian ministries were former NSDAP members, compared to 30.4 per cent of those employed by the Deutsche Reichsbahn in Thuringia (pp. 230–1).

[8] See Norman Naimark, *The Russians in Germany: A History of the Soviet Zone of Occupation, 1945–1949* (Cambridge, Mass.: Harvard University Press, 1995).

[9] On doctors and pastors, see the very interesting analysis by Christoph Kleßmann, 'Relikte des Bildungsbürgertums in der DDR', in Hartmut Kaelble,

the effects were often not quite what was intended (with very young and rapidly trained *Neulehrer* thrust in front of classes found to be repeating what they had themselves so recently learned as schoolchildren or students under the Nazis); moreover, many former schoolteachers were soon reinstated, such that, for example, around one-quarter of former Nazi teachers in Saxony who had lost their jobs had been reinstated by 1951.[10]

Moreover, the introduction in 1947 of a distinction between 'active' and 'nominal' Nazis, the termination of general denazification in 1948, and the prioritization of willingness to contribute to the new (socialist) future over a compromised past, soon brought about a degree of tentative conformity to the new circumstances in the Soviet zone. Uppermost in most people's minds, here as in the West, were worries about sheer physical survival, the whereabouts and well-being of loved ones and, in the case of refugees, the search for a new home. These concerns were further overlain by the impact of Soviet occupation itself, in particular the very widespread experiences of rape and burglary.

The effects of denazification processes in both East and West Germany were such as to block any honest soul-searching: most Germans were more concerned with a combination of sheer physical survival and the scramble for place in the new political circumstances of the post-war world. Thus for most people rationalization and repression were more common responses than genuine confrontation with issues of guilt and exoneration. The re-education efforts of, particularly, the British and Americans, may have influenced a few minds at the time and, more importantly, helped form the contours for a new liberal public culture, mightily assisted by prominent and critical German writers, journalists and publishers;[11] but even exposure to the horrifying revelations in the press

---

Jürgen Kocka and Hartmut Zwahr (eds), *Sozialgeschichte der DDR* (Stuttgart: Klett-Cotta, 1994). Doctors had had a disproportionately high NSDAP membership, reaching as high as 80 per cent of Thuringian doctors in the wartime years, 84 per cent of the medical faculty at Halle University, and 87 per cent among faculty professors; there was very little denazification of the medical profession after 1945 because of the drastic health situation (see p. 257; on light denazification of pastors, see p. 263).

[10] In the Soviet zone as a whole, around 72 per cent of the 28,000 teachers had belonged to the NSDAP. See Joachim Petzold, 'Die Entnazifizierung der sächsischen Lehrerschaft 1945' in Jürgen Kocka (ed.), *Historische DDR-Forschung* (Berlin: Akademie Verlag, 1993), p. 88; for figures on Saxony see pp. 102–3.

[11] See e.g. Nicholas Pronay and Keith Wilson (eds), *The Political Re-education of Germany and her Allies* (London: Croom Helm, 1985); Manfred Heinemann (ed.), *Umerziehung und Wiederaufbau* (Stuttgart: Klett-Cotta, 1981);

of former atrocities, as brought out in documentary films on the concentration camps (such as *Todesmühlen*) or through daily reports of evidence given in the Nuremberg Trials, did little to effect any widespread or active engagement with the issue of complicity in the horrific past that was being displayed. The very fact that only a handful of evil men were being brought to some form of legal justice only served to underline the essentially exonerating view that it was a small gang of criminals who had led the majority of innocent Germans astray.

Land of heroes? The disappearance of victims and perpetrators in the GDR

By the 1950s, the vast majority of the German people – on both sides of the Iron Curtain – appeared to have a relatively clean bill of political health. Exoneration for those willing to play their allotted roles within the new political parameters was available in both East and West. Clearly there were important differences, but collusion in a myth of innocence for the masses was perhaps more important than the widespread generalization about collective amnesia.

In the GDR, the new political elites were genuinely former anti-Nazis, consisting of those who had escaped or survived Nazi persecution. The dominant elements at the apex of GDR politics were predominantly those Moscow-trained Communists who had also managed to survive Stalin's purges, although former Social Democrats and Communists with rather different pre-1945 experiences (exile in the west, emergence from concentration camps) also played important roles. They genuinely believed in the urgency of creating a better Germany, of overthrowing the fascist past for ever. As far as their own roles were concerned, there was a real (if often idealized) basis for the founding anti-fascist myth of the GDR. But along with the (in most cases well-deserved) myths of heroism and resistance of the communist leaders went the myth of innocence of the workers and peasants.

What is important here is the fact that, for all their private memories and potential feelings of guilt, it was a myth which appears to have gone down relatively well with the vast mass of the East German population. Recent social historical research does not appear to show up denazification in particular, or the Nazi issue in general, as a live topic of current popular concern in the

Günter Pakschies, *Umerziehung in der britischen Zone* (Weinheim and Basel: Beltz Verlag, 1979).

GDR of the 1950s.[12] Far more important were concerns relating to the present: fears of a third world war, hopes for reunification, grumbles over wages, food shortages, restrictions on travel, closed borders with the west, and so on. 'Overcoming the past' was simply not much of an issue for the vast majority of East Germans who had far more trouble 'coming to terms' with the present.

It was in any event complicated by SED misuse of the term 'fascism' to apply not so much, or not only, to genuine former Nazis, but to anyone who criticized the self-professedly anti-fascist state of the GDR – in other words, to apply both to genuine sympathizers with western democracy, including social democrats, as well as to real former Nazis and other right-wing ideological opponents. In their constant battles against the 'class enemy' at home, the GDR regime sought to portray anyone who criticized or sought to escape from the GDR as influenced by or siding with the 'fascists', used almost indiscriminately to describe anything to do with western democracy as well as the Nazi past. It is certainly the case that periodically, and particularly when provoked by specific incidents or centres of unrest, the SED investigated real evidence of former Nazi affiliations and activities among members of the East German populace. But as far as the projected image and public picture was concerned, the 'workers and peasants' of the GDR were, after the immediate period of denazification and social transformation was over, collectively innocent. Any evidence to the contrary was merely evidence of enemy activities and infiltration of 'agents provocateurs' or 'saboteurs' from the west. In the simplistic view projected officially by the SED, the West was the real home of former Nazis: hence Nazism was scarcely an issue on the domestic front.

Indeed, if former fellow-travellers in the GDR were prepared to engage their energies in constructing the new society, and were sufficiently useful to the regime for its own purposes, they could do very well out of the situation. Thus for example former Gestapo informers who were prepared to turn into informers for the new East German state security service (Stasi) were amply rewarded; similarly, pre-1945 political splits could be exploited by the SED for the co-option of new supporters.[13] Those belonging to essential

[12] Cf. e.g. Mark Allinson, *Faith, Hope and Apathy: Popular Opinion in Thuringia, 1945–1968* (Manchester University Press, forthcoming; UCL PhD thesis, 1997).

[13] e.g. Gerhard Lotz, an informer first against the Confessing Church for the Nazis, and then a Stasi informer successfully influencing both policy and personnel decisions within the Thuringian church for the SED. Lotz provides a good illustration of the more general issue of the ways in which the SED used

professions with a high degree of expertise, such as medical doctors, were rewarded with relatively high salaries and perks (although their children were disadvantaged with respect to higher education) in order to counteract any temptation to flee to the West.[14] One of the bloc parties, the NDPD (National Democratic Party of Germany), had indeed been expressly founded in order to incorporate former Nazis in the new regime. The SED had to work with what it found, and a willingness to cooperate and make a positive contribution was in general sufficient to outweigh any previous complicity. The myth of innocence might have been at least a welcome hiding place for individuals who were not among those designated to have been sufficiently complicit to be interned in former concentration camps or removed to prisoner-of-war camps in the Soviet Union by the communists after the war.

Perhaps the greatest difference between the 'historical pictures' propagated in the two states had to do with official perceptions of the victims of Nazism. In the very early years of the GDR, Jews (and other politically less than correct groups) more or less disappeared as official victims, to be replaced by 'fighters against fascism' as heroes of the resistance. Thus, for example, the early post-war organization for 'Victims of Fascism' (*Opfer des Faschismus*) was at first most concerned with the KPD, excluding both Jews and Jehovah's Witnesses from its brief.[15] It was soon taken over by the formation of the *Vereinigung für die Verfolgten des Naziregimes* (VVN, the Association of those Persecuted by the Nazi Regime), which made a legal distinction between 'resistance worthy of recognition' and that which was to be 'devalued' (*anerkennenswerten und entwerteten Widerstand*).[16] A purge of VVN members in 1950 excluded 1,200 of the 9,000 members, in the main those who were politically out of line (such as those unorthodox communists dubbed 'Trotskyists', as well as Social Democrats now termed 'Schumacher agents' working for the West), as well as former

---

conflicts between former pro-Nazi 'German Christians' and anti-Nazi members of the Confessing Church to split the Protestant churches and increase communist infiltration and control; cf. M. Fulbrook, *Anatomy of a Dictatorship* (Oxford: Oxford University Press, 1995), ch. 4.

[14] Cf. Kleßmann, 'Relikte'.

[15] See Olaf Groehler, 'Integration und Ausgrenzung von NS-Opfern. Zur Anerkennungs- und Entschädigungsdebatte in der SBZ Deutschlands 1945 bis 1949', in Kocka (ed.), *Historische DDR-Forschung*. (It may parenthetically be remarked that Groehler was subsequently revealed to have been an informer for the Stasi, but it is not my view that this adversely affected his presentation of certain basic facts in this article.)

[16] Ibid., p. 126.

conservative opponents of Hitler associated with the 20 July Plot, and the Jehovah's Witnesses. Those who had been persecuted by the Nazis on grounds of 'race' were almost entirely excluded.[17] In the general context of a wave of official anti-semitism in the communist bloc states following the Slansky Trial of 1952, there was greater repression of Jews in the GDR. The VVN was disbanded and replaced by the *Komitee der antifaschistischen Widerstandskämpfer* (Committee of Anti-Fascist Resistance Fighters); by 30 March 1953 around one-third of Jews previously remaining in East Germany had fled the GDR.[18] Although this wave of official anti-semitism on the domestic front relaxed in 1956, the notion that in the Nazi period there had been only active political resistance, carried on by communists who were now the leading force in the GDR, and the concomitant demotion of what were seen as passive victims, continued as a key myth throughout most of the GDR's history.[19]

Thus the SED externalized the enemy and internalized the victim as heroic opposition. At the same time, the lukewarm and partial character of Western denazification was highly important for the GDR in the SED's attempts to show that West German capitalism represented a true continuity in terms of personnel as well as socio-economic structure with the more overt fascism which had preceded it. The SED did its utmost to portray the West as not only the natural home of ex-Nazis, but also the current and politically dangerous base for continued Nazi or 'fascist' activities. A large number of pamphlets and smear campaigns were devoted, not only to uncovering the sins of the past among members of the West German elite, but also to showing how they perpetuated their 'revanchist' campaigns in subtle and insidious ways in the present. In a series of 'Brown Books' (*Braunbücher*) the East Germans sought to reveal the brown (Nazi) pasts of West Germans in high places; the 1965 catalogue proved such a best-seller that by 1968 they had

[17] Ibid., p. 127.

[18] Mario Keßler, 'Zwischen Repression und Toleranz. Die SED-Politik und die Juden (1949 bis 1967)' in Kocka (ed.), *Historische DDR-Forschung*, p. 153. Keßler suggests (without any definitive evidence) that, in the meantime, many former Nazis who shared the communists' explicit anti-semitism may have felt to some degree rehabilitated; see p. 160. See also the general overview of the role of Jews in GDR society in the Introduction to Robin Ostow, *Jews in Contemporary East Germany* (London: Macmillan, 1989).

[19] This view about the past was of course linked with aspects of continuing SED politics, including anti-Zionism, policies towards Israel, and refusal to acknowledge any responsibility to pay reparations. The official stance on these matters began to soften only in the later 1980s.

produced a third, updated edition.[20] The East German smear campaigns were, however, only one element in the complex processes
of confronting the past in West Germany.

The absent nation? Public penance and strictly limited liability in the West

A variety of factors combined to produce the uneasy and faltering
processes of confronting the past in the West, which in the end
amounted to a pious public confession of collective responsibility
for acts which had been committed, in the passive voice, on the soil
of Germany, in the name of the German people, but apparently not
by any (or many) members of the German people.

Both domestic politics and foreign policy considerations played
key roles in Adenauer's Germany, which was a time of by no means
foreordained successful western integration and political stabilization. The first two years of the new government of the Federal
Republic were marked by energetic attempts in some quarters to
gain the reduction of sentences and/or the release from imprisonment of those who remained incarcerated.[21] Although Adenauer
resisted calls for a 'general amnesty', he trod a delicate line in a
highly sensitive political situation. Fine distinctions were drawn
between a very small group of perpetrators and the mass of those
to be exonerated. The perpetrators who, on this view, genuinely
deserved punishment were now designated as consisting of, on the
one hand, no more than a handful of evil individuals – Hitler,

---

[20] Nationalrat der Nationalen Front des Demokratischen Deutschland:
Dokumentationszentrum der Staatlichen Archivverwaltung der DDR (ed.),
*Braunbuch. Kriegs-und Naziverbrecher in der Bundesrepublik und in Westberlin:
Staat, Wirtschaft, Verwaltung, Armee, Justiz, Wissenschaft* (Berlin: Staatsverlag
der Deutschen Demokratischen Republik, 3rd edn, 1968). Some West Germans
were sufficiently irritated by this to produce their own version concerning
alleged former Nazis still active in high places in the GDR: Olof Kappelt,
Braunbuch DDR: Nazis in der DDR (Berlin: Elisabeth Reichmann Verlag,
1981), dedicated to 'the democratic youth of middle Germany [a right- wing
'revanchist' term for East Germany, implying the borders of 1937] who have
been continuously subjected to a dictatorship since 1933'. The Introduction by
Otto von Habsburg is a vehicle for a sustained diatribe against the 'totalitarian'
GDR; it claims that any NSDAP membership while young cannot be dismissed
as a *'Jugendsünde'* (youthful error) in the GDR (unlike in the Federal Republic)
because to continue to serve a dictatorship shows they have not learned from
their mistakes.
[21] For the following, see esp. Brochhagen, *Nach Nürnberg*; Frei, *Vergangenheitspolitik*; Ulrich Herbert, *Best* (Bonn: Dietz Verlag, 1996).

Himmler, Heydrich and a few others – and, on the other hand, the lower-class thugs, the 'asocials' or innate criminals, who had been the sadistic elements actually running the concentration camps (in the process confirming a long-held conservative nationalist disdain for the lower-class elements in Nazism). In between, on this view, were the very large numbers of those who had merely followed orders, the so-called 'desk perpetrators' (*Schreibtischtäter*), the professional men and the members of socially elite groups who had served in the army and in the organization of the system of terror, who were, as mere 'accessories' ('rendering *Beihilfe*'), effectively exonerated. The concept of 'victors' justice' (*Siegerjustiz*) was employed to imply that these men were unjustly being accused on political grounds of having committed acts which were not in themselves criminal, but were perfectly 'normal' aspects of the conduct of warfare, in the interests of a perfectly proper political cause.

Such a distinction having been made, the path lay open for the reintegration of hundreds of thousands of these accessories to the crime. In 1951, the the so-called '131 Law' (based on Article 131 of the Basic Law) was passed, ensuring continuity of employment or retirement on full pensions for former Nazi civil servants. Such legalized reinstatement was a notable act of collective amnesty.[22] And in 1956 Adenauer scored a considerable domestic political success by obtaining the release and return of German prisoners of war from the Soviet Union, making absolutely no distinction between those who might have been unjustly imprisoned for a whole variety of unrelated reasons and those who were certainly candidates for war-crimes trials. All were, in the West German view, now returning heroes of the Cold War. They were, too, now allotted new roles as heroes of the *Aufbaugeneration*, the generation that built up the new prosperous West Germany from the ruins (the ultimate causes of which need not be explicitly recognized).

The Federal Republic thus delivered up a few sacrificial lambs, in the form of the concession that there actually were some criminals who deserved to stand trial. The mass exoneration of the remainder was an important element in the political integration of potentially disaffected right-wingers in the early years of West German democracy. There were very strong pressures from a number of small right-wing parties, as well as from the (supposedly liberal) FDP (Free Democratic Party), for such exoneration. And for most of the less politically minded population, a prevailing sentiment of

---

[22] For a detailed indictment by a West German journalist, see e.g. Friedrich, *Die kalte Amnestie*.

'building for the future' combined with a sense that the Nuremberg Trials had already effectively 'dealt with' the past. Moreover, the fact that the East Germans were using the issue of the Nazi past as a focus of their anti-western campaigns tarred any concern with Nazi guilt with the brush of communism. The Cold War not only displaced the real issues very markedly, but also provided many conservative West Germans with a degree of ideological continuity and remarkable political self-righteousness across the divide from an anti-communist dictatorship to an anti-communist democracy.

There were of course very clear breaks: the election of the ageing Konrad Adenauer as the Federal Republic's first Chancellor signalled a return to the traditions of Weimar, albeit in relatively conservative garb. The new political parties made an explicit break with the heritage of Nazism, and sought to resurrect the more democratic traditions of Weimar Germany or at least to make more or less genuine professions of democratic faith (and those that did not were constitutionally banned, such as the Socialist Reich Party in 1952). Some of the West German politicians, such as SPD leader Kurt Schumacher, had genuinely suffered bitterly from Nazi persecution.

But what is perhaps most striking about the first two decades of the Federal Republic's existence is not only the relatively high degree of continuity in personnel in the higher reaches of many areas of West German life, but also the extraordinary degree of toleration and indeed elevation to high public office of men who, if not exactly guilty of war crimes, were at best political opportunists and immoral trimmers. The East German smear campaigns and accusations may often have fabricated the evidence and overstated their case; but their exaggerations should not blind us to some of the mundane realities of murky and highly revealing compromises in top places.

Take, for example, Adenauer's chief aide in the Chancellery: one Hans Globke. He was the civil servant who wrote the official commentary for Hitler on the Nuremberg Race Laws of 1935, which removed full citizenship rights from Jewish Germans (as defined by the Nazis) and made possible the further removal of Germans with Jewish ancestry or religious affiliation from the community of humanity – the essential precondition for that ultimate indifference which, as Ian Kershaw has put it, effectively paved the path to Auschwitz.[23] Not only Globke, but also other

---

[23] In the view of two American historians, Dennis Bark and David Gress, Globke's role in the prelude to genocide can be defended on the basis that a 'fanatical Nazi in Globke's position undoubtedly would have controlled

officials who had advised the Nazi regime on racial legislation, such as Rudolf Bilfinger (associated with the Wannsee Conference discussions which coordinated the details of the 'final solution') enjoyed high positions in the Federal Republic; Bilfinger held a top position in the administrative court of Baden-Württemberg in Mannheim.[24] Theo Oberländer, Adenauer's Minister for Refugees, was a former member of the Waffen-SS. He claimed that his first-hand experience of fighting Bolshevism and his eyewitness knowledge of Soviet atrocities before 1945 superbly equipped him to continue the fight against communism, on behalf of refugees and expellees, in the 1950s. He finally had to resign in face of the GDR's campaign culminating in 1960 in a trial condemning him, in his absence, to lifelong imprisonment.[25]

The Federal President from 1959 to 1969, Heinrich Lübke, according to another SED smear campaign coordinated by Albert Norden, had been involved in designing concentration camp barracks and construction work using slave labour. Although it is now clear that the SED falsified some of the evidence, it is also clear that the Federal Republic was willing to tolerate for a decade, as its supreme figurehead and ceremonial representative of the country, a man who had been sufficiently conformist to work quite happily in a group employed by Hitler's top minister Albert Speer on the construction of an underground armaments factory, including designing the barracks for the forced labourers and concentration camp inmates who worked there. Hardly a war criminal, but also hardly a hero of the resistance: just a standard swimmer with the prevailing political tide, who, moreover, was exceedingly tardy in recalling the

---

enforcement stringently and...would thereby have caused many more deaths'. Having played a significant role in the run-up to around six million murders can in their view clearly be forgiven if one could point to 'the thousands or perhaps tens of thousands of German Jews who were able to leave Germany thanks to the interpretation of the Nuremberg Laws that Globke provided'. D. Bark and D. Gress, *A History of West Germany* vol. 1: *From Shadow to Substance* (Oxford: Basil Blackwell, 1989), p. 248.

[24] *Braunbuch*, pp. 80, 326–7.

[25] On Oberländer, see e.g. the East German indictment in Committee for German Unity (ed.), *The Truth about Oberländer: Brown Book on the Criminal Fascist Past of Adenauer's Minister* (Berlin, 1960); and the attempt on Oberländer's behalf to rehabilitate his reputation, by Siegfried Schütt, *Theodor Oberländer. Eine dokumentarische Untersuchung* (Munich: Langen Müller, 1995), which portrays him as a principled conservative Christian and almost hero of the opposition (on the flimsy basis that he once annoyed Himmler, who allegedly remarked that he 'should be put against a wall and shot'). Carlo Schmid's comment about his capacity for conformist opportunism seems more apposite.

details or mounting any kind of public defence when attacked.[26] Equally indicative of an extraordinary strand of conservative opinion, surviving for a quarter of a century after the war, was the fact that Willy Brandt, who became Chancellor in 1969, was tarred in some quarters as a 'traitor' to Germany because he had worked against Hitler in the Norwegian resistance.

There were also notable continuities at lower levels in West German public life, which provided easy fodder for the East German campaigns. According to the SED's Brown Books, over 800 Nazi lawyers were active in West German courtrooms. More than 520 former Nazi diplomats and other officials were employed by Bonn's Foreign Ministry, including former Nazis acting as Bonn's ambassadors across the world. Professors, experts, newspaper editors (such as Hermann Starke, Chief Editor of *Die Welt* and formerly editor and author of anti-semitic pieces for the Nazi *Deutsche Allgemeine Zeitung*) and others involved in West German public life were alleged to have played at best ambiguous and somewhat contaminated roles in the Third Reich.[27] Even the main-stream television and radio stations came into the East German firing line for giving air time to refugees' and expellees' organizations, and broadcasting programmes devoted to keeping alive flames of nostalgia for 'lost homelands in the east' and refusing to recognize post-war boundaries as final.[28]

Even if it is accepted that a quantity of the GDR mud-slinging was politically motivated and exaggerated propaganda based on

[26] See Rudolf Morsey, *Heinrich Lübke: Eine politische Biographie* (Paderborn: Ferdinand Schöningh, 1996); Hubert Georg Quarta, *Heinrich Lübke – Zeugnisse eines Lebens. Versuch einer biographischen Darstellung* (Buxheim, Allgäu: Martin Verlag, 1978). Lübke is exonerated by Bark and Gress, *A History of West Germany*, vol. 2: *Democracy and its Discontents, 1963–1988* (Oxford: Basil Blackwell, 1989), pp. 139–40. Clearly apologists such as Bark and Gress did not think there was much latitude for deciding how far to cooperate with or resist the Nazi regime. Similarly, according to H. A Turner, Lübke's chief crime was primarily 'his inept response to East German disclosures'. H. A. Turner, *The Two Germanies since 1945* (New Haven: Yale University Press, 1987), p. 96. See also Michael Balfour, *West Germany: A Contemporary History* (London: Croom Helm, 1982), p. 228. The Austrian Waldheim affair of the 1980s, with late and partial admissions of having been present in the wrong places but not of guilt, was in some respects similar.

[27] *Braunbuch*, pp. 116, 247, 251–2, 406, and *passim*.

[28] See e.g. such diatribes against 'revanchism' and the 'murderers of tomorrow' as Nationalrat der Nationalen Front des Demokratischen Deutschland (ed.), *Neo- Nazismus in der Bundesrepublik: Massenmedien* (no place, no date [*c*. autumn 1967]), in which the Springer press (producer of the right-wing tabloid newspaper *Bild*) is accused, among other things, of resorting to Goebbels as its source of inspiration and propaganda techniques (pp. 22–4).

selected documents to which the West was denied access, quite a lot of the mud was sufficiently well founded to stick. A glance at the most influential figures in West German industry and economic associations in the 1950s and 1960s reveals, even for the most sober western scholars, a lengthy list of men – including well-known names such as Flick and Krupp – who had been closely associated with industrial concerns directly exploiting slave labour. Hermann Abs was a member of the Supervisory Board of I.G. Farben, representing the Deutsche Bank, and in full knowledge of the way in which its Buna plant at Monowitz exploited the slave labour of those 'selected' on the 'ramp'. After the war, Abs's banking expertise and international contacts were sufficient to save him from denazification, and to ensure a profitable future in the financial world of the Federal Republic.[29] The profits made by I.G. Farben and similar concerns through the abuse of prisoners fed into the rapid economic growth of the 1950s and 1960s. The I.G. Farben successor companies, BASF, Hoechst and Bayer, went from strength to strength with apparently very little thought for the ambiguous legacy of their parent company, which had not only exploited slave labour but had also used prisoners for unethical 'experiments' with its untested medications, and, in ultimate irony, had even produced the Cyclon B gas with which the exhausted labourers were eventually to be killed.[30] Moreover, even if the Brown Book figures require a little revision, it is certainly the case that hundreds of thousands of lawyers, civil servants, teachers and entrepreneurs who had been at best time-servers in the Third Reich (and at worst actively complicit in its functioning and capacity to carry out its genocidal programme) were able to retain their positions of power and privilege or take up new lives and make the best of new chances in the new democratic regime.

Clearly the prominence of former Nazis in West German public life was in part a matter of generation and time: at some stage, all those who had sustained the Third Reich, even as very young adults, would be pensioned off. Nevertheless, these men played a major role in setting the Federal Republic on certain tracks and courses of action, in framing decisions and impregnating political culture for the best part of two decades or so. This is not to suggest

[29] Tom Bower, *Blind Eye to Murder* (London: Granada, 1983), p. 22.

[30] Cf. *Braunbuch*, pp. 28–9. It has to be said that many German companies, such as Volkswagen, *did* recognize a degree of responsibility and sought to make amends by 'compensation' payments. However, on any conceivable scale, real 'compensation' for inhumanity, torture and murder was in principle impossible.

that vast swathes of post-war West German elites were died-in-the-wool former Nazis, let alone erstwhile vicious war criminals. It is, however, to suggest that many of the people who held prominent positions in the early decades of the Federal Republic's history had been at least passive accomplices in sustaining the Nazi regime, and were less than enthusiastic about picking over its entrails. They had a vested interest, at the very least, in portraying Hitler as an evil madman who had nearly single-handedly taken over an innocent country and had done dark things which only a tiny circle of close henchmen had known about. Perhaps the most insidious response was a downplaying of their role in Hitler's state, combined with bitter criticism of those who had even raised these embarrassing vestiges of a tainted past. Moreover, it has to be said, in defence of West German democracy, that the sorts of appointment listed above were also the object of massive critique from left-liberal quarters in the Federal Republic, in many cases ensuring the eventual resignation of the individuals concerned.

Perhaps the greatest difference between the 'historical pictures' propagated in the two states had to do with official perceptions of the victims of Nazism. In the West, public and legal exoneration of former fellow-travellers in the early years was to some degree counterbalanced by Adenauer's attempted act of public reconciliation with the former victims (or at least, their surviving representatives).

In contrast to the GDR, in the West 'victims' were identified primarily as Jews, who were placed on a special historical pedestal (while other victims, such as the Roma and Sinti, were for a long time largely ignored and forgotten). Although his stance was characterized by a degree of prevarication and a marked unwillingness to upset domestic German opinion by even talking too much about Jews, Adenauer did eventually adopt a very explicit position of officially accepting responsibility and seeking to make amends by both moral and financial restitution. The notion of 'restitution' (*Wiedergutmachung*) is of course a monstrous understatement or misnomer: there could be no 'making good again' for those millions who had been brutally murdered, or who had been physically and psychologically scarred by their treatment, or for survivors and relatives. An only slightly cynical view might suggest that 'restitution' was more about establishing the moral stature and international political credentials of the new West German democracy than about real reparations to the victims of Nazism. Simplifying only a little, one could say that state-ordained 'philo-semitism' was to some extent a mirror image of anti-semitism, in that it still categorized Jews as different and special; however, now one had to be (often exaggeratedly) nice to them and about them, rather than nasty.[31]

The culmination to several years of debate about 'restitution' was Adenauer's very revealing statement to the West German Parliament on 27 September 1951, 'Reconciliation with the state of Israel and with Jews throughout the world' (*Aussöhnung mit dem Staate Israel und den Juden in aller Welt*).[32] Its opening passage clearly locates the issue not in any moral context but rather in terms of *Realpolitik* and particularly foreign opinion:

> Recently, world attention has been variously concerned with the position of the Federal Republic with respect to the Jews. Here and there doubts have been raised as to whether, in this significant matter, the new state is being guided by principles that can do justice to the frightful crimes of a previous epoch, and can set the relationship of the Jews to the German people (*Volk*) on a new and healthy basis.[33]

Note that the 'crimes' linguistically appear to have been committed by nothing more substantial than 'a previous epoch', and that 'Germans' and 'Jews' are firmly distinguished as separate categories. The distancing from any active responsibility for perpetration of the crimes continues in a later passage:

> The federal government, together with the great majority of the German people, are aware of the immeasurable suffering that was brought upon the Jews in Germany and in the occupied territories in the time of National Socialism. The vast majority of the German people rejected the crimes which were committed against the Jews and did not participate in them...But in the name of the German people (*Volk*) unspeakable crimes were committed, which impose upon us the duty of moral and material compensation.[34]

Again there is the telling absence of any active perpetrators, and the elusive use of the passive tense: the 'immeasurable suffering' has somehow 'been brought upon' the Jews 'in the time of National Socialism'; the 'unspeakable crimes' have simply 'been committed

---

[31] See Frank Stern, *The Whitewashing of the Yellow Badge: Antisemitism and Philosemitism in Postwar Germany* (Oxford: Pergamon Press, 1992).

[32] Adenauer's speech and the contributions of other members of parliament are reprinted in Dietrich Rollmann (ed.), *50 Reden aus dem Deutschen Bundestag 1949–1983* (Stuttgart, Bonn: Burg Verlag, 1983), pp. 97–102.

[33] Ibid., p. 97.

[34] Ibid., p. 98.

in the name of the German people', but not, apparently, actually *by* any of them.[35]

In one fell swoop, Adenauer was able both to provide official sustenance for the story of exoneration and innocence, while yet conceding the existence of an anonymous crime and gaining moral credit for assuming responsibility for it. In this conjunction we see the typical antimonies and ambivalences that were to characterize subsequent public attempts at 'overcoming the past' in West Germany. On the one hand, there was an explicit acceptance of historical and general responsibility for acts undertaken in the name of the German people in the past – a willingness to take on the burdens of the past, an incorporation of collective shame, if not any real admission of guilt, into West German official political culture. This was without any doubt expressed in concrete economic and constitutional arrangements, from the reparations just mentioned to the generous constitutional provisions for asylum-seekers from unjust regimes, for example. Acceptance of responsibility thus deeply imprinted itself on West German parameters of public and political life. But, on the other hand, it was always tempered in conservative circles, to a greater or lesser degree, by a striking hesitancy with respect to condemnation of at least Nazi fellow travellers and even on occasion perpetrators.

Defining the perpetrators: the war-crimes trials

Millions had claimed after the war, when forced to confront the horrors of the concentration camps, that they had 'never known' anything about it. In fact, millions of Germans had known why people were being shipped on overcrowded trains to the east, and why the trains had returned empty; they had known the broad outlines of what the euphemistic term 'final solution' really meant, even if they had not known the exact scope or precise

---

[35] An account of the restitution issue which is very sympathetic to Adenauer's role is given by Hans-Peter Schwarz, *Konrad Adenauer*, vol. 1 (Oxford: Berghahn, 1995; German orig. 1986), pp. 641–9, although Schwarz also gives appropriate weight to the issue of the *Realpolitik* considerations which conveniently ran in the same direction as Adenauer's moral inclinations. Schwarz highlights the general financial context, including the issue of assuming Reich debts which were concurrently being negotiated on behalf of the German Government by Hermann Abs; he mentions Abs's opposition to any significant level of restitution payments, but does not here refer to his background. Adenauer is presented throughout as sitting on high moral ground.

details.[36] On their own doorsteps they had seen the treatment of forced labourers, had witnessed slave labourers marching past to work in *Außenstellen* (satellites to concentration camps) and had, if they had eyes and ears, known only too well the general tenor of the regime's policies. However, in their memories, in their post-war interpretations and re-significations, they had somehow only partially glimpsed, not really perceived, that something awful was happening; and that something awful was happening when everything was awful, in times of total war, when all one's personal preoccupations and worries were sufficiently engrossing that one had no energy left to know or worry about the fate of others who had, somehow vaguely, somehow when one was absent, simply disappeared.

The brutal and sadistic details of the ways in which these policies were carried out in practice had been brought to public attention in horrific detail in the early post-war enforced confrontations with the concentration camps and the Nuremberg trials. There was then something of a lull in the mid-1950s; when the successor trials started in 1958, Germans appear to have been shocked anew, to have only just discovered, again, what had been done in their name. It is perhaps always the case that the bringing to public attention of the almost unimaginable inhumanity and brutality of Nazi torture and cold-blooded murder results in ever-renewed shock; certainly every generation has to confront it anew, and even for those steeped in this sort of material each new illustration or piece of evidence has the power to arouse shocked emotion, a renewed incapacity to comprehend or explain. But it is also possible that there were the beginnings of a sea change in West German political culture, helping to explain the public reception of the trials, particularly in the early 1960s.[37] These inaugurated – or were accompanied by – both a massive shift in historical consciousness, as a younger generation coming to maturity in the 1960s radically queried the actions and inactions of their parents' generation, and a significant change in the character of historical research and writing on the Third Reich (topics to which we shall return in subsequent chapters). In what follows, some lengthy extracts will be reproduced to provide some illustrations of the nature of the trials.

Up until 1958, pursuit of Nazi war criminals in Germany had been what could at best be (generously) described as half-hearted.

---

[36] For details of just how much was known about the Holocaust both within Germany and among the Allies and neutral countries during the war, see e.g. Walter Laqueur, *The Terrible Secret* (Harmondsworth: Penguin, 1980).

[37] For ruminations along these lines, see e.g. Herbert, *Best*, pp. 492–3.

However, in 1958, the trial in Ulm of the *Einsatz-Kommando* Tilsit brought to light, not only the horrific details of the early stages of extermination by the *Einsatzgruppen* which had escaped notice in the Nuremberg Trials, but also the sheer scale and difficulty of the collation of sufficient evidence and witnesses to bring cases to prosecution.[38] After considerable pressure from former victims, a central office (the so-called *Zentralstelle der Landesjustizverwaltung-en*) for coordination of cases across *Länder* was set up in Ludwigsburg under Erwin Schule, who had been chief prosecutor in the Ulm trial, and the pursuit of evidence began at least a little more energetically, although the staff of the Ludwigsburg office was pitifully small in relation to the size of the task.

A series of trials were then mounted, which between them provided something of an insight into the range of Nazi practices of brutality, torture and extermination. In June 1958 the trial of Sommer (KZ Buchenwald) was opened in Bayreuth, and the trials of Sorge and Schubert (KZ Sachsenhausen) started in Bonn. In June 1959 the trial opened of Unkelbach (Czenstochau ghetto), providing something of a pre-taste of the later discussions of ghettos.[39] These brought to public attention acts of almost unbearable inhumanity and brutality in the testimony of witnesses who had, in many instances, found their own memories too painful to bear and had hardly spoken of these matters in the preceding thirteen years. In the Buchenwald trial, for example, details were given of the cold-blooded selection and murder (by shooting in the back of the neck) of twenty-one Jewish Germans on 9 November 1939, the first anniversary of *Kristallnacht* (the 'night of broken glass'). The Sachsenhausen testimonies provide chilling evidence of sadistic torture, often resulting in death, of Germans who had been imprisoned for a wide range of reasons – Jehovah's Witnesses, members of a Catholic youth group attached to the Centre party, former Social Democratic Members of Parliament, lawyers and others, some arrested on political and others on 'racial' grounds. They show, among other things, just what a total absurdity it was for postwar Germans to divide their history and memories into those of 'Germans' and those of 'Jews': the real divide was between Nazis on the one hand, and those who opposed them or whom the Nazis designated as enemies, on the other. Yet the Nazi exclusion of

[38] H. G. van Dam and Ralph Giordano, *KZ-Verbrechen vor deutschen Gerichten*, vol. 2 (Frankfurt am Main: Europäische Verlagsanstalt, 1966).
[39] See H. G. van Dam and Ralph Giordano (eds), *KZ-Verbrechen vor deutschen Gerichten*, Dokumente, vol. 1 (Frankfurt am Main: Europäische Verlagsanstalt, 1962).

'enemies of the people' appeared to have anchored itself sufficiently firmly in the minds of most former fellow-travellers that
they accepted a historically produced and now internalized sharp
dividing line.

By 1963 a total of around 141 different trials, both large and small,
had taken place, covering both individual actions and mass exter-
minations. Critics pointed to the leniency of sentencing, the general
ignorance of the significance of particular statements in evidence,
the legalistic blinkers which focused attention only on details of
specific incidents or individual acts rather than seeing the broader
picture, the recourse to pleas of 'overwork' in failing to follow
leads, which cumulatively meant that only a small fraction of the
more than 31,700 Germans on the western Allies' list of wanted war
criminals were brought anywhere near 'justice'.[40] They also pointed
to the mental climate or general atmosphere in which the judges
were operating, which often made it difficult for them to pass harsh
judgements on their compatriots. Hermann Langbein sought to
characterize the mentality of many members of the West German
judiciary by suggesting what a typical judge might implicitly be
saying:

> Well, you know how it was, one simply had to go along with it at the
> time. You can only really understand these actions if you lived
> through the times then. Nowadays people like to present things as
> if only criminals belonged to the Party at that time. But we know that
> many honourable men exercised functions in the Party. Is it not the
> case that to pass judgement on people who wore National
> Socialist uniforms and obeyed orders, is effectively also to pass
> judgement on all who at that time had faith in the Führer and in
> greater Germany; would this not also be a judgement on ourselves?[41]

But the issues could no longer so easily be evaded.

The two big trials of the early 1960s really brought the question of
how to interpret Nazi crimes to major public attention: the Auschwitz trial in Frankfurt and the Eichmann trial in Jerusalem. Hannah
Arendt's famous portrayal of the latter in her 'Report on the Banality

---

[40] Hermann Langbein, *Im Namen des deutschen Volkes. Zwischenbilanz der
Prozesse wegen nationalsozialistischer Verbrechen* (Vienna: Europa Verlag,
1963), esp. pp. 19–34. The Appendix lists the trials and their outcomes, as far
as known, with specific names and sentences. See also e.g. Jürgen Weber and
Peter Steinbach (eds), *Vergangenheitsbewältigung durch Strafverfahren? NS-
Prozesse in der Bundesrepublik Deutschland* (Munich: Olzog, 1984); and Adal-
bert Rückerl (ed.), *NS-Vernichtungslager im Spiegel deutscher Strafprozesse.
Belzec, Sobibor, Treblinka, Chelmno* (Munich: dtv, 1977).

[41] Langbein, *Im Namen des deutschen Volkes*, p. 142.

ot Evil' is scathing in the extreme, not only about Eichmann himself but also about contemporary German reactions to the past.[42] Arendt portrays Eichmann not as a devil incarnate, an epitome of evil out- side of normal humanity, but rather as a somewhat pathetic crea- ture, of limited mental abilities, prone to confusion, with a poor memory and an inability to express himself, taking comfort in clichés right up to the moment of his execution. Perhaps more inter esting for our purposes are her comments on what she perceives as key reactions of the Germans to the digging up of their past:

> The attitude of the German people toward their own past...could hardly have been more clearly demonstrated: they themselves did not much care one way or the other, and did not particularly mind the presence of murderers at large in the country, since none of them were likely to commit murder of their own free will; however, if world opinion – or rather, what the Germans called *das Ausland*, collecting all countries outside Germany into a singular noun – became obstinate and demanded that these people be punished, they were perfectly willing to oblige, at least up to a point.[43]

The parallel with Adenauer's move for reparations to the Jews can hardly be overlooked: if world opinion demanded restitution on the one hand, punishment on the other, then the Germans must deliver – and all the better if they gained in moral stature by so doing.

Arendt also has harsh comments about excessive indulgence in an essentially self-serving expression of guilt among innocent mem- bers of a younger generation: she talks of

> ...how spurious these much publicised guilt feelings necessarily are. It is quite gratifying to feel guilty if you haven't done anything wrong: how noble! ...The youth of Germany is surrounded, on all sides and in all walks of life, by men in positions of authority and in public office who are very guilty indeed but who *feel* nothing of the sort. The normal reaction to this state of affairs should be indigna- tion, but indignation would be quite risky – not a danger to life and limb, but definitely a handicap in a career. Those young German men and women who every once in a while...treat us to hysterical out- breaks of guilt feelings are not staggering under the burden of the past, their father's guilt; rather, they are trying to escape from the pressure of very present and actual problems into a cheap sentimen- tality.[44]

[42] Hannah Arendt, *Eichmann in Jerusalem: A Report on the Banality of Evil* (Harmondsworth: Penguin, 1994; orig. 1963).
[43] Ibid., pp. 16–17.
[44] Ibid., p. 251.

This is intriguing as an insight on the part of a particularly acute contemporary observer, although obviously something of an over-generalization.

The Auschwitz trial, which took place in Frankfurt from 20 December 1963 to 20 August 1965, was even more revealing of widespread attitudes to the past – among the judiciary, witnesses, and the general public, as well as on the part of the former murderers. Let us just consider a few aspects which, from a distance, appear particularly striking in this context.

The trial was not the first to bring those involved in the crimes of Auschwitz to account for their acts. Around 617 people (including Rudolf Höss, whose testimony was quoted at the start of this chapter) had already been tried in Poland for Auschwitz crimes.[45] Coming to its conclusion a full twenty years after the end of the war, it is already remarkable how late any West German efforts were to deal with this particular case that had become the epitome of Nazi evil. Nor were former SS men in Austria or the GDR available to stand trial in the Federal Republic. Juridically, as in the earlier trials, individuals stood trial for individual acts, rather than for general participation in the machinery of mass murder. Thus, irrespective of the length of time they had spent sustaining the work of Auschwitz in one capacity or another, if the evidence of their own personal involvement in any specific case of brutality or murder was in any way inconclusive, they were pronounced 'innocent'; if precise evidence was there but sparse, then they received very mild sentences.

In general, the sentences were extraordinarily mild, given the scale of the crimes involved. Karl Höcker, for example, was found guilty of assisting mass murder in three specific instances, in each of which around 1,000 people were murdered. For his part in helping to kill an estimated 3,000 human beings, Höcker received a total sentence of seven years' imprisonment.[46] A similar sentence was given to Dr Willi Funk for his role in six demonstrable cases of assisting murder, each case involving around 1,000 people; thus a total of around 6,000 murders was again rewarded with a mere seven years in prison. The grounds for (even greater) leniency are also in some cases noteworthy. Emil Hantl, who came away with a mere three and a half years imprisonment for the forty-two instances in which he was proved to have assisted in murder, had the following 'mitigating' factors:

[45] The figure is given in Hermann Langbein, *Der Auschwitz-Prozeß. Eine Dokumentation* (Vienna: Europa Verlag, 1965), vol. 2, p. 993.
[46] Ibid., p. 876.

Hantl is a primitive person. He was not intelligent enough to find a way out of the situation into which he had got himself in Auschwitz. It appears to have been shown that he had greater reservations about carrying out crimes than did his co-defendants.[47]

When it is well known that even Himmler was physically sick on witnessing mass killings, the notion that Hantl's 'greater reservations' about carrying out acts that were then, nevertheless, carried out, should in some way constitute grounds for mitigation almost to the point of non-punishment is virtually beyond belief.

It is also of interest that the myth was completely exploded that SS men were only obeying orders which it was totally impossible to refuse. Many examples were brought forward of individuals who had refused to serve in Auschwitz, or on the 'Ramp' where selections for gassing took place, and that there had been no serious adverse consequences for them personally as a result of their refusals. A lawyer from the *Zentralstelle*, Hinrichsen, who had been systematically investigating cases relating to so-called *Befehlsnotstand* (having to obey orders under duress) for several years, presented his unequivocal conclusion: 'I could find no case in which the failure to obey criminal orders would have brought with it any danger to life or limb of the person in question.'[48] Refusals were perfectly possible; those who were responsible for carrying out the cold-blooded crime of organized mass murder did have a choice. 'Obeying orders under duress' was a post-war invention as a convenient line of defence and exoneration.

Equally interesting is the fear of giving evidence on the part of some witnesses, who still had to build their lives among the survivors and relatives of their tormentors from the past. Consider the following very revealing exchange:

Witness: I would like to stop giving evidence. I have a good job, I don't want to say any more.
Chairperson: We have a duty to pursue the truth. Why should giving evidence result in any difficulties for you?
Witness: In the train on the way here, all the passengers were saying that one should just let things well alone, we're only giving ourselves a bad name abroad, all this should have been done a long time ago. People visiting my workplace are of the same opinion.
Chairperson: You said in the inquiry that you had been beaten and

---

[47] Ibid., p. 898.
[48] Ibid., p. 833.

trodden on for two hours by Boger.
Witness: I can't say any more. I forget everything so quickly.
Juror: You live in Stuttgart. Doesn't the family of the defendant Boger also live in Stuttgart?
Witness: I don't want to do any harm to Boger.
Judge Hummerich: How long have you been living in Stuttgart?
Witness: One year.
Hummerich: Are you afraid of losing your job? Are you afraid of revenge?
Witness: Maybe subconsciously.[49]

Clearly a combination of public reactions and private pressures led this and no doubt other potential witnesses to opt for a quiet life rather than the pursuit of a very belated – and half-hearted – 'justice'.

It cannot have been very pleasant to have been a witness in any event. Not only was there the anguish of having to re-live, recreate in the imagination, terrible memories which many survivors had repressed or denied over the preceding years. There was also the ordeal of the trial itself, in which many witnesses were subjected to horrendous and demeaning cross-examinations. Some of the defence lawyers repeatedly and viciously sought to cast aspersions on the veracity of witnesses' testimonies on political grounds, particularly when the witnesses were of left-wing persuasions, or came from a communist bloc country and might be being kept under observation by the communist regime under which they lived. Certain defence lawyers also pointed to any conversations or contacts among witnesses – some of whom were former comrades from Auschwitz reunited for the first time in two decades – as evidence of 'conspiracy' to fabricate a case for the prosecution. As one witness put it, rather bitterly, these tactics actually reminded him of Auschwitz: 'If two prisoners talked to each other there, then the SS could sniff a conspiracy.'[50]

While the Auschwitz trial undoubtedly illustrated the difficulties of Germans standing in judgement over themselves, nevertheless a public statement had in effect finally been issued. The new German state was, in principle, unequivocally condemning the acts sanctioned by its predecessor, even if, in practice, the punishment for these acts was extraordinarily lenient. Moreover, after the gruesome and minute reconstruction of detail required by the process of law, with its insistence on proof beyond any reasonable doubt of

[49] Ibid., pp. 843–4.
[50] Ibid., p. 858.

the exact nature of every act of torture and killing, there was no longer the possibility of camouflage and dissembling. Even where not guilty verdicts were reached, the reconstruction of detail was an invaluable exercise from the point of view of historical record. Nor, in the face of this sustained barrage of evidence, could Germans any longer even pretend to engage in collective amnesia. For themselves, and for the world, the crimes of Auschwitz had been laid open for all to see.

Contested cultural representations

Even so, knowledge of the 'facts' is by no means the same thing as insertion of these facts into a broader framework of understanding and interpretation. Reactions of shock and horror do not necessarily bring with them a complete framework of explanation. To think these things through (perhaps the real meaning of '*Vergangenheits-bewältigung*'), to sift and raise for discussion alternative interpretations, to try to *understand* who could or could not have done what, who was really to blame, was very often carried out in the cultural sphere – in drama, literature and film.

As we have seen, the trials of the late 1950s and early 1960s began to bring the questions of responsibility for the past very much more to the forefront of both public and private debate in West Germany. Similarly, the publication of the Diary of Anne Frank in the mid-1950s had served to dramatize and bring home to a very wide number of people the real horrors of the curtailment of innocent life. In the following decades, these issues remained a recurrent concern in the public sphere in the Federal Republic, with more muted echoes in the GDR. Here, without any attempt at either comprehensive coverage or detailed interpretation, we shall take a brief illustration of the ways in which historical pictures (*Geschichstbilder*), with different presentations of heroes, victims and villains, could be presented to the broader public. Such cultural representations often had far greater impact on popular interpretations of the past than did the writings of professional historians (considered further in chapter 5 below).

Rolf Hochhuth's play about Auschwitz, *The Representative* (*Der Stellvertreter*) provoked a storm of controversy when first performed in Germany in 1963.[51] In some respects, however, the controversy about this play was interestingly displaced – or rather, the issues which the play raised were issues which did as much to

[51] Rolf Hochhuth, *Der Stellvertreter* (Hamburg: Rowohlt, 1963).

confirm parts of the pre-existing (and relatively comfortable) historical picture as to challenge them.

Hochhuth was highly critical of the role of the quiescent Pope, who, despite full knowledge of the fate of the Jews, refused to issue a public condemnation even when his own Italian Jews, many of them good Catholics, were marched past his window on their way to deportation to Auschwitz. This condemnation of the Pope caused outrage in many quarters of West Germany's Catholic establishment, with some members of audiences standing up and walking out in protest.

Yet in other respects Hochhuth essentially repeated a familiar story of other-worldly evil and the possibility of redemption through sacrifice. The person of 'the Doctor' (Mengele), Auschwitz's angel of death, is cast as a Mephistopheles figure, the epitome of evil personified, almost beyond any plane of humanity with which one could identify, bringing shudders even to those ordinary people who surround him and assist him in his work. The Doctor figure is far from the 'banality of evil', the ordinariness of everyday mass murder, portrayed by Hannah Arendt in her account of Eichmann. Hochhuth thus basically underlines the 'small gang of criminals' version, the 'evil men taking over Germany' view of history. The victims we see, and are asked to empathize with, are not Germans but Italian Jews – Jews again as 'other', not 'one of us', however much we are provoked into anguished human empathy with their fate. In the person of Gerstein, a member of the Confessing Church who risked his own life to inform foreign diplomats and churchmen about the Holocaust, as well as doing his best to hide a Jew and to save his life against the odds, the figure of the 'good German' is reinforced. Gerstein's heart is clearly in the right place, and he is doing all he can – but the odds are stacked against effective action, not least because, in order to be in a place even to try to be effective, one had to conform, one had to wear the uniform. And, in the ultimate self-sacrifice of Riccardo, an Italian Catholic who seeks in frustration (and in vain) to stand in for the inaction of the Pope, we have the possibility of redemption. Despite the dramatic and depressing end, in which evil appears triumphant in Auschwitz on the stage, this is essentially a modern morality play in which we know that ultimately evil is not of this world, that satanic forces are not part of normal life, and that good will ultimately triumph, in part through and because of the self-sacrifice of one man.

The play nevertheless raised the issues to public attention, possibly in a more compelling and provoking, and certainly more condensed, emotive and immediate way than the trials. Hochhuth also, in a number of dialogues, succeeded in airing accessibly the complexity of some of the issues and challenging the plausible-sounding reasons for sail-trimming among men of high office.

It contrasted markedly with a near contemporaneous representation of the Holocaust as part of a system, in which the roles could in principle be filled by anybody, in Peter Weiss's dramatization of the Auschwitz trial in his play, *Die Ermittlung*.[52] This briefly achieved great official acclaim when performed in theatres throughout the GDR (as well as West Germany) in late 1965. In the main, however, the imaginative representation of the recent past in the GDR, through more orthodox films and novels, was at this time one of barely believable triumphalism, in a simplistic version which had little real popular resonance.[53]

Enough has perhaps been said to illustrate the main themes and patterns of the diverse early attempts at 'overcoming the past' in practice in the two German states. Although there are multiple threads, and no single, simple chronology, there were key contrasts between the characteristic designations of victims, villains and heroes in the two states; and (as we shall see in subsequent chapters) there were major fractures between state-ordained pieties and popular perceptions within each state. Interestingly, one of the important contrasts is that of salience versus indifference: the past was increasingly an inescapable, highly sensitive issue in the West, in a way which it was not in the East.

A myth of 'innocence' (essentially personal in the West, collective in the East) rather than 'collective amnesia' is perhaps a better phrase for general approaches to the past in both German states in the 1950s. One could perhaps claim that in the Federal Republic (give or take an unavoidable political scandal or two) there was a tacit agreement at least among the dominant conservative elites to put the past behind them for perhaps at most a few years in the mid-1950s, say between the last of the euthanasia trials in 1953 and the reopening of the juridical process of working through the past in 1958. For these few years, perhaps, there were virtually no perpetrators: crimes had been committed by a very few individuals, or more collectively in the passive voice, and the victims had been restituted. There was even a degree of ambivalence, in the early years, about finding acceptable 'heroes' of the resistance, given that

---

[52] Peter Weiss, *Die Ermittlung* (Frankfurt am Main: Suhrkamp, 1965).
[53] See e.g. Erica Carter, 'Culture, History and National Identity in the Two Germanies' in M. Fulbrook (ed.), *German History since 1800* (London: Arnold, 1997).

many still felt that opponents of Hitler had been traitors to the fatherland in time of war; the conservative elites associated with the July Plot eventually were called upon, somewhat inappropriately, to fill the role of 'good Germans' and ideological forerunners of the Federal Republic. Whatever else there was not, there were certainly no communist heroes as far as the West was concerned. But, given both the domestic democratic conditions and the importance of international opinion (including what was perceived as the important Jewish lobby in the USA), pressures not to allow the past to die were able to find a voice, even if the results were often partially deflected by a prevailing and politically dominant conservatism. The circle of perpetrators was limited to a few acceptable targets of ostracism and condemnation; the role of victims was allotted to those who had already been ousted from the community of Germans, and were far away in Israel, America or elsewhere (while the taken-for-granted 'national community' remained shrunken to the racially defined and limited circle of 'ethnic Germans'). In the GDR, far from forgetting the past, the SED had a direct political interest in simply relocating it: the perpetrators had gone west, the victims were redesignated or disappeared (as a category if not in reality), the resistance fighters lived on and enjoyed power in the new antifascist state. The tracks which had been laid in the early decades were key parameters for later reshapings and re-presentations of an unresolvable past.

4

Awkward Anniversaries and Contested Commemorations

It has been suggested that shared memories, a myth of a common past, form integral elements in the construction of a strong sense of collective identity. In the case of that collective identity which seeks to be a nation, these historical myths should be ritually and regularly re-enacted in such a way as to form powerful common bonds across society, and across generations. Not so in Germany, as we shall see.

Whether in the form of imaginative representations in drama, novels and film, or public participation in anniversary events and ceremonies, or reconstructions and commemorations in politicians' speeches, or other modes of conscious memorialization, Germans trod through a minefield of exploding sensitivities, in which no simple and widely accepted story about the nation's common past could ever be enacted. In the GDR, the official message was always both positive, and consciously produced with specific political intent; yet it often backfired miserably as far as widespread popular resonance was concerned. In the Federal Republic, all public representations were fraught with taboos, surrounded with controversies, subjected to acute debate, analysis and critique.

Memorialization

Revulsion against Nazism was always placed in a wider framework of both explanation and evaluation. The GDR regime knew what story it wanted to have told, and which elements were to be emphasized or downplayed. The heroes were clearly designated, both in general and in particular. All over the GDR, memorials to anonymous Soviet liberators were in evidence – massive statues of manly figures gazing a little vacantly into the heavens, confirming the story of 8 May as the 'day of liberation'. A more specific, individualized hero was the communist leader Ernst Thälmann (who had stood against Hitler in the 1932 presidential elections), who secured posthumous fame by being martyred under the Nazis. He had innumerable streets, schools, squares named after him, and even the Young Pioneers youth group, the 'Ernst-Thälmann Pioniere'. There were also countless less obvious memorials and plaques across the GDR dedicated to a relatively wide range of groups of victims: concentration camp inmates who had died on the death marches at the end of the war, prisoners working in *Außenlager*, forced labourers from a variety of countries, victims of the euthanasia programme, and less well-known local heroes of the workers' movement.[1]

Memorials to Jewish victims and resistance fighters were harder to find. A prominent East German Jew, Irene Runge, finally managed to get the Herbert Baum opposition group a memorial in the centre of East Berlin in 1987 – but no mention was made on the massive, but rather un-striking, block of stone which served as the memorial, that this was a Jewish resistance group. Similarly, the women who successfully protested on the Rosenthalerstraße, also in East Berlin, against the deportation of their Jewish husbands, were not commemorated until after the collapse of the communist GDR. Their memorial was erected only after the political watershed of the *Wende* of 1989–90. Hence memorials too, in their presence and absence, underlined the ubiquitous message about the fight between left-wing political resistance and fascism, seriously downplaying if not entirely omitting racial aspects of Nazism.[2]

In West Germany, the aspects of the recent past which were selected for public memorialization were somewhat different. The conservative heroes of the 20 July Plot had their names

---

[1] For often quite moving details, see Anna Dora Miethe, Institut für Denkmalpflege in der DDR (ed.), *Gedenkstätten. Arbeiterbewegung, Antifaschistischer Widerstand, Aufbau des Sozialismus* (Berlin, Leipzig, Jena: Urania Verlag, 1974).

[2] The Preface by Walter Bartel (whose official position was *Leiter der Geschichtskommission beim Komitee der antifaschistischen Widerstandskämpfer in der DDR*) to Miethe, *Gedenkstätten*, does speak of the 'unzähligen Opfer des faschistischen Rassenwahns, der in der physischen Ausrottung von Millionen Juden gipfelte' (innumerable victims of fascist racial madness, which culminated in the physical elimination of millions of Jews; pp. 10–11); however, this verbal acknowledgement of the scale of the murder of Jews is not matched by physical representations in memorials.

posthumously honoured in street names (Stauffenbergstraße and so on); the young Catholic students of the White Rose group in Munich were commemorated in the Geschwister-Scholl-Platz, the square outside the university building where they had been caught distributing pamphlets (as a result of which they were later executed). Left-wing communist resistance was virtually absent from the official landscape, until local historians in the 1980s began piecemeal reconstructions. Thus the names were swallowed up into the taken-for-granted banalities of everyday life (in which most people have no idea about the origins or significance of street names, but at least know how to spell them when confronted with the textbook story). West German and other sculptors and artists engaged in a variety of attempts at representing the unrepresentable, disappearance – including sculptures which literally disappeared below the ground.[3] But the ambivalences and political contentiousness of West German memorial culture were evident in virtually every instance.

If recent history did not provide much sustenance for a stable and uncontested sense of German national identity, what of the more distant past?

Although concentration camp visits were to some extent compulsory parts of East German political education, through both school visits and the Free German Youth group (FDJ), young East Germans were also invited to share in other aspects of their heritage. Initially certain princely and public buildings (such as the old royal *Schloss* on Berlin's historic central avenue, Unter den Linden) were simply demolished, but in the course of time many historic buildings eventually became the 'property of the people', for the people to enjoy exhibitions or to walk in the parks and gardens which had formerly been the prerogative of the rich and powerful, such as Sanssouci in Potsdam. Particularly in the late 1970s and 1980s, emphasis began to be placed on the restoration of sites associated with selected German cultural figures, such as J. S. Bach and Martin Luther. With the help of West German cash, East German churches and religious buildings began to be restored. Meanwhile, their own historic city centres – partly for want of political will, partly for want of the material means – tended to crumble and disintegrate through a combination of wartime bomb damage and subsequent neglect. Vast new housing estates and residential 'new towns' were cheaper to construct at a time of desperate housing shortage, and preservation of the German heritage was scarcely at the top of any

[3] Cf. James Young, *The Texture of Memory: Holocaust Memorials and Meaning* (New Haven and London: Yale University Press, 1993).

communist priority list in the early decades of the GDR. By the 1980s environmental pollution and economic collapse both accompanied and conflicted with new concerns with heritage. As we shall repeatedly see, feeling bad about the present was for many East Germans a concomitant of not needing to feel bad about the past.

In West Germany, benefiting from the astonishingly rapid postwar economic recovery, enormous attention was paid to the preservation and reconstruction of (frequently pedestrianized) historic city centres, medieval walls, castles, and the like. The tourist trade rapidly cashed in on romanticized versions of the Rhine, the Black Forest, the eccentric nineteenth-century castles of King Ludwig II of Bavaria, and so on.

Opinion surveys in the West repeatedly showed greater pride in long-distant heroes, particularly in the cultural sphere, where the *Land der Dichter und Denker* could arguably claim to have made major contributions in the spheres of philosophy, literature, music, religion. In 1984, for example, when asked about 'all the things one can be proud of as a German' (*worauf man als Deutsche alles stolz sein kann*), 71 per cent of West Germans answered 'Goethe, Schiller and other great writers', who came out joint top with 'the beautiful landscapes' (*die schönen Landschaften*). The 'bravery of German soldiers', at 33 per cent, somewhat suspiciously (in the present context) scored slightly higher than 'German resistance' at 30 per cent; both defeated Prussia, which came an ignominious second to last, with only 18 per cent confessing to pride in the Prussian heritage (barely beating into last place, with a paltry 17 per cent, medieval Germany and the Hohenstaufen emperors.)[4]

There were clearly many issues which were still problematic about the longer cultural heritage in the West. For example, a constantly reiterated debate among West German intellectuals revolved around the issue of the allegedly 'apolitical' German, who – from Luther through Kant to Thomas Mann in his early incarnation – retreated from the problematic realm of politics into the more ethereal spheres of the spirit, effectively abdicating responsibility for this world to princes, autocrats and dictators. Such debates exploded at regularly repeated intervals in one form or another; what is interesting, to an outsider, is the frequent combination of an implicit teleology (how do we explain Hitler, even if what we are ostensibly looking at is Lutheran theology, Kantian

---

[4] Elisabeth Noelle-Neumann and Renate Köcher, *Die verletzte Nation. Über den Versuch der Deutschen, ihren Charakter zu ändern* (Stuttgart: Deutsche Verlags-Anstalt, 2nd edn, 1987), p. 60.

philosophy, the modern novel, or whatever), and the presupposition of some quintessential German cultural identity that reappears across centuries and generations. In other words, even in the democratic and pluralist conditions of the West, the appropriation of the longer-distant past as 'heritage' was an integral aspect of debates over current identity. And, interestingly, among left-liberal circles a fairly strong sense of identity as a *Bundesbürger* ('citizen of the Federal Republic') was developed precisely in opposition or counterpoint to these alleged legacies of the past, stressing, for example, the moral duty to disobey orders which are felt to be contrary to the dictates of conscience.

'National days': the celebration of the nation?

If the surviving physical remnants of the past are partly a matter of chance – which bit of Germany happened to have what sites on its soil – they are also, as we have seen, very much also a matter of political choice. To renovate, restore and present for display, or to reappropriate for other unrelated purposes, or to neglect entirely – these are all results of political decisions and actions. The leeway for conscious construction of public memory is, if anything, even greater when it comes to the construction of new forms and means of commemoration, in concrete or symbolic shapes – the erection of memorials, the designation of certain days as days of remembrance, the orchestration of rituals and ceremonies. Moreover, particularly in respect of regularly repeated ceremonies and rites of remembrance, on particular anniversaries, we have a superb example of willed collective self-representation. Days of atonement and reconciliation, days of celebration, tell us a great deal about the values and emotions supported by at least those who organize and stage the ceremonies; about the interpretations propagated by those in a position to mount such efforts. Economic and political power is here translated into symbolic power, the power – if the staging is successful – to construct perceptions of and attitudes towards the past, in the interests of a particular version of identity in the present.

Thus, to examine the contours of public memory, we need to employ an anthropological approach to the (at least officially) projected self-understanding of society, examining the values, pieties and taboos expressed through rituals, high days and holy days, the politically designated 'sacred calendar', with its ceremonies and symbols. The 'making present' of the past comes in part through the ways in which it is memorialized. This is not purely a matter of relatively dry, educative, pedagogic aspects – the presentation of artefacts and remnants in museums – but is also emotive and evaluative: the presenting of heroes and victims, the processes of mourning, grief and celebration. The two German states had the same past, with the same significant days – yet the signification of this past was very different.

One way of illustrating the difficulties of telling a widely shared story about a national past is through the analysis of anniversaries. Here, if anywhere, the resonance of a politically constructed and universally enacted (even if often only by omission, such as having a day off work) 'collective memory' should be apparent. Moreover, such regular or calendar-driven forms of remembering may help to shape what is remembered, how it is signified, and what is forgotten. Some dates are marked on an annual cycle, with perhaps a routinization of celebration, even if changing meanings over the years. Others are linked to specific years or anniversaries. The salience of all such dates may change over time, as they are invested with different meanings.

The German states had singular difficulties with their anniversaries. Anniversaries took on a peculiarly politicized significance in both East and West, often in contradistinction to one another. The annual calendar of public ritual was never a simple matter of routine leisure, indulgence, and unexamined sense of community along the lines of the American Thanksgiving Day in late November, or Independence Day on the Fourth of July, or the slightly more controversial but still widely accepted Bastille Day in France, let alone the entirely unexamined and generally meaningless 'Bank Holidays' in Britain scattered almost arbitrarily on Mondays close to formerly important religious or folk holidays (Whitsun, May Day). Rather, even for anniversaries where both states agreed the need for commemoration, there was always competition and contested interpretation.

'National days', even in the democratically legitimated West Germany, tended mainly to be 'difficult days', not days of triumph and celebration. Only the date commemorating the East German uprising of 17 June 1953 constituted anything approaching a celebratory 'national' holiday in the West – but in the sense of celebrating a rather complex, post-war, peculiarly West German sense of identity, defined both by democracy and by an initially, at least, more painful national division.

The strikes and demonstrations by thousands of East Germans had been sparked by changes in the communist government's socioeconomic policies but, given the intrinsic links between specific policies and the political system as a whole, rapidly developed into a broader set of protests against the system as such.[5] For the fledgling democracy of the Federal Republic (which incidentally signally failed to intervene with any practical support for the demonstrators, fearing potential international combustion), the demonstrations were interpreted as a vindication of its own existence as a better Germany. Traditional anti-communism, inherited from the Third Reich and before, was easily co-opted and camouflaged in a new celebration of western democracy against the 'totalitarian' system in the East. Thus 17 June was declared a national holiday in the West, and the central avenue running through West Berlin's leafy Tiergarten, from the highly symbolic 'Victory Column' to the equally symbolic Brandenburg Gate marking the boundary before entering East Berlin's main avenue, Unter den Linden, was renamed the 'Straße des 17. Juni'.

Thus 17 June was a prime candidate for an 'acceptable' anniversary, celebrating West German democracy and commitment to overcoming division. It has been argued that there was a crucial shift in the meanings imputed in the Federal Republic to this date over the years: while in the 1950s it served as a lively representation of real desires for reunification with the East, and hence implicitly also against the Federal Republic's own westernization, by the 1980s the day had been 're-functionalized' (*umfunktioniert*) as a ritual day celebrating West Germany's own sense of an established, superior and well-anchored democracy with only lip-service being paid to the theme of reunification.[6] Whatever the twists and turns in the coloration and precise interpretation of this day over the decades, West Germany's self-celebration was at the same time a commemoration of national division and an explicit rejection of the GDR.

For East Germany, too – where, needless to say, it was not formally marked or remembered – 17 June had multiple layers of meaning. It was a searing and complex experience for those who had striven in vain to achieve change by popular protest; while for

[5] There is by now a rapidly growing literature on 17 June. See e.g. the classic account in A. Baring, *Der 17. Juni 1953* (Stuttgart: Deutsche Verlags-Anstalt, 1983; orig. 1965); and the more recent (and conflicting) post-*Wende* interpretations of T. Diedrich, *Der 17. Juni in der DDR. Bewaffnete Gewalt gegen das Volk* (Berlin: Dietz Verlag, 1991); Armin Mitter and Stefan Wolle, *Untergang auf Raten* (Munich: C. Bertelsmann, 1993); M. Fulbrook, *Anatomy of a Dictatorship* (Oxford: Oxford University Press, 1995).

[6] Paper delivered by Edgar Wolfrum, of the Free University of Berlin, to a conference on 'The Crisis Year 1953 and the Cold War in Europe' (Zentrum für Zeithistorische Forschung Potsdam and the Woodrow Wilson Foundation, Potsdam, Nov. 1996).

those who had suppressed the uprising, it served as a traumatic reminder that political stability could not be taken for granted.[7] As Lutz Niethammer put it, on the basis of his oral history interviews, in which virtually all respondents in one industrial centre of erstwhile unrest mentioned 17 June in great detail: 'In the history of Bitterfeld, 17 June is *the* experience, a shock which had dug itself all the deeper into everyone's memories because it was totally repressed from public memory and therefore, without being aware of it, stamped its mark on the party's perception of the grass roots.'[8] The ruling SED's party reports are, throughout the years, full of fear about a possible repetition of the unrest; and in the revolutionary autumn of 1989, as the SED regime was on the brink of ultimate collapse, the Stasi chief Erich Mielke was heard to ask, 'will 17 June break out tomorrow?'

The nearest equivalent to a 'national day' relevant to its own specific political system in the GDR was 17 January, the anniversary of the death of the two left-wing German socialists, Rosa Luxemburg and Karl Liebknecht, who had been murdered by Free Corps units in January 1919. But this day too was fraught with dangers and difficulties for a regime seeking to celebrate and memorialize a moment in history the meanings of which were essentially contested. That all the politically articulate elements of the population did not share the official interpretation of this day became only too evident on 17 January 1988, when, despite measures to prevent any alternative placards appearing at the demonstration, protestors still managed to display a banner with an entirely subversive quotation from the official national heroine, Rosa Luxemburg, to the effect that 'Freedom is always the freedom of those who think differently'.[9] When massive secret service activity and armed police presence is necessary to allow the official line to be enacted in public, and numerous arrests, imprisonments and unwilling exiles follow, the 'national day' can hardly be described as one of unadulterated and easy representation of national identity.

Another traditional left-wing holiday, 1 May, was officially celebrated in the GDR with great public fanfare and the display of military might traditional in communist states. But these ceremonies, by all accounts, were empty rituals as far as most East German workers were concerned; a day on which they had to perform

[7] Cf. Manfred Hagen, *DDR – Juni '53* (Stuttgart: Steiner, 1992).

[8] Lutz Niethammer et al., *Die Volkseigene Erfahrung* (Berlin: Rowohlt, 1991), p. 55.

[9] For further details, see Fulbrook, *Anatomy of a Dictatorship*, pp. 238–9.

routine political obeisance by showing up with the work brigade, and were relieved to be able to slip away for a beer once they had put in a showing.

The construction of an acceptable cultural heritage?

Nothing in the GDR was or could be apolitical. The SED was in a constant state of seeking to transform consciousness, to produce the (extraordinarily elusive) 'socialist personality', to manipulate popular consciousness in the interests of strategic goals. The celebrations of anniversaries relating to 'great men' (with strikingly few exceptions such as Rosa Luxemberg, they *were* always men) were events mounted from above in order to manipulate those below, with greater or lesser degrees of success. In the 1950s, for example, a series of anniversaries celebrated great German cultural heroes – Goethe (1949), Bach (1950), Beethoven (1952), Schiller (1959 and more or less annually), Handel (1959) – emphasizing the GDR as the home of German *Kultur*, to some extent in opposition to the contemporaneous (and clearly inferior) Americanization of West Germany.[10] At the same time, old German military heroes were – rather surprisingly – also wheeled out: Gneisenau, Scharnhorst, and other implausible Prussians, who had recently been denounced as representatives of 'Prussian-German militarism' were suddenly resurrected and redeployed in 1952 to prepare East Germans for the introduction of a redesignated 'patriotic' and 'defensive' remilitarization in the GDR.[11]

Even in the more technocratically orientated and wilfully 'modern' 1960s, distant elements of German history could in some way be instrumentalized as allies of the SED's cause. Let us take a moment to consider in a little more detail, as a revealing and important example, an individual who, on the face of it, appears to be an implausible candidate for legitimation of the communist, atheist, GDR – the religious reformer Martin Luther. The 450th anniversary in 1967 of the start of the Reformation was in fact an often overlooked prefiguration of the later rehabilitation of Luther. While Luther was officially still historically denounced as a reactionary supporter of the princes against the peasants, the

---

[10] Cf. Alan Nothnagle, *Building the East German Myth* (Ann Arbor: University of Michigan Press, forthcoming), ch. 3.

[11] Cf. Maoz Azaryahu, *Von Wilhelmplatz zu Thälmannplatz. Politische Symbole im öffentlichen Leben der DDR* (Gerlingen: Bleicher Verlag, 1991), pp. 135ff.

population of the GDR was nevertheless still very much more religious than it later became. Moreover, the Protestant Churches of the GDR still belonged to the last remaining all-German organization, the EKD (the German League of Evangelical Churches); the state was at this time busy trying to persuade the East German churches to break their remaining all-German links.[12] Joint celebrations of the Reformation were mounted by church and state (with the latter controlling all the choreography and guest lists), as the state sought to move a faltering step further in its attempt to co-opt the predominantly Lutheran Protestant churches of the GDR.

The state's aims in these 'celebrations' (which had next to nothing to do with Luther, as far as the communist regime was concerned) were quite clear: it sought 'in a specific manner to contribute to the firming up of the historical and political consciousness of the GDR population' and 'in making use of what is primarily a church occasion, to strengthen the common bonds of Marxists and Christians and, using this particular event, to further the state consciousness of confessionally rooted citizens, in that the Reformation ceremonies will be carried out together, but with a clear demarcation of world views', as well as 'further developing the process of differentiation within the church leadership of the GDR'.[13] On the regime's view, the 1967 celebrations were a considerable success: 2,561 foreign tourists from capitalist countries brought in a total of 440,000 marks; the (still all-German) church organization was prevented from celebrating the Reformation within a western framework of interpretation, and West Germany was defeated in its claim to sole representation of Germans (*Alleinvertretungsanspruch*); and the celebrations allegedly strengthened the 'development of a live sense of historical and political consciousness among the population'.[14]

It is quite clear that, throughout the first two decades of the GDR's existence, the SED was engaged in a process of seeking to co-opt traditional elements of German culture – its 'heritage' – in the service of the communist state. Objects for adulation or commemoration were sought, not for purposes of genuine and honest confrontation and engagement with complexity and ambiguity, but rather for an often one-sided appropriation in pursuit of a particular campaign or cause, whether it be remilitarization, a degree of

[12] I have analysed relations between church, state and people in greater depth in *Anatomy of a Dictatorship*, ch. 4.
[13] Bundesarchiv Potsdam, O-4 458, Staatssekretariat für Kirchenfragen, Information no. 2/68, 22 Jan. 1968, 'Analyse der Vorbereitung und Durchführung des 450. Jahrestages der Reformation 1967', fos 1, 2.
[14] Ibid., fos 4–5.

national cultural pride within an international socialist context, or
the deflection of West German claims to all-German hegemony.
Without going into any detail of East German cultural policy, it is
perhaps fair to say that the policy-makers themselves were genuinely committed both to a desire to transform culture and social/
historical consciousness, on the one hand, and by their own
upbringing within traditions of respect for German high culture,
on the other. It was notable how official occasions would be marked
by very serious 'enjoyment' of classical concerts, for example.
Something of the antimonies and ambiguities of working-class
organizations in Imperial and Weimar Germany lived on in the
GDR, where a desire for 'self-improvement' through engagement
with the classics was held to be part of the socialist tradition. And,
despite the cynicism with respect to the Christian churches which is
manifest in many of the confidential state and SED documents
concerning religious policy, many of the older generation carrying
out these policies had themselves been brought up in a context of
religious practice and education (if not belief) and therefore had a
line of communication and dialogue with their more Christian
compatriots.

The situation changed to some extent after the conclusion of
Ostpolitik, in that the GDR had now officially obtained international recognition and was seeking to construct a more specific
'GDR national consciousness'. The flowering of an apparent concern for the whole of German history, which was very striking to
external observers of the GDR in the late 1970s and 1980s, might at
first appear a little strange in this context. Notables previously
dubbed reactionary but of whom the GDR populace were now
once again allowed to be proud included Frederick the Great
(whose statue returned to its place on Unter den Linden) and
Bismarck.

It is sometimes suggested that the East German resurrection of
great cultural heroes in the 1980s had to do with the obvious
economic difficulties and the alleged need for greater cultural legitimation at a time of economic recession and the collapse of material
legitimation.[15] It is also, on occasion, suggested that the GDR had
an eye to the trouble that the neighbouring Polish regime was
having with Solidarity in 1980–1, and their awareness of the close
links between church, nation and political opposition in Poland,
which they sought to defuse in the GDR. But the resurrection of the
'whole of German history' in the later 1970s and 1980s in the GDR

[15] Cf. e.g. Harold James, *A German Identity* (London: Weidenfeld and
Nicolson, rev. edn, 1990).

was not an entirely new phenomenon: the SED had already tried to gain political legitimacy through cultural sympathy from the very earliest years. Moreover, it was in constant competition with West Germany for the signification of the past. The terms of this competition had changed somewhat, but not completely, with the official recognition of the GDR as a separate state: the underlying and persistent battle to represent both the legitimate successor to the whole of the German past and the signpost and pathway to a better and more glorious future was still essentially the same.[16]

More importantly, perhaps, the international cultural context of the competition had also changed. The later 1970s and 1980s saw the boom, across the western world, of what became known as the 'heritage industry': from theme parks on native American Indians or colonial history in the USA, through historical documentaries, films and TV soaps, to serious exhibitions and interactive museum exhibits, engagement with the past was opening up to popular consumption in ways that could not be ignored even in the GDR. History was sufficiently central to communist politics that parts of it could not be written out of the political script; and the themes which would attract attention and popular significance in the West could not, in a time of more porous borders and enhanced communications (not least through television), be ignored.

In this context, the decision to confront head-on the more thorny or reactionary elements of German history is hardly surprising. The rehabilitation of Frederick the Great and Bismarck in the GDR have to be placed in the context of the West German reconsideration of Prussia, with the mounting of a massive exhibition in West Berlin in 1981 and the publication of highly popular books by West German 'high culture journalists' such as Sebastian Haffner and Marion Gräfin Dönhoff which re-examined the heritage of Prussia for German identity.[17] In the West German efforts, attempts were made to evaluate the ambiguities and multi-faceted character of Prussia's legacy for modern Germany. There was an explicit rejection of the simplicities of previous tendencies to denounce Prussia for 'negative' legacies such as militarism, discipline, unquestioning obedience to authority, asceticism and the like. The West German exhibitions took place in a broader historiographical context in

---

[16] See further ch. 5 below.

[17] See e.g. the exhibition 'catalogue', *Preußen – Versuch einer Bilanz* (Hamburg: Rowohlt, 1981); O. Büsch and W. Neugebauer (eds.), *Moderne Preußische Geschichte* (Berlin: Walter de Gruyter, 1981); Sebastian Haffner, *Preußen ohne Legende* (Hamburg: Stern, 1979); Marion Gräfin von Dönhoff, *Preußen – Maß und Maßlosigkeit* (Berlin: Wolf Jobst Siedler Verlag, 1987).

which Prussia was no longer equated with the whole of German history, or seen as the epitome and driving force of German history. In the East German context, these historiographical debates also took place, but in a more muted and politically constrained fashion.

There were also, of course, in each instance particular political considerations to be taken into account. The Luther example provides a good illustration. The Luther celebrations of 1983 not only put other historical luminaries into the shade; they also overshadowed even the celebrations devoted to the major ideological forefather of the GDR, Karl Marx, who had died exactly one hundred years earlier. The preparations for the 1983 Luther year went back well before either domestic economic difficulties or political turbulence in Poland became so apparent: the 'Luther-Jubiläum' was already being discussed at the state/church summit in March 1978, and the general strategy behind it, as we have seen, went back well into the 1960s.[18] But it attained heightened significance in a period when the Church was already deeply split, between those state-sustaining Protestants such as Manfred Stolpe – who genuinely appeared to believe he could support both church and state without betrayal in either direction – and the more subversive undercurrents of dissent which were swirling around on the margins of the Church.[19] The state sought both to contain the energies of committed Christians, and to marginalize those peace and human rights activists who were destabilizing the political compact, by a subtle campaign of taking over and incorporating the symbols of the church, appropriating them for the more general GDR cultural heritage.[20] At the same time, the GDR regime sought to raise its international profile and reputation for religious toleration, as well as attracting foreign tourists – and hard currency – in far greater numbers than the more modest celebrations of 1967. In other words, it sought to capitalize in every possible way – domestic and international, political, cultural and financial – on the accident of having the most historic and important sites of the Protestant Reformation on its geographical soil.

Other celebrations were in even more direct competition with the West: the 750th anniversary of Berlin, in 1987, for example, could not avoid the fact that the city celebrating its 750th birthday was

[18] Cf. e.g. Bundesarchiv Potsdam, O-4 970, 'Bericht über das Gespräch des Generalsekretärs des ZK der SED und Vorsitzenden des Staatsrates der DDR, Genossen Erich Honecker, mit dem Vorstand der Konferenz der Evangelischen Kirchenleitungen in der DDR am 6. März 1978'.

[19] Cf. Fulbrook, *Anatomy of a Dictatorship*, chs 4 and 8.

[20] Cf. e.g. Martin-Luther Komitee der DDR, *Martin Luther und unsere Zeit* (Berlin, 1980).

radically divided. In West Berlin, again, economic resources and historical expertise combined to produce a lavish and sophisticated exhibition presenting a range of aspects of Berlin's past for debate and critical engagement.[21] East Germany was no less able to call on expert historians in the service of the cause: but the outcome, such as the little official booklet, *750 Jahre Berlin. Thesen*, produced by the committee of historians and politicians, was neither on the scale of the western publications nor, in its manifest distortions and manipulation of history for political purposes, as compelling.[22] Here, as in other respects, we see the over-instrumentalization of history as arguably counter-productive: while some of it might be swallowed by the gullible and those with no access to alternative information or points of view, the manifest politicization of the message might produce more cynical responses among those inclined to disaffection or exposed to other material. Moreover, the raising to public consciousness of the all-German heritage was ultimately to boomerang in sustaining a sense of all-German belonging among the population of the GDR.

Awkward anniversaries

The situation was no easier with respect to days which were significant from the more recent common past of the two German states, and which had to be marked in overt competition with each other, showing how each German state had allegedly 'overcome' the reprehensible Nazi past better than the other. Certain days commemorated crimes committed in the name of Germans (such as 9 November, the anniversary of the pogrom against the Jews in 1938 known as *Reichskristallnacht*); others signified the end to atrocities (D-day Normandy landings, liberation of particular concentration camps, and particularly, the end to hostilities in Europe on 8 May 1945). The first of these entails a confrontation with what Germans did to those they designated as inferior, outcasts, leading eventually to the cold-blooded mass murder of millions of human beings; the second entails addressing the end of the Nazi regime and the total military defeat of Germany. To employ a massive understatement: neither of these provides anything even

---

[21] G. Korff and R. Rürup (eds), *Berlin, Berlin. Die Ausstellung zur Geschichte der Stadt* (Berlin: Nicolai, 1987); see also Geoffrey Giles, 'Berlin's 750th Anniversary Exhibitions' *German History*, 6 (1988), pp. 164–70.
[22] Komitee der Deutschen Demokratischen Republik zum 750–jährigen Bestehen von Berlin (ed.), *750 Jahre Berlin. Thesen* (Berlin: Dietz Verlag, 1986).

approaching a possible basis for national pride and memories of a glorious past, as would be possible in the memorial days of states with less problematic constructions of national identity. Rather, they entail commemoration of Germany's most evil hour, and can only provide the basis for an ambivalent pride in the present as the utter rejection of the past – not an easy feat, when a sense of continuity is of the essence of identity. Even in this respect, the ways in which the days were marked could never be easily accomplished, and the manner in which commemorations were actually accomplished was deeply contentious.

Unlike declared national holidays, these dates were not marked by official ceremonies annually, but only gained heightened attention in particular years: thus 8 May, or 9 November, gained increased significance when the year marked a decade (or similar) after the original date of note. The commemorations of the end of the war, for example, were particularly significant in 1965 and 1985; the commemoration of the *Kristallnacht* was particularly noted on its fiftieth anniversary in 1988.

Let us take, as a particularly revealing example of the contrast between the two states, the case of the commemoration of 8 May 1945 on its fortieth anniversary in 1985. At this time, the division of Germany and the existence of two quite different German states looked as though it would be a permanent feature of the geopolitical landscape of Europe for the foreseeable future. An analysis of the very different forms of public presentation of the same date from a common past serves to illustrate the dramatic differences in the political appropriations of the past – not only between the two states, but also, particularly, within West Germany. Thus what should have been a common historical heritage was bitterly contested, not only across the ideological gulf of the Iron Curtain, but within the uneasy and fractured consciousness of the Federal Republic.

The political instrumentalization of the past was always effected – at least as far as the outward and public face of the commemoration was concerned – most easily in the GDR.[23] The official day of 'liberation', 8 May, could be marked in an unequivocal manner and was the focus of massive political efforts. In 1985 the fortieth anniversary was celebrated with great public fanfare. The official brochure for this occasion, *Upholding the Antifascist Legacy*, was produced in many foreign-language versions for maximum

---

[23] This is not to suggest that there were not complex internal political debates and struggles over the forms and manner of commemoration, which, however, are not our concern here.

international consumption and public impact. It reiterated the by now familiar themes: the Soviet Union, along with the antifascist armies and resistance fighters of other nations, had paved the way 'for the peoples' liberation from the fascist yoke and saving human civilisation'. The Soviets and their allies had not exactly defeated the German people (who had in fact experienced it rather in this way), but rather had 'liberated' them. It is worth presenting a lengthy extract, which exemplifies the style of the document, to underline this point:

> The fascists had drummed into the German people's brains that defeat in the war would be tantamount to the end of their existence. But in actual fact liberation by the Soviet Union offered the German people a great historic chance. Finally it had become possible to tread the path envisaged by their best representatives throughout the centuries, and for which the fighters of the antifascist resistance had fought in deep clandestinity, in the hell of concentration camps and jails and under the bitter conditions of exile – the path of peace and friendship among nations, humanism and social progress.
>
> The fateful question arose: Would the German people use the historic chance they were being offered? Conditions for this did exist. The ideas of national freedom, the cause of peace and democracy had not died completely even during the darkest years of fascism. They had from the start found a home and incarnation in the antifascist resistance movement. The Communist Party of Germany had fought a determined and consistent struggle against fascism from the very moment it began to emerge, being the key force of German resistance. It preserved the honour of the German people side by side with social democrats, Christians and resistance fighters from middle-class circles.[24]

The pamphlet conveniently omitted mention of the years 1939–41: the Hitler/Stalin mutual non-aggression pact, with the agreement to divide the Polish booty between them. These years were simply lost from public history in this context – one of the infamous 'blank spots' on the historical map. It also conveniently forgot entirely to mention the Jewish and other 'racial' victims of Nazi persecution. It once again located the erstwhile fight against fascism in its Nazi guise with the contemporary fight 'for peace' in the world: it concluded with a ringing call 'to all sensible, humanist and peace-loving people to form a worldwide peace alliance'.[25]

---

[24] *Upholding the Antifascist Legacy* (Dresden: Verlag Zeit im Bild, 1985), pp. 4–5.
[25] Ibid., p. 47.

What is to be noted here are the prominent omissions: what was simply not available for popular historical consciousness, particularly among the generations who were too young to have personal memories of the Nazi period, or who were born later. The sheer absence of certain themes, topics, made them not available at all – what you do not know about cannot be debated.

This grotesque over-simplification contrasts markedly with the cluster of clumsinesses surrounding West German commemorations in the mid-and later 1980s, which between them illustrate the range of positions and sensitivities involved in the West German community of the agonized soul.

In the run-up to the fortieth anniversary of the end of the war in Europe, the two conservative leaders of the USA and the Federal Republic engaged in an extraordinary series of bungled negotiations.[26] For his part, Chancellor Helmut Kohl was desperately concerned to achieve a sort of 'final reconciliation' between the erstwhile enemies, comparable to that of reconciliation achieved by shaking hands with the French leader at Verdun, on the anniversary of the Normandy landings the previous year. By finding some 'site of memory' which would allow honouring the German dead as well as those who fought against them, he hoped to achieve a symbolic rehabilitation of the German nation, which would finally provide the sought-for *Schlußstrich* under the Germans' problematic past. The concentration camp at Dachau had first been mooted, then withdrawn; later, the military cemetery at Bitburg (also home of an American airbase, symbolizing their post-war role in the maintenance of peace in Europe and the partnership with West Germany in the Cold War) was chosen as a convenient location for Kohl to meet with the US President and former movie actor, Ronald Reagan. At the time the site was chosen, neither Kohl nor Reagan was aware that the cemetery contained the graves, not only of former German soldiers, but also members of the Waffen-SS.

Two sets of controversy then blew up. One had to do with the morality of a visit that included only the former oppressors, and not the former victims; the other had to do with interpretations of the character of the oppressors. The first was ostensibly resolved by Reagan and Kohl finally agreeing – after a lot of moral outrage and international uproar along the way – that a visit to the site of the Bergen-Belsen concentration camp should also be fitted into the programme. The meaningless rituals of the public rhetoric of

[26] See esp. the account and the wealth of reprinted documents in Ilya Levkov (ed.), *Bitburg and Beyond. Encounters in American, German and Jewish History* (New York: Shapolsky Publishers, 1987).

penance and shame were to be acted out here, while the reconciliation was to be effected at Bitburg. The problem of the SS graves
remained (for at this point virtually no one outside a very small
circle of scholars was prepared to concede that ordinary soldiers in
the German Wehrmacht might also have been tainted by involvement in atrocities on the eastern front).

Reagan made the first massive public blunder here. In a typically
meandering and ungrammatical statement at a White House press
conference in Washington on 18 April 1985, Reagan emitted his
own view of the German past:

> I think that there's nothing wrong with visiting that cemetery where
> those young men are victims of Nazism also, even though they were
> fighting in the German uniform, drafted into service to carry out
> the hateful wishes of the Nazis. They were victims, just as surely
> as the victims in the concentration camps. And I feel that there is
> much to be gained from this, and, in strengthening our relationship
> with the German people, who, believe me, live in constant penance,
> all those who have come along in these later years for what their
> predecessors did, and for which they're very ashamed.[27]

Far from distancing themselves from this bizarre rewriting of history (comparable, incidentally, in some respects to the East German
version of the common people as dupes in uniform), prominent
members of Kohl's government underlined it. In a letter of 19 April
1945 to the members of the US Senate, the Chairman of the parliamentary group of the CDU/CSU (the conservative Christian Democratic Union and its Bavarian ally, the Christian Social Union) in the
Bundestag, Alfred Dregger, produced a comparable mixture of
historical distortion, plays on emotional identification, and political
manipulation:

> On the last day of the war, 8 May 1945 – I was 24 years old at the time
> – I defended with my battalion the town of Marklissa in Silesia
> against attacks by the Red Army...My only brother, Wolfgang,
> died in the Kurland pocket on the Eastern front in 1944, I do not
> know how. He was a decent young man, as were the overwhelming
> majority of my comrades.
>   If you call upon your President to refrain from the noble gesture he
> plans to make at the military cemetery in Bitburg I must consider this
> to be an insult to my brother and my comrades who were killed in
> action...I ask you whether such an attitude is compatible with our
> shared ideals of decency, human dignity and respect for the dead? I

---

[27] Repr. ibid., p. 39.

ask you whether you regard as an ally the German people which was subjected to a fascist dictatorship for twelve years and which has been on the side of the West for forty years?

... There are forces which would like to abuse the commemoration of 8 May 1945 to undermine the German-American alliance. We should not further their endeavours.[28]

Pause to consider this West German declaration of support for Reagan's viewpoint for a moment. What strands of interpretation does it represent?

There are notable similarities both with the historical picture presented by Ernst Nolte and Andreas Hillgruber in the *Historikerstreit*, and with the model of totalitarian dictatorship (discussed further in chapter 5 below). German soldiers on the eastern front were noble defenders of the last bastions of western civilization against the Asiatic hordes of the Red Army. German civilians at home were the innocent and unwilling subjects of a faceless 'fascist dicatorship' (quite the GDR model, too!) which no one appears to have supported and for which no one was responsible. And anyone attempting to cast any slurs on the German character is implicitly acting as a fifth columnist, undermining the western alliance as upholder of 'freedom and democracy'. Historical veracity must be jettisoned in the interests of present politics.

Living in a democracy, however, made it possible for West Germans of other political persuasions to challenge this interpretation. Peter Glotz, General Secretary of the SPD, immediately responded to Dregger in a letter of 23 April:

> Until now I did not believe that we would encounter another West German politician who would so thoughtlessly proclaim the fable of a small minority of deceivers and a large majority of decent Germans. You present our history...as if it were impersonal fate... What is equally shocking is the unconcealed undertone of blackmail in your letter.[29]

But Chancellor Kohl himself persisted in the determined effort to achieve a posthumous denazification of German soldiers, including members of the Waffen-SS. In a statement to the Bundestag of 25 April, in which he adroitly invoked the impeccable political credentials and memory of former SPD leader Kurt Schumacher, Kohl pointed out that those Nazis who had been fortunate enough not

[28] Repr. ibid., p. 95.
[29] Ibid., p. 104.

to have died in the war had been subsequently exonerated and integrated into the Federal Republic, including nearly 900,000 surviving members of the Waffen-SS. He renounced all claims to human capacity to make decisions on political and moral grounds by asserting that 'the extent of such involvement [in the Hitler Youth (HJ), or as soldiers, civil servants, etc.] was in many cases determined solely by one's age, by one's personal circumstances or by the arbitrary decisions by the rulers.' He continued the attempt at the denazification of the dead by posing the rhetorical question (without even a question mark): 'Does it truly fall to us to judge people who were involved in that injustice and lost their lives, while we respect the others who were perhaps no less involved but survived and have since then rightly made use of the opportunities that life has afforded them, who have served the cause of freedom and our republic by participating in the political parties.'[30]

The Bitburg and Bergen-Belsen visits went ahead as planned, with the appropriate utterances being made in each site of memory – but the damage had been done. On the day itself, members of Jewish organizations attended to mount alternative ceremonies in protest against the historical exoneration of the perpetrators. Menachem Rosensaft, a son of Holocaust survivors and born in Bergen-Belsen in 1948 when it was a camp for displaced persons, spoke forcefully of the way in which 'one of the holiest sites in the world' had been 'desecrated' by Reagan and Kohl:

> Bergen-Belsen has today been exploited for the political interests of these two men, and the sanctity of this place has been violated.
>
> For forty years, no one has dared to stand here for any reason except to mourn, to commemorate, to remember and to vow that the horrors of Nazism, of the Third Reich, will never be repeated, and that the murderers will never be forgiven.
>
> Never, until today, has anyone dared to use these graves as part of an attempt to rehabilitate the SS...[This is] an appalling effort to achieve a reconciliation with the ghosts of Nazi Germany.[31]

But by the time the protestors were attempting to 'reconsecrate' the ground of Bergen-Belsen, Kohl and Reagan were back at Bitburg, waving their magic wands over those who died in the service of Nazism. Posthumous amnesty and eternal salvation was at hand, as Reagan pronounced, with regard to one of the German soldiers

---

[30] Repr. ibid., p. 108.
[31] Ibid., p. 136.

who had died shortly before his sixteenth birthday: 'Perhaps if that 15–year-old soldier had lived, he would have joined his fellow countrymen in building the new democratic Federal Republic of Germany devoted to human dignity and the defense of freedom that we celebrate today.'[32]

This attempt at mass exoneration of the German people – collective innocence to replace collective guilt – proved to be a massive blunder. Germany's official moral stature in the eyes of millions of people internationally was only rescued by the speech to the German Parliament made on 8 May by the Federal President, Richard von Weizsäcker.[33] He reminded his audience of the great diversity of ways in which Germans had experienced 8 May 1945 – as a day when illusions were shattered, when exhaustion and anxiety about family and friends were combined with fears about an uncertain future, when some were able to return to their homes while others had been forced to leave their homeland forever. But, even if Germans only fully realized this later, it was ultimately a day of liberation with the possibility of a new start for Germans. Weizsäcker's speech combined remarkable empathy and understanding for a range of experiences and feelings – touching sensitively on the impossibility of forgetting for victims and survivors (not only Jews, but also Sinti, Roma, homosexuals, the mentally ill, those who resisted or were persecuted for a whole variety of reasons), and gently surveying the roles of women, of refugees and expellees, of those who were children at the time or born later. In its political and moral range, its willingness to accept historical responsibility in combination with authentic personal memories and emotions, its refusal to engage in over-simplifications and its clear-sighted confrontation with current political realities, this speech was a remarkable performance. The urge to remember and understand the past, to celebrate the opportunities that had been granted in the Federal Republic, was also the challenge to combat intolerance, to work for freedom and peace, to reject complacency and 'look truth in the eye'. This speech was on a very different intellectual and moral plane to the attempted political instrumentalization of the past in Bitburg.

But it took an individual of the calibre of President Richard von Weizsäcker to hit just the right moral tone. All the old sensitivities

---

[32] Ibid., p. 169.
[33] Repr. in full in *Erinnerung, Trauer und Versöhnung. Ansprachen und Erklärungen zum vierzigsten Jahrestag des Kriegsendes. 8. Mai 1945–8. Mai 1985* (Bonn: Presse-und Informationsamt der Bundesregierung, Reihe Berichte und Dokumentationen, 1985), pp. 63–82.

were inflamed again, a mere three years later, when it came to the fiftieth anniversary of the pogrom against the Jews (*Kristallnacht*). On 10 November 1988 the CDU parliamentary floor leader Philipp Jenninger delivered such an inappropriately calibrated speech that some of the parliamentary delegates walked out in protest, and Jenninger himself was subsequently forced to resign.[34] In part, Jenninger had clearly internalized the conceptual categories of the Nazi period; in part, he had over-empathized and too elaborately reproduced the anti-semitic feelings of the time. Jenninger began his speech with the extraordinary remarks:

> Ladies and gentlemen! Jews in Germany and all over the world are thinking today of the events of fifty years ago. We Germans too remember that which took place half a century ago in our country . . .
> . . . On the invitation of the Central Council of Jews in Germany, many of us took part yesterday in the memorial occasion at the synagogue in Frankfurt am Main. Today, we have now come together in the German Bundestag, in order to commemorate, here in parliament, the pogroms of 9 and 10 November 1938, because we Germans, not the victims, want to clarify our understanding of our history and the lessons for the political moulding of our present and future.[35]

Here, it is quite striking how Jenninger – apparently quite unself-consciously – reproduced the radical distinction between 'the Jews' and 'we Germans' that had been effected by the Nazis, betraying not even a glimmer of understanding that – until their forcible ejection from the racially defined Nazi *Volksgemeinschaft* – thousands of Germans viewed themselves as Jewish Germans, Germans of Jewish descent or Jewish faith (or Christian, or not religious practitioners at all), and that the stigmatization and casting out on 'racial' grounds was politically imposed and contentious. The clarities of racial stereotypes apparently lived on in Jenninger's world view, unaffected by any enhancement of historical understanding or political education in the fifty years since the events being commemorated. Moreover, the curiously impersonal phraseology – 'we Germans remember that which took place half a century ago in our country . . .' seemed at least linguistically to exonerate 'us Germans' from being the subjects or active perpetrators of the crimes

---

[34] The speech is reproduced in its entirety in Astrid Linn, '. . . *noch heute ein Faszinosum* . . .' *Philipp Jenninger zum 9. November 1938 und die Folgen* (Münster: Lit Verlag, 1990).
[35] Ibid., p. 28.

committed against those other 'victims'. (Shades of Adenauer's speech of 1951 clearly hovered behind Jenninger's script.)

A marked empathy with the reasons why many Germans supported Hitler's anti-semitic policies, at least in the early, non-genocidal phases, also apparently lived on rather clearly in Jenninger's mind. A very lengthy passage of his speech was devoted to remembering how 'Hitler's triumphal march' in foreign policy and the dramatic changes in domestic policy appeared 'like a miracle', concluding that 'most Germans...in 1938 had good reason to believe that in Hitler they could see revealed the greatest statesman in our history'.[36] Not contenting himself with what sounded remarkably like lingering on fond memories of Germany's greatness (note the use of the possessive 'our' history), Jenninger went on to expound the Nazi position on the Jews, barely distancing himself even with a shadow of inverted commas or contemporary aside from the sentiments expressed:

> And, as far as the Jews were concerned...Had they not perhaps deserved to be shown some limits? And above all: did not the propaganda – apart from a few wild excesses, not to be taken seriously – actually correspond in essential points with one's own speculations and convictions?[37]

Jenninger's identification or empathy with 'most Germans' continued, as he expounded on the reasons why anti-semitism had appeared broadly acceptable, concluding that capitalism, large cities, and all that they brought with them, 'appeared just as "un-German" as the prominent participation of Jews in liberal and socialist groups'.[38]

Having made German complicity in the Nazi past sound eminently reasonable, Jenninger finally brought himself back to the world of post-war official penance and piety. While Germans were not collectively guilty – each must ask himself or herself individually what their role had been – they were now, in a sense, collectively good:

> Many Germans let themselves be dazzled and seduced by National Socialism. Many Germans, in their indifference, made the crimes possible. Many themselves became criminals. Everyone must individually answer for themselves the question of guilt and its repression...
>   ...Ladies and gentlemen, keeping memory awake and accepting

[36] See ibid., pp. 32–3.
[37] Ibid., p. 34.
[38] Ibid., pp. 35–6.

the past as a part of our identity as Germans – this alone promises us ... liberation from the burden of history ... Against the background of the catastrophic false tracks of our recent history, a particular ethical responsibility springs from us almost of necessity.[39]

This was ritual commemoration of the Nazi past for the purposes of political and moral expiation in the present.

It would perhaps not be unfair to suggest that, although West Germans eventually engaged in much public hand-wringing and institutionalized guilt with respect to the Nazi period, for at least the first quarter of a century after 1945 this dark blot on the visible landscape of memory tended to sink almost invisibly – for those who were not urged, or had no reason to seek it out – between the sanitized present and the romanticized and further distant past. When it reappeared on the horizon, it was always contentious: there was no easy and simple set of responses to German history, no uncontested narrative that could be imposed on the inescapable remnants of the past. In the East, by contrast, the public heroization of the recent past always rang a little false with at least older members of the population; but the attempt to reappropriate – in constant competition with Western representations – the longer-term cultural heritage paradoxically only underlined a contested all-German national past at the expense of a specific GDR identity.

[39] Ibid., pp. 42–3.

5

The Past which Refuses to Become History

This chapter explores the changing facets of the past as presented through the works of its official detectives, interpreters, and 're-presenters', the professional historians, in East and West Germany over time. There are a variety of overlapping, conflicting and contradictory strands on each side of the Wall. However, if a generalization can be made (for all the qualifications in the pages to follow) it is this: historians in the Federal Republic did little to dent, and quite a lot to contribute to, the culture of heightened sensitivity about recent history, associated with a diffuse sense of collective shame, that was built up in so many other facets of West German public life; while by contrast historians in the GDR generally buttressed the official picture of the GDR as a land of heroes, the highest point of German history, where shame would be almost tantamount to treason.

Yet professional historians carried with them the cachet of 'telling the truth' about the past. It is therefore important first to reflect briefly on the nature of history as an intellectual enterprise.

One widespread lay view is that good history consists in producing an accurate narrative. This provides a chronological framework, establishing causation, development and outcome, with appropriate illustrative detail and imaginative reconstruction of events and personalities along the way. When such a craft is exercised with skill, it provides a compelling interpretation which engages the reader, and imparts an air of considerable authenticity. This rather straightforward view is held, not only by readers willing to engage in the 'suspension of disbelief' common to other forms of creative representation, but also by many practising historians of note.[1] It is a view which has come under massive critique from a variety of theorists drawing insights from certain strands of literary theory and philosophy, often collectively brought under the somewhat opaque label of postmodernism.[2]

Even without conceding a postmodernist view, however, closer consideration reveals that matters are somewhat more complicated than the lay view of objective truth might lead one to suppose, and that not even the apparently simplest historical account can escape processes of selection, conceptualization, interpretation and creative re-presentation, which themselves rest on wider, often only implicit assumptions. In principle, one might think it should be possible to build up a synthesis leading to an ever-fuller, more accurate, nuanced and detailed picture of the past. In practice, however, such an ideal process rarely takes place, for both 'good' and 'bad' reasons.

The 'good' reasons have to do with the fact that history deals with concepts which are doubly constructs of the human imagination, not inanimate entities (as are the entities which are captured in the – also constructed – theoretical concepts in natural science, such as atoms, neutrons and quarks). They are not in some way natural 'givens', but are often the focus of very real political and moral disagreement, and hence may be what has been called 'essentially contested'. There is, in other words, no theory-neutral data language to describe the human, social world, and interpretive paradigms or metatheoretical assumptions are not readily susceptible to empirical refutation. Alternative conceptual frameworks may confront each other without any real mutual engagement.

---

[1] Classic bombastic and by now notorious versions of a 'common-sense' and 'craft' notion of history include Arthur Marwick, *The Nature of History* (Basingstoke: Macmillan, 3rd edn, 1989); Geoffrey Elton, *The Practice of History* (London: Fontana, 1969); Geoffrey Elton, *Return to Essentials* (Cambridge: Cambridge University Press, 1991).

[2] This is clearly not an appropriate place to embark on a major theoretical engagement with current controversies about the nature of history. For some guides into and contributions to these debates, see e.g. Joyce Appleby, Lynn Hunt and Margaret Jacob, *Telling the Truth about History* (New York: W. W. Norton, 1994); Richard J. Evans, *In Defence of History* (London: Granta, 1997); H. Kozicki (ed.), *Developments in Modern Historiography* (Basingstoke: Macmillan, 1993); Keith Jenkins, *Rethinking History* (London: Routledge, 1991) and *On 'What is History?' From Carr and Elton to Rorty and White* (London: Routledge, 1995); John Tosh, *The Pursuit of History* (London: Longman, 2nd edn, 1991); Hayden White, *The Content of the Form: Narrative Discourse and Historical Representation* (Baltimore: Johns Hopkins University Press, 1987). My own views on the 'nature of history' are developed in my forthcoming book *Historical Theory* (London: Routledge).

Thus historical accounts are couched in conceptual and theoretical frameworks which are themselves social and historical artefacts. We perceive the past through particular spectacles: we pose questions, define categories and look for relations, in ways dependent on certain more general assumptions about the constituent elements of the social world and the ways in which it changes.

Some questions may be generally important to a particular age, irrespective of political standpoint (Max Weber, for example, thought that explaining the rise and dynamics of modern capitalism had to be a major issue for both its supporters and its opponents). Certain questions clearly appear more important, and cast a particular slant over the past, under some conditions than others. Thus the rise, and indeed celebration, of the unified nation state was the central question for historians in Imperial Germany; Prussian traditions and German nationalism took on very different connotations after the descent into the Third Reich, which for obvious reasons became a key concern for historians after 1945. Nevertheless, the conceptual framework within which mutually agreed general topics are analysed may vary widely with theoretical paradigm, intellectual traditions and personal standpoints (consider, for example, the precise definition and empirical operationalization of an apparently innocent little concept such as 'class'). Certain categories are accepted as valid and fruitful in some theoretical frameworks, while they may be ignored or rejected in other approaches. In the GDR, the state-supported version of Marxism provided a particularly explicit set of categories of analysis and theories of historical change (progressive stages of history, development through a combination of class struggle and changes in the forces of production, and so on) which were rejected by western historians of other theoretical persuasions. In the Federal Republic, for all the diversity of other possible theoretical perspectives, to be a self-confessed Marxist was to invite charges of the taint of communism.

It is also important to remember that historians are themselves a distinctive historical group, with a particular social profile. Historians work as part of a profession which is trained and employed, which undertakes research and publishes, under distinctive historical conditions and constraints. As we shall see, the key difference between history writing in the two Germanies was not quite as simple as some westerners would have liked: as they saw it, in the GDR history was simply an ideological arm of the state, while in the West history was the pristine presentation of 'objective truth'. Rather, the difference lay for the most part in the conditions for research and debate, and the relative possibilities for revision of views in the light of real debates and new evidence.

Historical writing also requires not only empirical research, but also a flight of the imagination. To understand human action in the past, we have to seek to enter the minds of those who have gone, who very often had radically different ideals, values and goals from our own. To bring the understanding we have gained to readers in the present requires an act of imaginative reconstruction and interpretation, of condensation and re-presentation. In this act of translation, nuances may be altered or lost, emphases may be changed or distorted.

The intended audience of historical accounts matters greatly too. The products of historical research may be appropriated for political purposes, they may unconsciously reflect political attitudes, or they may be actively produced with certain intended political effects in mind. Debates within specialized professional circles clearly differ in level of sophistication, qualification and detail from the popularized or simplified versions in coffee-table histories or school textbooks. Given the confrontational, front-line context of the two Germanies, the politicization of history – to different degrees in each state – was clearly highly relevant for conscious purposes of political education (and many people felt, after a dozen years of subjection to Nazi propaganda, rightly so).

There are also less good – or at least less theoretically rooted – reasons. Since historical consciousness is so closely linked with current political and national identity, it can readily be harnessed to political functions. Even if, for reasons there is not space to go further into here, history is not about a perfect mimetic rendering of 'reality', this does not logically lead to a position of total relativism: there are quite clearly degrees of falsity, of omission or inappropriate perspective, of unwitting or wilful distortion. In both East and West Germany in particular, given the acute contemporary relevance of the past, history has often seemed to be less a would-be 'objective science' than a minefield of political, theoretical and interpretive controversy, with different nuances on each side. But there were degrees and variations in each case – more so, given the pluralist context of debate, in the West than in the East. Genuine shifts of perspective and improved approximations to more appropriate models of the past can be discerned. In the GDR, even the apparent dramatic shifts towards a broader, more all-encompassing historical perspective in the later years were to some extent rooted in pre-planned and politically grounded tactics; and yet some of the apparently ideologically conformist work was of real, if partly camouflaged, significance. Here, we can only select out a few aspects and illustrations of key developments which are relevant in the wider context of history and national identity in Germany.

Theoretical contrasts and common functions in the early years

In both German states, during the 1950s and early 1960s, East and West German historical traditions diverged markedly in terms of personnel, politics and prevailing theoretical approaches. Nevertheless, as we shall see, there was an extraordinary mirror-image symmetry about the ways in which the interpretations of professional historians sustained the broader historical pictures we have already met in the political and public sphere, in terms particularly of the identification of villains, victims and heroes, and the location of the present in the long sweep of German and European history.

In the very early post-war years, there had still been a diversity of historians and historical approaches in the Soviet zone of occupation. East German historian Alexander Abusch's *Der Irrweg einer Nation* (actually written in Mexican exile) was in some ways compatible with West German historian Friedrich Meinecke's *Die Deutsche Katastrophe*.[3] But very soon the political battle lines began to emerge, and West and East German traditions became more clearly differentiated.

As in other spheres of activity, things began to be tightened up in the Soviet zone in 1948: non-Marxists were subjected to increasing pressure, and many were excluded or left for the West. Abusch's rather pessimistic account (the so-called 'misery theory' of German history) was attacked by the Central Committee of the SED in October 1951.[4] In its place came a range of somewhat more positive interpretations. Just as the notion of a 'German road to socialism' expounded by Anton Ackermann in 1946 had been rejected, so too there was no longer to be a peculiarly 'German road to Nazism'.[5] Rather, a more general view of progressive stages of history common to all capitalist societies took its place.

The Marxist view of history lent Germany a certain advantage in that the stage theory of history inevitably entailed the struggle of 'progressive' (= good) and 'reactionary' (= bad) forces in every age.

[3] Alexander Abusch, *Der Irrweg einer Nation. Ein Beitrag zum Verständnis deutscher Geschichte* (Berlin: Aufbau Verlag, 8th edn, 1960; orig. 1946); Friedrich Meinecke, *Die Deutsche Katastrophe. Betrachtungen und Erinnerungen* (Wiesbaden: Eberhard Brockhaus Verlag, 1946).
[4] See *Dokumente der SED* (Berlin: Dietz Verlag, 1952), vol. 3, pp. 581ff, for an emphasis on the need for more positive interpretations of revolutionary traditions in German history.
[5] Anton Ackermann, 'Gibt es einen besonderen *deutschen* Weg zum Sozialismus?', *Einheit*, 1 (Feb. 1946), pp. 22–32.

For all the historiographical developments over time in the GDR (on which more below), the general line of interpretation remained rather simple: Nazism was but one variant of the generic stage of 'fascism', explicable in terms of the development of imperialist monopoly capitalism. Thus in the Marxist view there was nothing intrinsically and always bad about *German* history specifically: Germany was not saddled with the liability of a *Sonderweg* (peculiar or special path to 'modernity'), whether conceived in cultural or socioeconomic and political terms. In other words, it was capitalism rather than anything specifically wrong with Germany which was to blame for Hitler. Since the working class, the ultimate winner of history, was currently in power in the GDR – or at least, the vanguard party was ruling on its behalf in a transitional period – it was perfectly possible to write a more positive version of German history in terms of the history of class struggles.[6]

This more positive view was expressed in the 1950s by a concentration on revolutionary upheavals and the struggle for freedom. It was possible to combine this view with a real, and quite emotive, patriotic love for the German fatherland. Jürgen Kuczynski's 1953 history of Germany since 1900 opened with an almost purple passage (as far as history textbooks go):

> Germany around 1900 – how beautiful was our land: just like today with its hills and valleys, its meadows and woods! Who does not love the Harz mountains and the Bavarian Alps, the North Sea and the Baltic, the valleys of the Main and the Elbe, the woods of Thuringia and the Mark?
>
>   And how many beautiful towns there were, that bore witness to the hard work and artistic sense of many generations of our *Volk*: Rothenburg and Nuremberg, Lübeck and Bremen, Weimar and

---

[6] For general views of the development of East German historiography, see e.g. Alexander Fischer and Günter Heydemann (eds), *Geschichtswissenschaft der DDR*, vol. 1, *Historische Entwicklung, Theoriediskussion und Geschichtsdidaktik* (Berlin: Duncker and Humblot, 1988); A. Dorpalen, *German History in Marxist Perspective: The East German Approach* (Detroit: Wayne State University Press, 1985); Konrad Jarausch (ed.), *Zwischen Parteilichkeit und Professionalität. Bilanz der Geschichtswissenschaft in der DDR* (Berlin: Akademie Verlag, 1991); Georg Iggers (ed.), *Marxist Historiography in Transformation: New Orientations in Recent East German History* (Oxford: Berg, 1991); Jan Herman Brinks, *Die DDR-Geschichtswissenschaft auf dem Weg zur deutschen Einheit* (Frankfurt an Main and New York: Campus Verlag, 1992). Post-*Wende* revisions of our understanding of East German historical science are currently being undertaken by Martin Sabrow, Matthias Middell and others. See e.g. Martin Sabrow and Peter Th. Walther (eds), *Historische Forschung und Sozialistische Diktatur* (Leipzig: Leipziger Universitätsverlag, 1995).

Dresden. Who can name all the houses and marketplaces, the town walls and fountains, that told of the culture of our *Volk*.[7]

But very soon the villains appear in this idyllic picture of Germany: alongside the millions of hard-working and creative workers, peasants and professionals 'there were also two tiny little, but also very important groups: the *Junkers* [landowners] and the monopoly capitalists'.[8] In the view presented here, the masses of the people are effectively innocent, the land is beautiful, love of the German *Heimat* is not only acceptable but even encouraged, positively evoked by the style of writing; and, by implication, the only blots on the German landscape are the vicious landowners and monopoly capitalists. Once they are ousted, all will be well.

Similarly, Ernst Engelberg's 1958 celebratory address (*Festrede*) on the occasion of the fortieth anniversary of the November revolution of 1918 was effectively a paean of praise to the traditions of communist struggle, which, although thwarted by the half-hearted compromises of the Weimar Republic, found ultimate fulfilment in the foundation of the GDR.[9] There can be little doubt that both these historians were deeply convinced by and committed to the interpretations they expressed here.

The basic moral of these and other writings of this early period was – for all the differences of topic and style – essentially simple. The German people – workers and peasants – were an innocent *Volk*; the ills of German history did not arise from the peculiarities of any specific *German Sonderweg* – whether defined in cultural, political or socioeconomic terms – but from the oppressing imperialist capitalist classes (both agrarian and industrial). The amnesty that had been given the Nazi *Mitläufer* (fellow travellers) in terms of denazification and rehabilitation was effectively echoed in an amnesty in historical interpretation. The heroes were the KPD and its allies. Although the July Plotters had momentarily received a degree of respectful attention in 1945–6, through the 1950s they were presented in ever more negative terms, as 'anti-soviet', 'imperialist' and 'anti-national': by 1959, the definitive verdict was

[7] Jürgen Kuczynski, *Die Geschichte unseres Vaterlandes von 1900 bis zur Gegenwart* (Berlin: Dietz Verlag, 1953), p. 7. Note the use of the word *Vaterland* in the title – which would have very different connotations if used by a Western nationalist German.

[8] Ibid., p. 8.

[9] Ernst Engelberg, *Die Deutsche Novemberrevolution 1918/19. Festrede anläßlich der Feier zum 40. Jahrestag der Novemberrevolution veranstaltet von der Karl-Marx-Universität am 7. Nov. 1958* (Leipzig: Verlag Enzyklopädie Leipzig, 1959).

that 'the events of 20 July 1944 cannot be spoken of as antifascist struggle'.[10]

For the most part, the Holocaust was not discussed in the historiography of the GDR in the 1950s.[11] Insofar as the racist aspects of the Third Reich were mentioned, they were still subsumed under the overriding critique of capitalism. In a lecture at a conference occasioned by the Eichmann trial in 1961, for example, Jürgen Kuczynski explicitly mentioned anti-semitism and the murder of six million Jews.[12] But the explanation of this mass murder was not sought, simply assumed as intimately and instrinsically rooted in capitalism. In the ensuing discussion, Wolfgang Heise 'pointed out that anti-semitism since 1917 had always been a form, a method for putting anti-communism into effect... only that which accorded with the interests of the monopoly was put into practice', while Ernst Engelberg 'showed...that anti-semitism was suited, as virtually no other false doctrine, to serve the criminal aims of German imperialism'.[13] The main focus was rather an analysis of the role of certain sectors of monopoly capital (particularly I.G. Farben) with its alleged interests in unleashing war – and, given the continuities of capitalist personnel and ideology in West Germany, the continuing dangers of a third world war in the present. The (remarkably bucolic) solution was clear: 'We only call for one thing, we life-affirming Germans in all parts of our fatherland: an end to the barbarian domination of monopoly capital, so that in the morning, when we go to work, and in the evening, when a useful day is drawing to a close, the happy tones of the bells of peace, the harmonic melody of humanity, accompany us.'[14]

These were the views of committed Marxist historians who, whatever periodic local frictions they might have had with the regime, were basically its intellectual pillars. Jürgen Kuczynski, for example, had the occasional clash with Ulbricht's government; but, as he himself later put it, he was always essentially a 'dissident

[10] Quoted in Ines Reich, 'Das Bild vom deutschen Widerstand in der Öffentlichkeit und Wissenschaft der DDR', in Peter Steinbach and Johannes Tuchel (eds), *Widerstand gegen den Nationalsozialismus* (Berlin: Akademie Verlag, 1994), p. 563.

[11] See e.g. Olaf Groehler, 'Der Holocaust in der Geschichtsschreibung der DDR' in Ulrich Herbert and Olaf Groehler, *Zweierlei Bewältigung* (Hamburg: Ergebnisse Verlag, 1992).

[12] Jürgen Kuczynski, 'Die Barbarei – extremster Ausdruck der Monopolherrschaft in Deutschland', *Zeitschrift für Geschichtswissenschaft*, 9/7 (1961), pp. 1484–1508.

[13] Heinz Heitzer's review of the discussion, ibid., p. 1635; see for the full report pp. 1632–8.

[14] Kuczynski, 'Barbarei', ibid., p. 1508.

faithful to the party line'.[15] As we shall see, Kuczynski's research institute was one of the few places where a degree of debate could be enjoyed by researchers (who, because of the separation of teaching and research, were not in any danger of exposing students to their views, it should be noted), and which, in some of the later social historical writing from colleagues at this institute such as Jan Peters, proved to be one of the most productive stables of East German historical research.

The situation for those with less politically amenable views became progressively more constrained. Political interventions in shaping a compliant historical profession more generally were quite direct during this early period. Ulbricht criticized the historians' theses celebrating the fortieth anniversary of 1918, while, at the 1958 Trier Historians' Congress, East German historians broke away from the *Verband der Historiker Deutschlands* and the new GDR *Deutsche Historiker Gesellschaft* was founded in its place.[16] This sort of institutional separation was paralleled in other fields of endeavour in the GDR, with the SED exerting pressure on all sorts of professional groups to mark their distance from the West.[17]

Less committed historians than Kuczynski and Engelberg were seriously worried by the constraints on their writing and thinking. The growing Stasi kept a close eye on historians of a 'bourgeois' persuasion who were less prepared to write history in this fashion and to celebrate the triumphs of the party of the working class. Clusters of historians who were potentially 'hostile to the state' were closely observed by the Stasi in, for example, the Martin-Luther University of Halle, the *Deutsche Institut für Zeitgeschichte*, the *Institut für Gesellschaftswissenschaften* at the Humboldt University in Berlin, the University of Leipzig, and elsewhere.[18] Several of those under Stasi surveillance at this time subsequently left for the West, including the Halle church historian Kurt Aland and the

[15] *'Ein linientreuer Dissident'*, used as the title of one of his many volumes of memoirs.

[16] The East Germans blamed a West German historian and former member of the NSDAP, Hermann Aubin, for splitting up the *Historikerverband*. Cf. Nationalrat der Nationalen Front (ed.), *Braunbuch* (Berlin: Staatsverlag der Deutschen Demokratischen Republik, 3rd edn, 1968), p. 351.

[17] There are, for example, striking parallels in the development of the – much more problematic and ideologically opposed – church/state relations in the GDR, with the formation of the East German *Pfarrerbund* and the 1958 Communiqué indicating a degree of separation from the West German 'NATO-church', although full institutional separation in this case did not happen until 1969.

[18] Cf. e.g. the reports by the Ministerium für Staatssicherheit (Stasi) in the Gauck-Behörde: MfS, ZAIG 118; ZAIG 119; ZAIG 137; ZAIG 158; ZAIG 169.

journalist and later historian of the GDR Hermann Weber.[19] By the late 1950s, the East German historical profession was becoming more streamlined, more politically conformist or constrained.

Its character was by then very different from that of the West German historical profession, which was predominantly conservative and nationalist (in a traditional sense) in character. As Winfried Schulze and others have pointed out, the West German historical profession of the 1950s showed remarkable lines of continuity with the historical profession in Hitler's Germany.[20] Only twenty out of 110 historians who had served under Hitler's regime were affected by denazification measures in Germany and Austria, and they were relatively easily 'disinfected' and reinstated in their old positions within a relatively short period of time. At the same time, out of 134 historians who had emigrated on political or 'racial' grounds, only twenty-one returned.[21] Those who did return were generally sympathetic to the prevailing conservative climate: the historian Hans Rothfels, for example, who had emigrated purely on account of his Jewish ancestry, was quite at home with the conservative views of men like Gerhard Ritter.[22] The continuities in methodological approaches and presuppositions were also notable; differences and debates largely took place within a relatively conservative overall world view. Of course one should not overgeneneralize: there were key differences, for example, between Catholic historians and the largely Protestant conservative nationalists; and there

[19] Kurt Aland belonged to the mostly Christian circle in Halle which, according to the Stasi report, consisted of several former NSDAP members as well as many who belonged to no political party. By the time of the report in 1958, this group had been meeting for about ten years, in the attempt to ensure that non-Marxist teaching and research could continue in Halle and to prevent SED and FDJ people from taking over the faculty. On the Halle group, see MfS, ZAIG 119, report of 11/4/1958. On Hermann Weber, see MfS ZAIG 432, no. 321/61 (21/6/61), 'Einzelinformation über das Renegatenzentrum "Der dritte Weg"'.

[20] On early post-war West German historiography, see esp. Winfried Schulze, *Deutsche Geschichtswissenschaft nach 1945* (Munich: Oldenbourg, 1989), and Ernst Schulin and Elisabeth Müller-Luckner (eds), *Deutsche Geschichtswissenschaft nach dem zweiten Weltkrieg (1945–1965)* (Munich: Oldenbourg, 1989). Cf. also my review of these books in 'German Historiography after 1945 Reconsidered', *Bulletin of the German Historical Institute London* (Feb. 1991), pp. 3–9.

[21] Winfried Schulze, 'Der Neubeginn der deutschen Geschichtswissenschaft nach 1945: Einsichten und Absichtserklärungen der Historiker nach der Katastrophe', in Schulin and Müller-Luckner (eds), *Deutsche Geschichtswissenschaft*, pp. 19, 20.

[22] Volker Berghahn, 'Deutschlandbilder 1945–1965. Angloamerikanische Historiker und moderne deutsche Geschichte', in Schulin and Müller-Luckner (eds), *Deutsche Geschichtswissenschaft*, pp. 245–6.

were – hotly contested and often marginalized – forerunners of later developments, as witnessed for example in the foundation of the Munich Institute of Contemporary History in 1950. But the prevailing climate of historical orthodoxy – the dominant views within the 'historians' Guild' or *Zunft* – was one in general accord with the politics of the Adenauer period.

In an interesting symmetry with East German views at the time, West German historians in the 1950s tended to present Nazism not as intrinsic to the long sweep of German history, but rather as a broader European phenomenon. Rather than employing the Marxist concept of fascism, however, which rooted Nazism in capitalism and hence the West, Western historians adopted the no less politically useful category of 'totalitarianism'. This interpreted the Third Reich as a form of modern one-party and one-ideology dictatorship resting on a combination of repression, propaganda and the manipulation of the masses. It equated Nazism with communism, and provided a reason for denigrating communist resistance to Hitler because it was allegedly in the service of an equally totalitarian cause. The association with modern mass politics, as in Gerhard Ritter's view, also had certain implicitly anti-democratic overtones.

Ritter's 1948 work became a classic, setting the parameters of a dominant historical picture which prevailed widely until at least the early 1960s. In it, Ritter provided a broad survey of German history up to the First World War. In this, there was little or nothing to explain the rise of Hitler. After the war was when it all began to go wrong, and it went wrong for reasons which had more to do with the emergence of the masses onto the historical stage in modernity than with anything specifically related to preceding German traditions:

> The system of 'totalitarian' dictatorships as such is not a specifically German development...The possibility...is given everywhere where, after the destruction of all traditional authority, there is an attempt at the unmediated popular domination of the 'uprising of the masses', without any incorporation of these masses in federal or corporate organs or through the traditions of old political elite groups.[23]

He goes on to emphasize that the existence of 'modern masses (*Massenmenschentum*), who are the fertile soil for the agitation of modern popular leaders (*Volksführer*) and for the erection of

---

[23] Gerhard Ritter, *Europa und die deutsche Frage* (Munich: Münchner Verlag, 1948), pp. 193–4.

"totalitarian" people's states (*Volksstaaten*) is not specific to German evolution'.[24]

Again in a curious symmetry with East German historians, West German historians also managed to parallel the collective amnesty for the role of the 'little people' in Nazi Germany. This was not through the Marxist theory of class guilt and class innocence (capitalists and *Junkers* versus peasants and workers), but rather through a demonization of those at the top of the Nazi pyramid of power, easily embodied in the totalitarian model with its emphasis on a combination of repression and dazzling seduction of the masses. With distinguished exceptions, such as Karl Dietrich Bracher's sociological and structural survey of the rise and character of the Nazi dictatorship,[25] there was a tendency to inflate the role of Hitler as a madman, a criminal surrounded by a small gang of evil henchmen, who had taken over an innocent country (the *Land der Dichter und Denker*) and led it down evil paths. Friedrich Meinecke, in his 1946 classic, states unequivocally that a 'club of criminals ruled us'; he represents Nazism as 'an age of inner foreign domination, the domination of a gang of criminals'; the Third Reich was 'the greatest misfortune that ever happened to the German *Volk* in its history'; Nazism managed 'for a limited time to force the German *Volk* onto the wrong tracks (*Irrweg*)'.[26] This view both served to condemn Nazism and Hitler as evil, while at the same time asserting that Nazism neither arose from long-term trends in German history, nor had any intrinsic relationship with the German people, who appear simply to have bumped into it and been blown off their proper course.

Ritter's analysis was very clearly provoked by a desire to exonerate Germany in the eyes of the outside world. For him, and for Meinecke, the specifically *German* 'catastrophe' (no mention of the catastrophes which Germans had thrust on other peoples) appears more to consist in the defeat and division of the German nation, and its stigmatized status in the eyes of the world, than in anything the Germans might have done to others. Germans were no worse than other peoples; they were 'blinded' by the early successes of the war, and did not see or did not want to see the 'abominable crimes (*Schandtaten*) of Hitler's domination by force in Europe' (incidentally the only, and highly elliptical, allusion by Ritter as to why Germany might have become singled out for particular shame).

---

[24]   Ibid., pp. 194–5.
[25]   Karl Dietrich Bracher, *Die Auflösung der Weimarer Republik* (Stuttgart: Ring Verlag, 1955).
[26]   Meinecke, *Deutsche Katastrophe*, pp. 144, 127, 142.

The solution for Ritter was to salvage Germany as a 'cultural nation', which required 'self-confidence instead of dejected self-doubt'.[27] For Meinecke, too, there was a similar construction of problem and answer: 'Our German state is destroyed, extensive German land has been lost to us. Foreign domination has become our fate for a long time to come. Will we succeed in saving the German spirit?' This is followed by an appeal (almost offensive in the circumstances) to the 'highest spheres of the eternal and the godly' which answer back promising 'hope'.[28]

The tone of the historical interpretation set by Ritter and Meinecke clearly paralleled the *Vergangenheitspolitik* ('politics of the past') pursued by Adenauer, with its emphatic demarcation between those few criminals who were to be excluded and punished, and the vast masses of German fellow-travellers who were to be exonerated and reintegrated. The 'problem' appears to be less what Germans had actually done than the consequent national defeat, occupation and division, and international stigma. There is little evidence of any willingness to seek the roots of these problems within German history or the actions of responsible German people.

There was at the same time a marked unwillingness to deal with the Holocaust proper (a term which was not itself used at the time). Meinecke passes over the mass murder of the Jews in a couple of sentences, in the context of discussing the Nazi welfare state, which he concedes took place at the expense of those who were excluded from the community of the *Volk*. Here again, the 'catastrophe' appears to have consisted more in the death of 'the last breath of western Christian cultured behaviour and humanity' than of six million real human beings.[29] Konrad Kwiet has pointed out that most of these historians – who had conformed in whatever ways required of them during the Third Reich – had themselves never actually even queried the existence of a 'Jewish question' which required 'solution', and had raised no objections when their Jewish colleagues were removed from their positions and forced to emigrate or disappeared in the east. It was clearly easier to leave what they considered to be 'Jewish history' to 'Jewish historians'.[30]

[27] Ritter, *Europa und die deutsche Frage*, pp. 199, 200.
[28] Meinecke, *Deutsche Katastrophe*, pp. 176, 177.
[29] Ibid., p. 125.
[30] See Konrad Kwiet, 'Die NS-Zeit in der westdeutschen Forschung 1945–1961', in Schulin and Müller-Luckner (eds), *Deutsche Geschichtswissenschaft*. It also now seems clear that even some of the more apparently 'progressive' social

But on the left too, as well as among conservative and perhaps intrinsically anti-semitic nationalists, there were good reasons for a degree of myopia here. Interestingly, even those Germans who had themselves experienced life inside a concentration camp as political prisoners were less than fully aware of the true extent and character of the extermination camps and the Holocaust proper. Thus Eugon Kogon's path-breaking early anatomy of the 'SS-state' was deeply rooted in his own experiences as a German political prisoner in a concentration camp designed primarily for detection rather than extermination. He was first prompted to this task by a request from the western Allies who were the liberators of Buchenwald, and in the latter part of 1945 turned the first report, based on his own experiences in Buchenwald (which fed into the Nuremberg Trials), into a more general full-length book on the system as a whole.[31] This volume is exceedingly valuable, not least because it is written with great analytic clarity but also from close personal experience. Nevertheless, it is written from the perspective of a survivor who documents in great detail patterns of terror and modes of survival in the everyday life of 'normal' concentration camps, rather than extermination centres; only a tiny fraction of the book is devoted to 'the fate of Jews' under the more general heading of 'group fates and special actions' (*Gruppenschicksale und Sonderaktionen*).

It was not until the war-crimes trials of the late 1950s and 1960s (particularly the Eichmann trial and the Auschwitz trial) that professional historians began to devote more attention to these matters, as in the *Gutachten* (expert testimonies) developed for these trials by historians at the Munich Institute for Contemporary History.[32] Up to this time, sheer ignorance affected the overall historical picture as much as any putatively wilful disregard for 'Jewish' history; and, as we have seen in discussion of the trials, for many of those very directly affected as former participants and witnesses,

---

historians of the 1950s, Theodor Schieder and Werner Conze, were more supportive of Nazi population policies than some of their latter-day pupils and admirers would like to concede. Cf. the debates of the Frankfurter Historikertag, 1998, as reported e.g. in the *Frankfurter Allgemeine Zeitung*, 14 Sept. 1998.

[31] Eugon Kogon, *Der SS-Staat. Das System der deutschen Konzentrationslager* (Frankfurt am Main: Verlag der Frankfurter Hefte, 3rd edn, 1948; orig. 1946), 'Einleitung'.

[32] Hans Buchheim, 'Die SS – das Herrschaftsinstrument. Befehl und Gehorsam', *Anatomie des SS-Staates*, vol. 1; Martin Broszat, 'Konzentrationslager', Hans-Adolf Jacobsen, 'Komissarbefehl', and Helmut Krausnick, 'Judenverfolgung', *Anatomie des SS-Staates*, vol. 2 (Munich: dtv, 1967), first produced for the Frankfurt Auschwitz trial in 1964.

memories were often too painful for any desire to engage in detailed historical exploration.

The notion that the Holocaust could in this way be almost completely absent from 'German history' is today astounding. Yet for a variety of perfectly understandable, if not always entirely laudable, reasons, West German historiography of the 1950s allowed both the German people as possibly culpable accomplices and the Jews as victims to disappear almost entirely from historical accounts.

In order to show that there were 'acceptable' traditions leading into West Germany (parallel to the GDR emphasis on communist resistance, progressive traditions, and their culmination in the GDR) the idea of an 'other Germany' was developed. The muted heroes – if there were any, but this was hardly a heroic literature – of West German accounts at this time were the men involved in the largely conservative, nationalist resistance of the July Plot of 1944. But even this proved to be a rather sensitive topic which was treated more often by former friends and associates seeking to preserve their memory, and more frequently in the popular media of newspapers, magazines, radio and film, than in books by professional historians.[33] Still, by emphasizing strategic and tactical mistakes made by Hitler, a degree of honour could be salvaged for the army (particularly helpful in constructing an acceptable heritage for the Bundeswehr). The fact that many (although by no means all) of those involved in the July Plot were members of a relatively traditional Prussian *Junker* and military elite also struck sympathetic chords. The earlier frisson or tension between the elites of Imperial and Weimar Germany and the upstart 'Bohemian Corporal', Hitler, reappeared in this historical dissociation. It was not until much later that a new generation of left-liberal historians pointed out just how little many of those involved in the July Plot actually sympathized with or understood democratic ideas.[34]

Thus, in the predominant West German historical picture of the 1950s and early 1960s, Nazism had more or less collided with the 'real' history of the German *Volk*, blowing it off course; the masses of the German people had been exposed to and blinded by Hitler's

[33] See e.g. Christian Toyka-Seid, 'Der Widerstand gegen Hitler und die westdeutsche Gesellschaft: Anmerkungen zur Rezeptionsgeschichte des "anderen Deutschland" in den frühen Nachkriegsjahren', in Steinbach et al. (eds), *Widerstand*. Toyka Seid points out further that Hans Rothfels's book on the opposition was written first in English, and subsequently translated into German; and that Ritter's book on Goerdeler failed to address broader issues which were too sensitive.

[34] H. Mommsen, 'Social Views and Constitutional Plans of the Resistance' in H. Graml et al., *The German Resistance to Hitler* (London: Batsford, 1970).

charms as a result of 'modernity' in the form of the collapse of traditional authority after the First World War; a criminal club had taken over Germany: some courageous and good (nationalist, conservative, authoritarian) men stood up to them; and finally, after bitter defeat and division of the fatherland (the real catastrophe), the new West German state sought to rebuild on the ruins by reiterating the virtues of traditional German culture in an effort to throw off international stigma. For all the public anguish about national humiliation, there was little evidence of a sense of real guilt or concern for real victims.

It is clear that, in the early post-war historiography of the two German states, the character of the historical professions became distinctively different, as did the constraints and conditions under which East and West German historians worked. Yet, despite radical divergence in the substantive interpretations of the common past, there were remarkable formal similarities in the effects of different substantive interpretations. The accounts highlighted certain heroes and villains: in the West, the villains were the small gang of criminals who had in effect hijacked Germany; the heroes were the traditional elites, conservatives, nationalists in a good sense, those who ruled because they were born to rule and who ruled on behalf of the people, the masses who could not be trusted. In the East, the villains were the monopoly capitalists and imperialists, a product not so much of Germany in particular as of the fascist stage of European capitalism in general; the heroes were the heroic communists who struggled on behalf of the oppressed and innocent people (who actually also could not be trusted; hence the Party had to rule in their name). Thus, for all their substantive differences, in the later 1940s and 1950s the interpretations presented in both German states served on the whole to remove the Third Reich from distinctive long-term peculiarities of German history in particular, and also, in large measure, to exonerate the masses of the German people from any real responsibility for the Hitler regime and its doings.

Towards the truth, the whole truth, and nothing but the truth?

Although there were always a handful of sociologically inclined historians in West Germany (such as Theodor Schieder and Karl Dietrich Bracher), dramatic changes in the atmosphere of West German historiography occurred in the 1960s. The publication of Fritz Fischer's re-examination of the origins of the First World War in 1961 exploded a variety of taboos.[35] It also opened the way for a more comprehensive analysis of the implications of domestic social and political tensions in Imperial Germany, and focused critical attention on long-term trends leading towards the Third Reich, which could no longer look quite so accidental.

The new interest in societal history was given a massive boost by the energetic and vigorous contributions of scholars associated with what became known as the Bielefeld School, most notably Hans-Ulrich Wehler and Jürgen Kocka. Wehler's deliberately provocative theses on Imperial Germany, elaborating a theory of the German *Sonderweg* or 'special path' to modernity, emphatically displaced the 'spanner in the works'/'demonic takeover by one charismatic man' historical pictures that had earlier been prevalent.[36] Despite their interest in social-structural history, the early writings of these historians soon came under attack for being over-elitist and functionalist: the history of Imperial Germany, for example, for a while appeared as if clairvoyant elites knew exactly what tricks to engage in to dupe the poor masses into nationalist conformity. But the underlying message – that the causes of Nazism must be sought, if not exclusively, then at least also, within longer-term aspects of German society, politics and culture, and that it could not be simply shrugged off as something that 'happened' to Germans – took hold in many, if not all, parts of the historical profession.

Meanwhile, the student movements and the resurrection of neo-Marxist theories in the 1960s not only challenged the prevailing public climate of defensive amnesia, but also brought attention once again to the more pan-European aspects of Nazism as a variant of fascism. Interest in western neo-Marxist theories firmly established capitalism as the culprit for many on the left, often with rather more sophisticated theoretical debates within Marxism than were possible on the other side of the Iron Curtain. But the debates were not always caried out on the highest intellectual plane: the dramatic and emotional clashes between generations and political positions within West German universities often led to a wild hyper-inflation in the use of the term 'fascism', which expanded to cover a wide variety of sins. Nevertheless, the stifling conformity of a conservative guild had been, if not broken, then at least fractured and challenged. It may be noted in passing that, when Gerhard Ritter

[35] Stefan Berger, *The Search for Normality* (Oxford: Berghahn, 1997) provides a stimulating if highly opinionated overview of this and other controversies, with a good guide to the detailed literature.
[36] English version in Hans-Ulrich Wehler, *The German Empire* (Leamington Spa: Berg, 1985).

published an expanded and revised version of his *Europa und die deutsche Frage* in 1966, he directed it now not so much against international stigmatization as against a younger generation whom he considered to be rejecting their fatherland. The self-pitying tone with respect to division of the fatherland, the sharp distinction drawn between Hitler and the German people, and their alleged lack of knowledge of the 'atrocities committed by Hitler's henchmen' are, if anything, even more emphatic in this new edition.[37]

In the 1970s there were developments in a diverse range of perspectives. There was – not just in Germany, but in the broader western historiographical arena – a proliferation of new theoretical approaches from alternative viewpoints, including the emergence of feminist history and the history of everyday life. Deeper understanding of non-organized workers, and non-elite groups, sought to show that the masses were not just puppets of elite manipulation (although on occasion there was a tendency to idealize the underdog). Similarly, the emphasis on a German *Sonderweg*, which firmly anchored the Third Reich in earlier disjunctures in German history, came under widespread attack by the early 1980s, with both theoretical and substantive research tending to undermine the premises on which it had been based.[38]

At the same time, new perspectives on the Third Reich itself were developing with more intensive empirical research into the character of popular opinion and everyday life. Research such as the 'Bavaria project', based in the Munich Institute of Contemporary History (*Institut für Zeitgeschichte*) under Martin Broszat, proved highly fruitful, initiating a spate of studies revealing the complexity of patterns of popular opinion and political dissent in the Nazi state. A wide variety of new interpretations by scholars such as Hans Mommsen and others began to show just how untenable a simple theory of totalitarianism was, and to delineate the complexity and multiplicity of structures of power in what increasingly appeared to be a 'polycratic' regime. Debates over the origins of genocide became increasingly sophisticated, as wider paradigms of interpretation – 'intentionalist' and 'functionalist' or 'structuralist' – were deployed to reinterpret the development of Hitler's anti-semitism into organized mass murder. German historians, at a

---

[37] Gerhard Ritter, *Das deutsche Problem* (Munich: Oldenbourg, 1966), particularly 'Vorwort' and 'Schlussbetrachtung'.
[38] A key text was David Blackbourn and Geoff Eley, *The Peculiarities of German History* (Oxford: Oxford University Press, 1984), who challenged both the normative assumptions and aspects of the substantive historical picture implicit in the *Sonderweg* thesis.

distance of a generation, participated in major debates which were by now taking place on an international scale.[39]

From local studies of shades of resistance and complicity in everyday life to analyses of the ideology and actions of ordinary soldiers on the eastern front, or the role of professional groups in alleged 'modernization' based in some form of economic rationality, received wisdoms (and implicit alibis) began to be challenged. Responses to challenges were frequently highly emotional and vitriolic: the issue of whether an interpretation was 'left-wing' or 'right-wing' appeared almost as (if not equally) important as any evaluation of fresh empirical evidence. There was an extraordinary emotional charge and contemporary political relevance to nearly all discussions.

These developments have sometimes been sketched as though what we have is simply a story of increasingly detailed knowledge and unfolding enhancement of historical understanding.[40] What is less often emphasized is the simultaneous, continuing reiteration of other views which stand in a direct line of continuity with earlier prevailing pictures. Writers such as Ernst Nolte, Andreas Hillgruber and Michael Stürmer, who were to become well known (indeed notorious) in the context of the 'historians' dispute' or 'historians' controversy' (*Historikerstreit*) of 1986 7 on which more in a moment – were propounding many of their views well before these hit the headlines of the national highbrow press. For example, Nolte's controversial views on the 'precedence', both chronologically and in some sense causally, of Bolshevik crimes over those of the Nazi racial extermination programme, which was to be a main focus of attention in the *Historikerstreit*, was adumbrated already in his 1973 book *Germany and the Cold War*.[41]

---

[39] This is obviously not the place for a major bibliographical footnote regarding the massive spate of relevant publications. For overviews and guides to the further literature in English, see e.g. Ian Kershaw, *The Nazi Dictatorship* (London: Longman, 3rd edn, 1993); M. Fulbrook (ed.), *German History since 1800* (London: Arnold, 1997), pt. 3; Saul Friedländer, 'The Extermination of the European Jews in Historiography Fifty Years Later', in Alvin Rosenfeld (ed.), *Thinking about the Holocaust* (Bloomington and Indianapolis: Indiana University Press, 1997); and, for some examples of recent developments, Michael Burleigh (ed.), *Confronting the Nazi Past* (London: Collins and Brown, 1996). See also esp. Ian Kershaw, *Hitler: 1889–1936: Hubris* (London: Allen Lane/Penguin, 1998).

[40] Which, I should make it clear, in some respects I think we do.

[41] Ernst Nolte, *Deutschland und der Kalte Krieg* (Munich: Piper, 1974). See for a brilliant, and scathing, analysis of Nolte's views, Hans-Ulrich Wehler, *Entsorgung der deutschen Vergangenheit? Ein polemischer Essay zum 'Historikerstreit'* (Munich: C. H. Beck, 1988), pp. 13–20.

Moreover, renewed versions of the historical pictures of the 1950s were constantly reinscribed into public consciousness through less abstruse, more accessible historical publications. 'Coffee-table history books' were a vital part of a mutually dependent combination of educated middle-class culture and capitalist publishing enterprises: lavishly illustrated history books sold in hundreds of thousands of copies, and lay, barely read but occasionally flicked through, on the coffee tables of the middle classes. While written by professional historians, these books directed at a wider popular market often simply repeated the emotional reactions and general historical pictures prevalent in the 1950s, without serious incorporation of the detailed social historical research of the 1970s and 1980s.

Let us take, for example, two prominent 'coffee-table' blockbusters on German history – the sort of volume which would lie on the tables of the professional classes in West Germany. The lavishly illustrated *Mitten in Europa. Deutsche Geschichte* (In the Heart of Europe. German History), is written by four prominent historians and runs to over 430 pages.[42] The other, *Geschichte der Deutschen* (History of the Germans) is written 'backwards' – starting with the present and working into the past – by one historian, Hellmut Diwald, and totals more than 760 pages.[43] Appearing in the late 1970s and early 1980s, these books symbolize the resurrection of history as a popular concern which was so evident at this time. Their titles mirror a certain unease about the subject matter of their histories: neither actually claims to be a history of 'Germany'. One evades the problem by using German as an adjective rather than a noun and using an exceedingly vague geographical expression (which also, incidentally, alludes to a particular and controversial interpretation of German history as seriously determined by its 'geopolitical location' 'in the middle'), while the other places the focus firmly on the German *Volk*, the German people, of whom it claims to be a history. Both seek vivid evocation of the past by the use of numerous illustrations and reproductions of original documents and other artefacts of history. They seek to convey a sense of the past to the widest possible audience, not to present new material for discussion among specialists.

In both of these coffee-table accounts, the absolute evil and total immorality of the Nazi crimes of genocide is stressed. But the roles

[42] Hartmut Boockmann, Heinz Schilling, Hagen Schulze and Michael Stürmer, *Mitten in Europa. Deutsche Geschichte* (Berlin: Siedler, 1984).
[43] Hellmut Diwald, *Geschichte der Deutschen* (Frankfurt am Main and Berlin; Ullstein, 1978).

of Hitler and the German people in relation to the Holocaust are treated in a way which is somewhat ambiguous, reinforcing a notion of general unease, shame without explanation. Michael Stürmer's treatment in *Mitten in Europa* is the more wide-ranging and nuanced, but even here Hitler is made to seem almost unrelated to German history: 'As though he came from a very long way away, a stranger in German history, Hitler pronounced that...' (and so on).[44] At the same time, a diffuse and exceedingly general sense of collective guilt is implied by the suggestion that all who saw, and looked away – even all who saw the yellow badge worn by Jews, let alone anything more sinister – were in some way 'implicated in the crime' (*in das Verbrechen verstrickt*).[45] The treatment of the Holocaust by Diwald (under a section heading using the Nazi term for 'Final Solution', *Die Endlösung*, without even attempting to remember to put it in inverted commas to signal distance) positively oozes with emotion. For Diwald, it is all too terrible to try even to put it into words, let alone seek to explain it. The two pages he nevertheless devotes to this topic emphasize Hitler's own madness and racist ideas; make no attempt whatsoever to enter a differentiated discussion of the roles of anyone else; briefly pass over serious attempts at broader explanation with a passing comment about the Allies after the war having destroyed (*vernichtet*) the documents which supposedly alone would have provided answers; and end with an abdication from any historical responsibility for sober explanation by wallowing in collective 'unbounded shame' (*abgründige Scham*) which must lead to 'falling totally silent' (*völliges Verstummen*).[46]

Less assiduous readers of a less instantly accessible general history, *Deutschland seit dem Ersten Weltkrieg, 1918–1945* (Germany since the First World War, 1918–1945), by Gerhard Schulz, might, however, be forgiven for not noticing that the Holocaust had happened at all. This general history, part 10 of the Vandenhoeck and Ruprecht history of Germany for the highbrow reading public (dense text, no illustrations), succeeds in summarizing the genesis, development and long-term significance of the Holocaust in precisely three sentences (in the original German), embedded in a detailed account of the war and almost impossible to locate on a

[44] Stürmer, *Mitten in Europa*, p. 357.

[45] Ibid., p. 358. Active opposition to Nazism is subsequently mentioned in a relatively balanced fashion (briefly mentioning the connections of the July Plotters with 'the churches, the conservative bourgeoisie and the workers' movement' – p. 362), but there is little interest in sketching patterns of popular opinion and dissent more broadly.

[46] Diwald, *Geschichte der Deutschen*, pp. 163–5.

casual perusal. The confusion, distortion, and evasion of the historian's task of allocating real historical responsibility for the Holocaust, while accepting a diffuse burden of guilt on behalf of German history, is remarkable.

The sentences are worth quoting in full to give a flavour of what was still served up as mainstream history for serious but non-specialist readers in West Germany, with its claims to objectivity and lack of political bias:

> The guidelines, against the principles of international law, which Hitler had already given out before the start of hostilities, and which were to 'deal immediately, effectively and with a weapon' with the political commissaries of the Red Army as 'the originators of barbaric Asiatic methods of struggle', were probably (*wohl*) not passed on by most army leaders, but occasioned considerable damage and announced the beginnings of the worst forms of the annihilation struggle (*Vernichtungskampf*): the procedures of the partisan fighting groups, the *Einsatzgruppen*, then the transportation, beginning in the autumn of 1941, of Jews from Germany and most of the occupied territories, their collection together in concentration camps, most of which lay in the 'Generalgouvernement', where they were forced into inhumane work performance, and in several specially erected camps, under great secrecy, were systematically murdered in great numbers. These events, for which SS-units were responsible, but which were ordered and organized according to plan at the highest levels – Himmler, SD-leader Heydrich, and Hitler himself – could be discovered only in the closing stages and in their full extent only after the end of the war. They explain the destruction of the majority of European Jewry and throw the greatest shadows on the most recent phase of German history.[47]

Note the striking features of this passage: the Holocaust is located (at least partly) in answer to Hitler's fight against Bolshevism; the army leadership is assumed to be innocent (note use of the word *wohl*); the crime of genocide, the mass murder of six million people, is passed over extraordinarily briefly, with barely a detail, other than to emphasize the 'great secrecy' of the deed; those responsible are the by now well-known small gang of criminals (SS, Himmler, Heydrich and Hitler); the Germans generally did not really know

---

[47] Gerhard Schulz, *Deutschland seit dem ersten Weltkrieg, 1918–1945*, in vol. 3 of *Deutsche Geschichte*, (Göttingen: Vandenhoeck and Ruprecht, 1985), p. 587. I have deliberately not tried to Anglicize my translation of this passage – which would read far more smoothly if I had subdivided the sentences into shorter ones – in order to indicate just how Schulz manages to recount the whole tale in such a breathlessly misleading way.

anything about it. All this in the first two sentences – which the third asserts constitute sufficient explanation of the Holocaust and its consequences for a stigmatized history. This breathtakingly brief gesture towards ritual public penance without any serious historical confrontation with the issues or even accuracy of detail is remarkable – but also rather indicative of the persistence of the self-exoneratory historical pictures of the early post-war period even forty years later.

By the 1980s there was, thus, a diversity of strands in West German historiography, both newer and older. In 1986 they exploded into public confrontation, in what soon became known as the *Historikerstreit*. Demands from a number of conservative historians, most prominently Ernst Nolte, Andreas Hillgruber, Klaus Hildebrand and Michael Stürmer, for a 'normalization' of past and a relativization of Germany's crimes, were met with heated counter-arguments by left-liberal historians and social theorists, including Jürgen Habermas, Hans-Ulrich Wehler, Jürgen Kocka, Hans Mommsen and Martin Broszat.[48]

The public controversy started when pieces published in 1986 by Hillgruber and Nolte aroused the critical attention of Jürgen Habermas. Hillgruber's two essays, printed together in a slim volume entitled *Zweierlei Untergang* (with the revealing subtitle 'The destruction of the German Reich and the end of European Jewry') presented a tendentious view of recent history: while the first sought in highly evocative language to elicit empathy for German soldiers and civilians battling to defend western civilization against the Bolshevik threat on the eastern front, presenting this as a wholly laudable aim in the continuing battle against communism; the second presented a dry essay on the Holocaust which made no connections between the prolongation of the war (as praised in the first essay) and the continuation of mass murder behind the front.[49] Nolte's article in the *Frankfurter Allgemeine Zeitung* on 6 June 1986 was, he claimed, the text of a speech he had been prevented from giving: in a series of rhetorical questions, with little

---

[48] The key texts of the controversy are reprinted in '*Historikerstreit*' (Munich: Piper Verlag, 1987), and in English translation in *Forever in the Shadow of Hitler?* (Atlantic Highlands, NJ: Humanities Press, 1993; trans. J. Knowlton and T. Cates). Among the spate of subsequent publications and critical commentaries, see esp. Hans-Ulrich Wehler, *Entsorgung der deutschen Vergangenheit?*; C. Maier, *The Unmasterable Past* (Cambridge, Mass.: Harvard University Press, 1988); Richard J. Evans, *In Hitler's Shadow* (London: I. B. Taurus, 1989).

[49] Andreas Hillgruber, *Zweierlei Untergang. Die Zerschlagung des deutschen Reiches und das Ende des europäischen Judentums* (Stuttgart: Siedler, 1986).

attempt at providing empirical evidence, Nolte suggested that the Holocaust was unique only in the technical means used, but that in other respects it was comparable to other twentieth-century atrocities, such as those committed by Stalin and Pol Pot; moreover, it was a form of defensive reaction to a prior 'Asiatic deed', the Gulag Archipelago.[50]

These pieces appeared in a context when conservative historians had already been assiduously concerned with the attempt to resurrect some pride in being German, some notion of 'normality' for German history. Michael Stürmer, for example, had advised Chancellor Helmut Kohl on his plans for a new museum of German history. In an article in the *Frankfurter Allgemeine* on 25 April 1986, Stürmer entered a plea for the reappropriation of history for the construction of national identity. As he famously put it, 'In a land without memory, everything is possible':

> Loss of orientation and the search for identity are like brother and sister. But whoever thinks that this has no impact on politics and the future ignores the fact that, in a land without history, the future is won by those who fill memory, stamp their mark on concepts, and give meaning to the past...

In Stürmer's view, the problem lies in the fact

> that all members of the different generations living in Germany today carry around with them different, even contradictory, pictures of the past and the future... The search for a lost history is not an abstract educational endeavour; it is morally legitimate and politically essential.[51]

This amounted to a remarkably non-objective attempt to provide a politically relevant version for the past for current political (and conservative) purposes.

The views given expression by Nolte, Hillgruber and Stürmer had long been prevalent among conservative circles but had, at least from the later 1960s, been to some extent taboo as far as public support by professional historians was concerned. In an article entitled 'A kind of settlement of damages', in *Die Zeit* on 11 July 1986, Jürgen Habermas presented a scathing critique of these 'apologetic tendencies'. He ended with a rejection of attempts to

---

[50] The text of this and the following short pieces mentioned are reprinted in *'Historikerstreit'*.

[51] Michael Stürmer, 'Geschichte in einem geschichtslosem Land', repr. in *'Historikerstreit'*, pp. 36, 38.

impose a single historical interpretration by governmental fiat (seeing history as a form of ersatz religious faith in a secular age, *'Geschichstbewußtsein als Religionsersatz'*), and made a plea for western values and 'constitutional patriotism' as the basis of West German identity.

In the storm which followed, numerous personal aspersions were cast, accusations and counter-accusations were flung about with abandon. The relativizing tendencies of Nolte and others, which located the Third Reich in the context of the (continuing) battle against communism, were strongly resisted by left-liberals such as Martin Broszat, Jürgen Kocka, Wolfgang and Hans Mommsen, Hans-Ulrich Wehler and others. This particular flare-up in the end served to produce more heat than light. But it has to be located in the broader contexts described above. Underlying all the debates, the specific arguments over points of detail, was the much wider issue: was it actually possible to treat the Third Reich 'normally', like any other period of history? Or was emotionality in fact – however understandable – an unnecessary hindrance to serious and dispassionate historical explanation?

This question was also being raised in related but arguably more fruitful dialogues. Martin Broszat, in an article of 1985, entered an urgent 'plea' for removing the Third Reich from the pedestal of unique reprehensibility and returning it to the realms of 'normal' historical interpretation.[52] Broszat wanted to argue against the treatment of the Third Reich as a 'special' case, where normal historical methods of empathy and even 'the pleasure of narration' are no longer valid. He sought to escape from the 'distancing' and 'stereotyping' which had become characteristic of historians' treatment of this period, and argued instead that it should be open for the analysis of *all* aspects of society, and open to the possibilities of continuities both pre-1933 and post-1945. While for the immediate post-war generation professed abhorrence combined with vagueness on details had played an important political role, new generations should be able to look at it in its entirety without repeating the tired shibboleths about the 'terror regime' and clichés of self-exculpation.

Broszat's plea came under attack from the Israeli historian Saul Friedländer, who argued that 'once a regime decides that groups ...should be annihilated there and then and never be allowed to

---

[52] Martin Broszat, 'A Plea for the Historicisation of National Socialism'; this and the ensuing debate between Friedländer and Broszat is repr. in English in Peter Baldwin (ed.), *Reworking the Past: Hitler, the Holocaust and the Historians' Dispute* (Boston: Beacon Press, 1990), pt 2.

live on earth, the ultimate has been achieved'.[53] This has several consequences: 1933 was an absolute break, the equivalent of a 'volcano' among 'hills' on the historical landscape; and for the victims, to speak of 'continuities' after 1945 can only sound like a cruel joke. While it is important to explore the shades of grey, the complicities of everyday life, as well as the obvious structures of power and repression, even to look away was to allow this crime to take place. Furthermore, in the current ideological climate, 'historicization' could lead, in certain quarters, to 'relativization . . . banalization, and ultimately . . . the elimination from human memory of its criminality'.[54]

This was clearly not what was intended by Broszat, but the point made by Friedländer was sharp. What constituted an 'objective' or 'scientific' approach from one perspective was itself a value judgement, devaluing the role of another perspective, the victims' memories, as 'mythical'. For the victims and those survivors who empathized with them, the Third Reich *was* on a unique plane, and 1933 and 1945 *were* absolute caesurae; any effort to 'normalize' and 'historicize' the Third Reich would be from the perpetrators' viewpoint, and would be to banalize and assist in covering up the enormity of the crimes, and the criminal character of the regime and society which inaugurated and sustained these crimes.

It was clear that 'normalization' could mean quite different things, with very different political implications: the conservative demand for a 'normalization' of German history as compared with other nations, suggesting that Germany was not uniquely evil, was geared to constructing an acceptable national identity for West Germany and freeing it from what right-wingers felt was the enormous burden of guilt. But collective exoneration or exculpation was not at all what Broszat had in mind. Rather, he wished to engage in more comprehensive historical analysis allowing more exact and refined evaluations of degrees of culpability, continuities and discontinuities.

These debates, raising as they did fundamental issues about the nature of historical inquiry where even professionals with a considerable area of common ground could disagree, indicate some of the difficulties with respect to this most sensitive and centrally relevant area of German history. Whatever else it was, West German historiography was not the straightforward bastion of value neutrality in pursuit of 'objective truth' some Westerners would have liked to believe, particularly when castigating their East

[53]   Ibid., p. 100.
[54]   Ibid.

German colleagues precisely for their overt political engagement in service of a very different cause.[55]

The peoples' own history?

In the GDR the explicit goal of historical writing was precisely to assist processes of the transformation of contemporary political consciousness. As Heinz Heitzer put it right at the very start of his concise history of the GDR, *DDR – Geschichtlicher Überblick* (first published in 1979): people read history 'to gain insights from the battles of the past and to draw inspiration from them to meet today's and tomorrow's challenges'.[56] Or, in the words of Walter Schmidt, people need to understand 'that, with the help of history, one is in a better position to understand the development of society in the present, the tasks of the future, and above all the policies of the Party of the working class'.[57] (Apart from the final comment about the politics of the party of the working class, this could almost have emanated from Michael Stürmer.) The difference was not so much that history was politicized in the GDR, but rather that the state did not permit the plurality of voices and approaches, the clashes of opinion and open debate, characteristic of the West. Moreover, for all the changes of approach and shifts in emphasis we are about to see, history was always closely tied to the perceived political interests of the SED, whether simply constrained and limited or more actively determined and informed by current political agendas. This meant that manifest and willed distortions, sins of omission and commission, are far easier to identify (and castigate) in the East than in the West (although they are far from lacking in some quarters in the West).[58]

[55] The extent to which, and/or the ways in which, history can in principle be 'objective' or 'value neutral', is itself a highly complex question which there is not the space here to pursue.

[56] Heinz Heitzer, *GDR: An Historical Outline* (Dresden: Verlag Zeit im Bild, 1981, trans. of 1979 German original), p. 7.

[57] Walter Schmidt, 'Geschichtsbewußtsein und sozialistische Persönlichkeit bei der Gestaltung der entwickelten sozialistischen Gesellschaft', in Helmut Meier and Walter Schmidt (eds), *Geschichtsbewußtsein und sozialistische Gesellschaft* (Berlin: Dietz Verlag, 1970), p. 21.

[58] See e.g. Hermann Weber, 'Die "Weißen Flecken" in der Geschichte', in Hermann Weber, *Aufbau und Fall einer Diktatur* (Cologne: Bund Verlag, 1991). I have made no attempt above to refer to the more extremist right-wing fringes of western publications, such as the Holocaust denial schools of history. These extraordinary distortions of the historical record were at least not supported –

In the course of the 1960s in the GDR, the focus on revolutionary moments and class struggles was broadened with the ambitious enterprise embarked upon by Jürgen Kuczynski and his colleagues on the history of the German working class. The eight-volume *Geschichte der Deutschen Arbeiterbewegung* was published in 1966; it was followed two years later by the first two general histories of Germany. It has to be admitted that Kuczynski brought refreshingly open perspectives to Marxist history: as he was to put it, with mildly humorous self-deprecation in the Preface to volume 1 of the *Geschichte des Alltags des Deutschen Volkes*, published in 1981: 'We Marxists still have great strides to make in our historical descriptions of class struggles... [We] often focus our entire attention just on the oppressed. As a result, there appears to be only one class that is doing all the struggling.'[59] But completing the picture of class struggles did not (yet) necessarily imply a more inclusive historical or empirically adequate picture: Kuczynski later had to concede that the total omission of any mention, in the relevant volume of his *History of Everyday Life*, of the disappearance of German Jews from German society under Nazism was a rather startling oversight (particularly on the part of a historian who was himself from a Jewish family).[60]

With the establishment of the GDR as an apparently permanent separate German state, enjoying a degree of international recognition and domestic stability, history in the GDR began to become an increasingly professionalized discipline, with a degree of distance from the immediate imperatives of politics.[61] It was also the case that the academic profession was in any event becoming more politically homogeneous and successfully shaped by political strategies and changing institutional patterns. As Ralph Jessen has pointed out, there were increasing numbers of academics who had come to realize that membership of the SED and political conformity was a better route to promotion than the writing of a heavy second dissertation (the traditional German *Habilitation*, replaced in the GDR by the 'Diss. B').[62] By the late 1960s, East

indeed quite the reverse – by the West German government. The SED – although with very different substantive objectives – was not always quite as scrupulous with respect to the rules of historical evidence.

[59] Jürgen Kuczynski, 'The History of the Everyday Life of the German People', repr. in Iggers (ed.) *Marxist Historiography*, p. 38.

[60] Jürgen Kuczynski, *Ein hoffnungsloser Fall von Optimismus? Memoiren 1989–1994* (Berlin: Aufbau Verlag, 1995), pp. 144–5.

[61] This is, in any event, the interpretation advanced by many commentators: cf. Heydemann, etc.

[62] Ralph Jessen, 'Professoren im Sozialismus. Aspekte des Strukturwandels der Hochschullehrerschaft in der Ulbricht-Ära' in Hartmut Kaelble, Jürgen

German academia was increasingly provincial and conformist; and historical research was in any event subjected to five-year planning and stringent political control.

In the 1970s, the conclusion of *Ostpolitik* was accompanied by a shift in historiographical approaches in the GDR. A theoretical debate on the distinction between '*Erbe*' and '*Tradition*' (legacy and tradition) provided the precondition for opening the whole of German history as a legitimate field of inquiry, while recognizing that only certain elements of the historical legacy were deemed to be positive.[63] This historiographical debate coincided with the shift in the definition of 'nation', to a class theory of nation, and the associated constitutional changes.[64] It also laid the foundations for some (apparently) remarkable new developments in East German historiography. How new these developments actually were we shall consider in a moment.

In the course of the later 1970s and 1980s, western observers were somewhat surprised to see the resurrection of what appeared to be 'bourgeois' and 'idealist' elements in GDR historiography. There was a renewed interest in the role of 'great men' in history, with the publication of the two-volume biography of Bismarck by Ernst Engelberg, and the accessible biography of Frederick the Great by Ingrid Mittenzwei.[65] In 1983, the centenary of the death of Karl Marx, commemorations of this great founding father of communism were almost overshadowed by the extraordinary rehabilitation of Martin Luther as a national hero, on the occasion of the quincentenary of his birth. As we have seen in chapter 4 above, the Reformation was now suddenly designated as the idealist precondition for Germany's 'early bourgeois revolution', the German Peasants War, and Luther took a place alongside the old hero of the Peasants War, Thomas Münzer, as a key forebear of the GDR.[66] The renewed

---

Kocka and Hartmut Zwahr (eds), *Sozialgeschichte der DDR* (Stuttgart: Klett-Cotta, 1994), p. 229.

[63] See Helmut Meier and Walter Schmidt (eds), *Erbe und Tradition. Geschichtsdebatte in der DDR* (Berlin: Akademie Verlag, 1988).

[64] See further ch. 7, below.

[65] Ernst Engelberg, *Bismarck*, vols 1–2 (Berlin: Akademie Verlag, 1985, 1990); Ingrid Mittenzwei, *Friedrich II. von Preußen. Eine Biographie* (Berlin: VEB Deutscher Verlag der Wissenschaften, rev. edn, 1982; orig. 1979).

[66] In English, see e.g. Max Steinmetz, 'Theses on the Early Bourgeois Revolution in Germany, 1476–1535', in R. W. Scribner and G. Benecke (eds), *The German Peasants' War 1525: New Viewpoints* (London: George Allen and Unwin, 1979). Münzer is still the real hero, providing an inspiring vision for a future German democratic republic, for which the conditions were not as yet ripe; but Luther clearly paved the way, uniting 'all classes and strata' against the papal church.

interest in Prussia as a field of historical investigation paralleled new approaches to the legacy of Prussia in West Germany in the early 1980s. There thus appeared to be striking similarities, not only in choice of topic, but also in approach: the *causal* role of ideas and great men had not previously been a notable feature of the materialist theory of history as interpreted in the GDR.

Even in the old and standard field of the history of the working classes and the labour movement, there were new theoretical approaches, again with startling parallels to developments in West German historiography in the 1970s and 1980s. The quotation given above from Jürgen Kuczynski, criticizing earlier Marxist history for being one-sided and simplistic, continues by arguing for a broader history from below; his remarks could almost have come from a variety of western protagonists:

> We pay too little heed as well to the fact that there were two kinds of class struggle... the momentous battles and the quiet, everyday struggle. Marxist historiography tends to concentrate on the momentous battles, of which it even then takes a one-sided view as noted above. Very little has been written about the everyday struggle, whether the reluctant toil of slaves and their small acts of sabotage or the diminished productivity of peasants carrying out their feudal obligations as compared with the efforts on their 'own' fields.[67]

In the broader field of social history, much research in the later period of the GDR could as easily have been published, in slightly different wrappings, in the West as in the East. Research on the peasants of the Magdeburg plain, on seating arrangements in eighteenth-century churches as a reflection of social and political structure, on marriage patterns and the formation of a proletariat in nineteenth-century Leipzig, were extraordinarily full of empirical detail and historical insight. Many East German historians adopted the 'sandwich principle': a rich and nutritious empirical filling could be safely topped and tailed by a little dry bread of Marxist-Leninist theory in the introductory and concluding sections.[68] There is no doubt that in the writings of historians such as Hartmut Zwahr or Jan Peters much valuable work was being done on topics in social history which were not directly relevant to present-day politics.

---

[67] Jürgen Kuczynski, 'The History of the Everyday Life of the German People', pp. 38–9.

[68] Cf. my review article, 'Historians and Historiography in the Former GDR', *Bulletin of the German Historical Institute London* (Nov. 1992), pp. 3–10.

This apparent broadening of approach was, however, not limited only to less politically sensitive periods of history: and where it more directly affected current politics and identity, it is a little more difficult to assess. Certainly it is the case that topics which were previously taboo were now on the acceptable historical agenda. The conservative resistance of the July Plot, for example, was now officially acknowledged on the occasion of its fortieth anniversary in 1984; by 1989 it had even acquired a place in school history textbooks.[69] At the same time, the account of Nazism presented by Kurt Pätzold and Manfred Weißbecker reinserted the role of the (admittedly misguided) German people in allowing Nazi anti-semitic policies to be carried out.[70] No longer was there a simplistic distinction between the monopoly capitalist 'fascists' and the innocent people: at first glance, Pätzold's account of the importance of popular indifference to the fate of the Jews appeared, on the face of it, to be quite compatible with the sort of research emanating from Martin Broszat and his colleagues. Western historians such as Konrad Jarausch and Georg Iggers greeted these developments with a degree of cautious enthusiasm.[71] As Iggers was to put it in a 1991 retrospective evaluation of transformations in Marxist historiography, 'in the last 15 years...such issues as that of the popular support of National Socialism and of the complexities of the anti-Nazi resistance, which went beyond the older doctrinal explanations, were cautiously approached.'[72]

However, while there were clear developments in terms particularly of choice of subject or topic, one must query the extent to which this apparent convergence with at least some strands among the diversity of Western approaches was real. The later developments in GDR history have been interpreted by some Western observers, rather cynically, as 'merely' a means of seeking to attain some degree of cultural legitimacy for the GDR at a time when its economic performance was visibly faltering.[73] It is also

---

[69] Reich, 'Bild vom deutschen Widerstand', (n. 10 above).

[70] See e.g. Kurt Pätzold and Manfred Weißbecker, *Hakenkreuz und Totenkopf* (Berlin: VEB Deutscher Verlag der Wissenschaften, 1981). But see also Dietrich Eichholtz and Kurt Gossweiler (eds), *Faschismusforschung* (Berlin: Akademie Verlag, 1980) for a restatement of orthodox views.

[71] Cf. e.g. Konrad Jarausch, 'Vom Zusammenbruch zur Erneuerung: Überlegungen zur Krise der ostdeutschen Geschichtswissenschaft', in Jarausch (ed.), *Zwischen Parteilichkeit und Professionalität*, pp. 16–17; Georg Iggers, 'Geschichtswissenschaft in der ehemaligen DDR aus der Sicht der USA', ibid., pp. 65–6.

[72] Georg Iggers, Introduction to Iggers (ed.), *Marxist Historiography*, p. 35.

[73] Cf. the discussion in ch. 4 above.

quite clear that some aspects of the shift were of considerable benefit to the state: the Luther anniversary celebrations, for example, brought in large amounts of western hard currency in the related tourist industry, given that virtually all the key historical sites associated with the Reformation – Wittenberg, where the ninety-five theses were nailed to the door; the Wartburg Castle, where Luther translated the New Testament of the Bible and allegedly threw an inkpot at the Devil, and other heartlands of the Reformation – were located on East German soil.

It is relatively easy to document the *coincidence* of the periodization of historiographical trends with wider political trends, particularly with respect to national identity claims. While still seeking reunification, and conscious of links with the West, the GDR pursued an interpretation of German history which saw all the progressive trends in German history leading to the GDR as the inevitable culmination of historical progress. West Germany had not fully overcome the past, but rather represented continuity with reactionary capitalist forces of the penultimate stage of history: the GDR, on the other hand, was on the final stretch towards communist perfection. When, however, *Ostpolitik* seemed to have confirmed the separation of two German states for the foreseeable future, the policy of constructing a new GDR-specific national identity was combined with an attempt to reappropriate the whole of the German past to provide emotional identification with the new state.

That, in any event, is the simple and functionalist narrative. But it is wise to remember the old maxim: correlation does not necessarily equal causation. To put the question perhaps a little more pointedly: although one can see functionality for a GDR 'national legitimation' of developments such as the *Tradition/Erbe* debate, and the appropriation of the whole of German history in 1980s, one must nevertheless ask whether the function *explains* these developments. This issue requires further exploration.

There are some interesting pointers to a much earlier political determination of the apparently radical shifts of the later 1970s and 1980s. (It should be remembered that, even if brochures and pamphlets can be produced very quickly, more substantial academic books are not readily written overnight!) Already in 1964 we have Ernst Engelberg – author of the later Bismarck biography – urging the importance of writing accessible and comprehensive historical accounts which serve the communist cause. In his address on the occasion of the refoundation of the Historical Section of the Academy of Sciences, Engelberg realistically assesses the attractiveness of much West German historical writing, to which even East Germans must have recourse as reference works. GDR history must begin to compete on the terrain to which West Germans have so far laid claim: not only 'representatives of democracy and socialism' but also

> depictions of Charlemagne, Otto I, Frederick the Great of Prussia, Bismarck, Hindenburg, Stresemann and other political exponents of the exploiting classes can make a magnificent contribution to expunging from historical consciousness false conceptions of Germany's past. The development of historical-biographical research, which so far has been a domain of the bourgeois historiography of West Germany, belongs among the most urgent tasks of planning and direction.[74]

Moreover, if we analyse some of the academic works which were the fruits of this change of emphasis, there continue to be some rather curious features. It may be helpful in this connection to consider for a moment the sense in which these developments can be considered to be 'Marxist'. The answer has to be somewhat differentiated.

Works published in the GDR clearly had to be Marxist in terms of openly professed values and sympathies; there is not the sort of hesitancy about expressing value judgements as is found in much would-be objective Western historiography. 'Good' and 'bad' are identified unequivocally, in a way that may be widely found in writings on Nazism in the West, but only in a more muted form, and with a degree of self-restraint, on most other topics among Western historians (with some notable exceptions on both the right and the left). It is also Marxist in the sense of assumptions about periodization, with use of, for example, an unexamined notion of 'late feudalism' rather than the more theory-neutral term 'eighteenth [or whichever] century'. It is Marxist with respect to particular concepts, especially the concepts of class and class struggle as organizing concepts for virtually all historical analyses.

There is therefore a framework of explicit values and metatheoretical framework. The question then has to be whether, or to what extent, this framework biases, predetermines or distorts the *explanations* which are advanced in many of the later academic historical writings of the GDR.

The materialist theory of history is not always, or even often, reduced to a simplistic 'base determines superstructure' mantra. In many of the works mentioned above, the complexity and detail

[74] Ernst Engelberg, *Der umfassende Aufbau des Sozialismus und die Aufgaben der Historiker* (Berlin: Akademie Verlag, 1964), p. 23.

of empirical exploration of the interrelationships between ideas, values, material interests, politics, are relatively compatible with many forms of western neo-Marxist as well as Weberian approaches to historical analysis. This is perhaps particularly the case with some of the social history writings dealing with the nineteenth century or earlier periods (Hartmut Zwahr, Helga Schultz).[75]

But this is far from always being the case, and was infinitely more difficult when discussing directly politically relevant topics. Consider for a moment the work of Kurt Pätzold on popular anti-semitism in the Third Reich. This was widely acclaimed as having broken an earlier taboo and opened up a new field in the GDR. However, when analysed more closely, the situation is rather more ambiguous.

In the Introduction to his (very useful) edited collection of documents on anti-semitism and genocide, Pätzold presents what is, on closer inspection, a somewhat distorted view.[76] In a curious adoption of Hitler's own conflation of Jewishness and Bolshevism, Pätzold manages to create an integral link between anti-semitism and anti-Marxism. In Pätzold's interpretation, racism and 'racial anti-semitism' are integrally linked with 'German imperialist interests in domination and expansion... The racial doctrine was above all an instrument of struggle against the German working class'.[77] Those sections of the population to whom anti-semitism appealed turn out to be the 'not-so-good' classes from the Marxist point of view, the 'backward sections of the population', such as the 'bourgeois and petty bourgeois strata'.[78]

In a positively astonishing statement, Pätzold assures his readers that facts need not get in the way of this interpretation. Appearances belie the underlying realities:

> Whatever appearance may be suggested by analysis of the origins, impulses, aims and goals of fascist racism and racial anti-semitism, it

---

[75] It has to be noted, however, that Helga Schultz also contributed to what she agreed subsequently were historically inaccurate 'Theses on Berlin', on the occasion of its 750th anniversary celebrations – and she even, somewhat emotionally, declared in public at a conference in Göttingen in 1996 that she had done this enthusiastically ('Ich hab es gern getan'.) See also now the published proceedings of this conference, re-evaluating the record and achievements of GDR historians: Georg Iggers, Konrad Jarausch, Matthias Middell and Martin Sabrow (eds), *Die DDR-Geschichtswissenschaft als Forschungsproblem* (Munich: Oldenbourg, 1998; *Historische Zeitschrift* suppl. 27).
[76] Kurt Pätzold (ed.), *Verfolgung, Vertreibung, Vernichtung* (Frankfurt am Main: Röderberg Verlag, 1984; orig. Leipzig: Verlag Philipp Reclam jun., 1983).
[77] Ibid., p. 8.
[78] Ibid., p. 16.

lies within the social field of imperialist interests in domination, power and profit. All the facts which provide evidence, before and after 1933, of the participation of petty bourgeois masses in the uniforms of the SA, the SS and the Hitler Youth, or out of uniform, do not affect the essence of fascist racism. Just as, in many places in previous centuries, groups of the population were aroused against minorities, tormented and murdered them, without seeing through to the fact that they were being manipulated, or knowing in whose interests, so too the fascist-influenced (*faschisierten*) petty bourgeois and workers were not aware of their real role.[79]

This passage accepts certain empirical evidence, but distorts it in order, first, to assert the 'imperialist-capitalist' theory of fascism; secondly, to continue to exonerate the common people, the workers and petty bourgeois who were carriers of the system; and thirdly, to devalue their essential humanity, in assuming that they were so easily manipulated that they were unaware of their true role. It thus simultaneously both exonerates and demeans the people, the innocent victims of such a degree of false consciousness that they clearly did not even know they were sustaining a system of mass murder. This demeaning view of the masses is directly compatible with the view of the people in the 'workers' and peasants' state', the GDR: here, too, they are not sufficiently mature to realize what is in their 'real' best interests, and therefore need the Party to rule on their behalf (as in the ubiquitous slogan 'Everything for the good of the people' – *Alles zum Wohle des Volkes* – even if against the expressed wishes of the *Volk* who have to be walled in for their own good).

This sort of concession to fact, only to reinsert it in a previously conceived and politically desired framework, is even more evident in the massive popular textbook history of Germany first published in 1974 under the title *Klassenkampf – Tradition – Sozialismus* and republished, on the occasion of the thirtieth anniversary of the GDR, as *Grundriß der deutschen Geschichte*.[80] Throughout, the innocent reader is allowed no opportunity to overlook the political and moral significance of the material presented. The alibi of the 'majority of the German people' who were thrown into uniform in Hitler's service is reiterated: the explanation is a combination of 'hate campaigns and terror' on the one hand, and being 'stultified' (*verdummt*) and 'blinded' on the other.[81] The fate of the Jews is

[79] Ibid., p. 19.
[80] Zentralinstitut für Geschichte der Akademie der Wissenschaften der DDR (ed.), *Grundriß der deutschen Geschichte* (Berlin: VEB Deutscher Verlag der Wissenschaften, 1979).
[81] Ibid., p. 471.

reduced almost to insignificance, easily overlooked in a work of this size, and firmly demoted in the midst of a paragraph about communist resistance:

> The fascists drew a net over Europe of concentration camps and extermination centres. Millions of people were deported into Germany as slave labour in factories and on the land. The SS, special *Einsatzgruppen*, the army and police units acted with particular brutality against communists and other resistance fighters. Millions of Jewish citizens were murdered in Poland and the Soviet Union, but also in other countries, according to a firm plan, incorporated within a system, and declared to be the 'Final Solution of the Jewish Question'. The fascist occupation regime was characterized by robbery and plunder, mass murder in 'factories of death', and brutal measures of repression against all progressive and humanist ideas and strivings, against the antifascist resistance.[82]

Both this passage, and the slant provided in Pätzold's gloss on the sources, read remarkably like the sort of picture presented in the concentration camp brochures and museum guides discussed in previous chapters; and, as we have seen, the 1985 commemoration leaflet did not even go this far.

It almost seems as if, in introducing previously taboo topics in order solely to reinsert them in older frameworks of interpretation, regime-sustaining historians were practising something akin to historical innoculation: introducing a small dose of the heretical virus together with its ideologically sound antidote, such that the GDR citizen's theoretical defences would be ready if inadvertently exposed to similar themes in western publications.

It has sometimes been assumed by western commentators that many of the academic historians who wrote the new and apparently more diverse, open forms of historical work may have experienced this as a form of 'liberation' or 'release' from earlier political constraints. It is true that for some scholars in the 1980s there was a genuine degree of increasing freedom of manoeuvre – which, it has to be said, was not always fully exploited. Many were professionals produced by, and having internalized the aims of, a state which was by now well-established and self-confident (and which had for the most part, indeed virtually to the very end, no inklings of its imminent demise). But it is also quite clear that at least some of them introduced – and politicians permitted the introduction of – new notes into the historiography of the GDR as part of a predetermined plan to compete with West German

[82] Ibid., p. 472.

historiography on common terrain, but with different interpretations.

An old joke in the GDR ran as follows. Question: 'What is the hardest thing to predict under communism?' Answer: 'The past'. There is (as with all jokes) a measure of truth in this. When history is conceived as a story of progress, then it is also a story of villains and heroes. And the evaluation given to particular villains and heroes can change with changing political interests. Those who were unexpectedly resurrected as heroes in the 1980s had earlier been castigated as the reactionaries of history, impeding the path of historical progress towards its glorious culmination in communist society. These later historiographical developments have to be set in the context of other aspects of GDR politics at the time, including the famed church/state agreement of 1978, which can now be seen as not so much as a step towards pluralism, but rather a form of co-option or *Gleichschaltung* of the churches by the state.[83]

With respect to the *substantive* interpretations advanced, one must also ask to what extent any particular account is 'distorted' by some political agenda. It is quite clear that many awkward aspects were downplayed or omitted, particularly in accounts designated specifically for overt political purposes. Some 'blank spots' are quite startling. But it would be a mistake to think that the blank spots or more political blinkers were only to be found on one side of the Wall.

What then of West German history? The writings on totalitarianism provide a classic version of a politically drenched concept deployed both to explain (away) and denounce. Assumptions about uniqueness and comparability of patterns in German history, whether a nineteenth-century *Sonderweg* or the European dimension of Nazism, also clearly have certain political implications. The real question is the extent to which empirical refutation of any particular paradigm is in principle possible. It would seem that the Marxist views elaborated in the GDR of 'underlying realities', irrrespective of 'surface appearances', represent rather formidable articles of faith which cannot be easily jettisoned in face of disturbing empirical facts, however much the latter may change. But the shifts in position over interpretations of Imperial Germany, or the *Sonderweg*, of many West German historians suggest a far greater degree of empirical openness and flexibility.[84]

[83] Cf. my account in *Anatomy of a Dictatorship: Inside the GDR, 1949–1989* (Oxford: Oxford University Press, 1995), ch. 4.
[84] This is of course to skirt very lightly over more fundamental issues, which there is not space to consider in detail here, such as the extent to which political

A very general point may also be made here about the filtering through of research to the teaching of history in the schools. Quite clearly, the teaching of history was bent to fit (changing) political purposes in the GDR. As Reinhold Kruppa put it, through the teaching of history schoolchildren will 'make the acquaintance of the revolutionary heritage of the popular masses, in particular the working class. Through a variety of ways and means they will be enabled to recognize interrelations and historical laws of social development and will be able to draw the lessons of history for the present and future.'[85] The West German government was similarly determined to ensure that, through education, its citizens should learn the lessons of history: not only (as in the GDR) to reject Nazism, but to value democracy in the western interpretation of this term. Thus textbooks made no pretence at 'value neutrality': they emphasized the abhorrent nature of the Nazi crimes of genocide, and the importance of learning to be good democratic citizens who would never let such evil deeds occur again. But, as we shall see, the impact was very often to create an obsession with a diffuse, ill-defined sense of collective shame – or a reaction against, even boredom with, this obsession – rather than a differentiated engagement with analysis of the past.

Historians often assume that their work plays a major role in shaping popular historical perceptions. But historical interpretations are neither themselves so free from contemporary political influences, nor necessarily translated so easily from the pages of history books into the contents of people's minds, as some professional historians might like to think.

Michael Roth has pointed to the way in which the representation of the past is not just about historical reconstruction and/or political appropriation (what he terms the 'empirical and...pragmatic investments in the past'); it is also about *piety*.[86] By 'piety' Roth means 'the placing of oneself in relation to the past in its otherness and potential connection to oneself... Piety is the turning of oneself so as to be in relation to the past, to experience oneself as coming after (perhaps emerging out of or against) the past. This is the

considerations determine the choice of concepts and theoretical frameworks of inquiry, the extent to which they affect the selection and depiction of material, and the ways in which the results of inquiry are deployed in order to present a particular historical picture with certain contemporary political implications.

[85] Reinhold Kruppa, 'Zur Weiterentwicklung des Geschichtsunterrichts an den allgemeinbildenden polytechnischen Schulen' in Meier and Schmidt (eds), *Geschichtsbewußtsein und sozialistische Gesellschaft*, p. 107.

[86] Michael Roth, *The Ironist's Cage: Memory, Trauma and the Construction of History* (New York: Columbia University Press, 1995), p. 16.

attempt at fidelity to (not correspondence with) the past.'[87] Roth employs this concept – which he admits 'has at best an awkward place in contemporary thinking about history'[88] – in a very personal manner when he discusses his own sense of Jewish identity in relation to Claude Lanzmann's film *Shoah*. He interprets *Shoah* as an 'act of piety' which makes it possible 'to dwell with loss, to suffer one's poverty, to be linked together in the presence of those absent and to give them...an everlasting name...[T]o incarnate the past, to name it, and to remain in the present.'[89]

This extraordinary expression of a deeply personal and authentic sense of piety, of relation to those who perished in the Holocaust, on the part of an American Jewish historian working in a profession more often characterized by confessions of 'value neutrality', even relativism and cynicism, is compelling. But such piety was infinitely more difficult for those who were complicit in the crimes of the perpetrators, or who wished to assure the post-war world that, while speaking in the name of the German nation, they rejected these crimes entirely, but still could not quite identify with the victims. Piety was one thing the West Germans sought to bring in shovelfuls, but always awkwardly tempered with misrepresentations and controversial appropriations. Virtually every ritual of remembrance was an attempted act of piety – but when it went amiss, in making the 'wrong' connections and identifications in Bitburg, or opting for empirical reconstruction rather than piety in Jenninger's speech on 9 November, then every vibration sent out the wrong signals. The public presentation of the past in West Germany was not and could never be a simple act of piety, but was always a contested, controversial and sensitive terrain.

Life was in this sense much simpler as far as the outward and visible signs of the past in the GDR were concerned: the SED clearly invested most heavily in the 'pragmatic' approach to political instrumentalization. But this was at the expense of both accurate reconstruction and authentic piety.

When does the past become history? One might answer, when it is no longer imbued with innumerable contemporary sensitivities, pieties, taboos – when it is no longer of vital contemporary significance. In Germany after Auschwitz, this has not yet come about. And, since the nation is unable to tell a collectively acceptable story about its own past, it has serious problems with developing a stable collective identity in the present that does not demand constant soul-searching and repeated attempts at redefinition.

[87] Ibid., p. 16.
[88] Ibid., p. 17.
[89] Ibid., p. 226.

6

Collective Memory? Patterns of Historical Consciousness

In the mid-1980s Auschwitz survivor Primo Levi wrote:

> Human memory is a marvellous but fallacious instrument...It is
> certain that practice (in this case, frequent re-evocation) keeps mem-
> ories fresh and alive...but it is also true that a memory evoked too
> often, and expressed in the form of a story, tends to become fixed in a
> stereotype, in a form tested by experience, crystallised, perfected,
> adorned, which installs itself in the place of the raw memory and
> grows at its expense.[1]

In horribly prophetic words (he was to commit suicide in 1987, a
year after publication of this book), Levi continues:

> The memory of a trauma suffered or inflicted is itself traumatic
> because recalling it is painful or at least disturbing: a person who
> was wounded tends to block out the memory so as not to renew the
> pain; the person who has inflicted the wound pushes the memory
> deep down, to be rid of it, to alleviate the feeling of guilt...[B]oth are
> in the same trap, but it is the oppressor, and he alone, who has
> prepared it and activated it, and if he suffers from this, it is right
> that he should suffer; and it is iniquitous that the victim should suffer
> from it, as indeed he does suffer from it, even at a distance of
> decades. Once again, it must be observed, mournfully, that the injury
> cannot be healed; it extends through time, and the Furies... perpet-
> uate the tormentor's work by denying peace to the tormented.[2]

---

[1] Primo Levi, *The Drowned and the Saved* (London: Michael Joseph, 1988;
orig. Italian, 1986), pp. 11–12.
[2] Ibid., p. 12.

Levi indicates here, with the anguish of his own experience, just what difficulties are raised by the memory of trauma. Yet the question of memory is a vital one which we must seek to address, however imperfect and tentative our comments will be.

There are key questions here. Did East Germans grow up in a guilt-free political culture? Were West Germans deeply affected by the all-pervasive culture of collective shame? What was the interplay between personal experiences, private stories, and the kaleidoscope of public representations of the past?

The concept of collective memory

First we need to look briefly but explicitly at what we mean by collective memory. Even individual memory is a notoriously difficult concept. We all experience our own, private sense of memory; and we are existentially aware of the fact that personal memory is crucial to our individual identities. We (selectively) remember our childhoods, our background, our past aspirations, achievements and failures; we remember relationships, we mourn losses, we face our own individual futures shaped by our perceptions of where we have come from, where we are going. And many of us have witnessed the anguish and loss of identity that is often a concomitant of illnesses such as Alzheimer's Disease or other dementias. We know, too, the tricks that memory can play, and the difficulties we may have – even as fully functioning, well-adjusted adults – with remembering certain events or facts. We know that our memories are not simple unrefracted reflections of the past, but are in part products of the present, both prompted and limited by surviving evidence, records, the memories of others, current conversations. There is by now a well-developed scientific literature on aspects of individual memory, discussing issues such as the differences between short-term and long-term memory, difficulties in retrieval or failure to register and encode.

The concept of 'collective memory' is even more problematic. There are a variety of approaches to this concept, first popularized by Maurice Halbwachs over half a century ago. Halbwachs used the (apocryphal) story of an Eskimo girl who was unable to present her memories in a new social and cultural context to argue that the essentially private, internal act of remembering can only take place within a collective social and cultural framework: 'No memory is possible outside frameworks used by people living in society to determine and retrieve their recollections.'[3] Halbwachs's view of 'society' was a great deal less totalizing than might be assumed: his work looked, for example, at religious collective memories, or at such small social units as the family, in which a 'framework of domestic memory' might be built up through shared secrets, anniversaries, ways of doing things known only to the family group.

There is clearly much mileage in such an approach, although many historians would now be more comfortable speaking of 'public discourses' about the past, rather than 'collective memory'. It is clear that the very terms and concepts through which people think are not personal – however personal and private the issue which is being thought about – but are themselves collective products of culture and history. In ways which seem quite extraordinary in relation to internal, individual memory, human beings are inextricably, inescapably, intrinsically constituted through their wider social and cultural environment. Moreover, perceptions of the past are deeply affected by experiences of the present. 'Real' memories are overlain by later reinterpretations: they are complicated too by taboos, by what it is permissible to remember, what must be repressed, what must be presented in a different light.

Some scholars have tried to adapt the concept by speaking not of 'collective' but rather of *'collected* memory'. James Young, for instance, prefers the notion of 'collected memory' as referring to 'the many discrete memories that are gathered into common memorial spaces and assigned common meaning . . . If societies remember, it is only insofar as their institutions and rituals organize, shape, even inspire their constituents' memories.'[4] Even this attempt to break down the concept is a little problematic: it may be admirable for Young's purposes, as an approach to the perception of multiple meanings, and changing significance, in memorials and sites of memory (aspects of which have been surveyed in preceding chapters); but it is less helpful when it comes to trying to tap into more inchoate, less visible forms of popular historical consciousness.

Even if we agree that what we are looking at is current discourses about the past, rather than some more metaphysical notion of a 'collective memory', there are methodological problems. Sophisticated sociological techniques for measuring 'historical consciousness', for example, may involve extensive surveys of representative

[3] Maurice Halbwachs, *On Collective Memory*, ed. and intro by Lewis Coser (Chicago and London: University of Chicago Press, 1992) p. 43.
[4] James E. Young, *The Texture of Memory. Holocaust Memorials and Meaning* (New Haven and London: Yale University Press, 1993), Preface, p. xi.

samples of the population, documenting knowledge of and attitudes towards particular historical events and periods; but, however interesting the findings, they tell us little or nothing about the real importance, the practical salience of such views for and in everyday life; nor do they necessarily capture the categories within which people think and talk, at home, in the pub, in the street. The more open-ended techniques of oral history or anthropology are more suggestive in these respects, but even they involve, to a greater or lesser extent, the bias of the presence of the observer and tend of necessity to involve only small samples from which it is difficult to generalize. Novels and autobiographies, which may emit a spurious sense of capturing authentic forms of consciousness and conveying a genuine flavour of the *Zeitgeist*, are by definition written by exceptionally articulate individuals; and although the shorter accounts provided in 'protocol' literature may be more revealing in some respects, they too are based on very limited numbers when one is trying to tap into 'collective' phenomena. Creative literature, drama and films may in any event do as much – or more – actively to shape than merely to reflect the terms of popular discourse about the past (which of course does not make them any less relevant for the topic).

Thus, we are faced with interrelated theoretical and methodological problems. We have the sense that something exists, is an important social phenomenon; but we have difficulties in providing a precise definition, and determining appropriate empirical indicators and methodologies for capturing and representing this phenomenon. This does not mean that the task is hopeless: merely that a variety and range of sources must be used, with a degree of awareness of the provisional and partial character of what we are saying – combined with a commitment to the view that saying something, however approximate and groping, is better than saying nothing at all. In the end, whatever we do, we are only examining facets of a broader question which we cannot hope to encompass in its entirety.

For all these cautionary comments, then, it is possible to achieve certain insights. We do have some definition of what it is we are after. The *subject* has to do with memories of an experience, a time, place, event that is of widespread significance for a particular generation or group. What we are interested in is a set of layers of experience, perception, and subsequent signification: initially, the 'authentic' memories or 'real experiences' of the relevant historical phenomena, as embedded in individual memories; secondly, the ways of categorizing, conceptualizing, describing, these phenomena – in other words, the social constructs which are used to label and classify them; and finally, the wider interpretive frameworks into which they are inserted as a means of rationalizing, reinterpreting, legitimizing, 'coming to terms with', the past; the stories which are told, the 'historical pictures' (*Geschichtsbilder*) into which the individual memories are reinserted and endowed with wider significance.

The first of these layers is quite discrete and peculiar to the 'worm's eye view', the individual's own experience – although many, perhaps millions, will have had very similar experiences, differing only in detail. (It is almost by definition this which makes the experience a potential object of *collective* memory, rather than purely private and individual memories.) The latter layers constitute a kind of 'collective conversation' about the past: the language, the terms of this conversation, the questions and stereotypical answers, are very much collective endeavours. Only those who lived through the experience in question will have authentic personal memories; but those who were not present at the time can participate in the 'collective memory' by an imagined reconstruction of the experience in question, and by taking part in the 'collective conversations' about it. 'Historical pictures' and collective 'discourses' about the past might perhaps be more apposite terms than 'collective memories'.

It is in this sense that the notion of patterns of collective memory is being used here. The plural is used intentionally: for there never was one single 'collective memory', one generally accepted 'conversation about the past', within either of the two German states. Differences, based in part in differences of class, gender and generation, but particularly in differences of political outlook and experience, are infinitely more striking than similarities. Former victims, survivors and their relatives, on the one hand, and their erstwhile oppressors and latterday sympathizers on the other, find it hard to inhabit the same mental terrain. There are dramatic generational contrasts between those who were adults during the Third Reich, and those who came to maturity in the very different political climates of the 1960s and after. Taboos and pieties overlay and colour previous memories and inherited tales. Memory is not simply given, passively present: an effort is required to reconstruct, in what has been termed 'memory work'.

Within each of these groups, there are, too, different aspects of the process of 'working through the past'. There is the cognitive level: seeking to understand and assign meaning to what happened in the past – which may at the time have been perceived only partially (in both senses) and which now needs to be placed in a radically altered political context, and a broader framework of

knowledge. There is also the more emotional (or 'affective') level:
seeking to express and work through a wide range of very difficult
emotions about this period, which was one of immense personal
tragedy in a very wide variety of ways. And even for those who had
(as Chancellor Kohl once put it with a degree of tactlessness) the
'fortune to have been born late', there are the legacies of living with
what their parents and grandparents had (or had not) done, as well
as empathetic emotional reactions which are almost inevitably
aroused by the confrontation with the facts of the Holocaust. Perhaps most disagreeably there is also a fairly widespread phenomenon which might be termed *Vergangenheitsbewältigung* ('mastery
of the past') as a widespread societal practice, a collective means of
seeking exculpation or absolution.

This chapter can only begin to scratch the surface of these complexities, to provide a few select examples to illustrate the range
and variations.[5]

Victims and perpetrators

Memory does not take place in a vacuum, but under specific historical circumstances. Countless thousands of Germans were forcibly
excluded from participating in collective memory as 'Germans', or
indeed even from being.

From many of those who had formed, and felt themselves to be,
part of the community of Germans before 1933, the possibility of
continuing to contribute to German society, culture and memory
was removed, against their will. Across the world, there are people
who fled from, or whose parents and grandparents fled from, the
Nazi system of terror. Their memories and the impact on their lives
and personalities should form part of this story; but it is a part
which more often contributes to the development now of other
cultures, other societies, and has for the most part been excluded
from what is deemed to be 'German' today.[6]

Those excluded from the *Volksgemeinschaft*, including not only
'racial' and political prisoners but also those classified by the Nazis
as physically or mentally unsuited to the 'Aryan' breeding stock,

---

[5] Here, more than ever, I am aware that a single chapter cannot possibly do
justice to the topic; it can only indicate some of the parameters of the question.

[6] See particularly works such as Lawrence Langer, *Holocaust Testimonies.
The Ruins of Memory* (New Haven and London: Yale University Press, 1991);
Aaron Hass, *The Aftermath. Living with the Holocaust* (Cambridge: Cambridge
University Press, 1995); Aaron Hass, *In the Shadow of the Holocaust. The
Second Generation* (London: I. B. Tauris, 1991).

and therefore sterilized or otherwise maltreated, were very often not only physically broken but emotionally hurt in ways which could never be 'overcome' or undone. To speak of 'memory', or 'historical consciousness', rather than an active struggle to live with the wounds and scars, the continuing legacy of the past, is almost tragically inappropriate for many victims of Nazi policies, wherever they subsequently settled.

Holocaust survivors sought to find ways of living in the world after the trauma they experienced: repeatedly telling younger generations, in the hope that such a thing could never be allowed to happen again.[7] Relatively few Jews felt able to try to make their post-Holocaust lives on German soil. A degree of exclusion, displacement, took place even for those who survived and emerged from hiding within Germany, and perhaps even more so for those who chose to return to Germany from abroad. They returned, as Hans Mayer put it, to 'a German foreign country'.[8] It was not a matter of simple reintegration, picking up the threads of lives that had been broken off; nor were responses of the remaining German population unaffected by their experiences. After twelve years of state-initiated separation, degradation, removal from German society and, for so many of the relatives and friends of survivors, from life itself, there could be no easy return to the integration characteristic of German Jewish life prior to 1933.

Frank Stern summarizes the immediate post-war situation thus: 'The general German mood towards the Jews was one of social distance, influenced both by pre-Nazi economic anti-Semitic stereotypes and arguments in favor of a "balance of victims", equating the Germans who died as a result of Allied air raids with the Jews murdered in Auschwitz.'[9] Although it was no longer state ideology, but rather absolutely taboo, high levels of anti-semitism were still prevalent among the population: perhaps around

[7] There is by now a rapidly growing literature on these themes. The late Rabbi Hugo Gryn, who settled in London, told of the personal and theological difficulties involved in answering the question 'What have I done that I deserved to be saved, and all those others perished? How can I make my life worthy of having been saved?' Aaron Hass, *The Aftermath*, emphasizes not only the suffering, but also the strengths and successes, of survivors. See also e.g. Aharon Appelfeld, 'The Awakening', and Lawrence Langer, 'Remembering Survival' in G. Hartman (ed.), *Holocaust Remembrance* (Oxford: Basil Blackwell, 1994).

[8] Quoted in Frank Stern, 'Breaking the "Cordon Sanitaire" of memory: The Jewish Encounter with German Society', in Alvin Rosenfeld (ed.), *Thinking about the Holocaust* (Bloomington and Indianapolis: Indiana University Press, 1997), p. 220.

[9] Ibid., p. 223.

one-third of Germans in the early post-war years were, to varying degrees, anti-semitic or racist. Commenting on declining percentages over the years, Bergmann and Erb argue that anti-semitism was not so much educated out as that it 'grew out'; in particular, the notion that there was a real 'Jewish question' which needed an 'answer' (if not the 'solution' adopted by Hitler) declined in salience with the passage of generations.[10] The new officially ordained anti-antisemitism was genuinely carried by only a minority of (usually left-wing) parties, intellectuals, the highbrow press, and was unstable in the highest places in both East and West Germany. As we have seen, a wave of anti-Zionism swept over the GDR in the early 1950s; and in the Federal Republic, 'restitution' carried with it a degree of barely suppressed irritation that the Jews (still stereotyped and perceived as 'other') continued to be a 'problem', now for German international stature.

Jewish communities did re-emerge, and seek to re-establish patterns of religious observance. Many non-practising Jewish Germans also sought, in one way or another, to reintegrate into German society; some were actively politically committed (on both sides of the border, but with particularly prominent examples of communists of Jewish background in the GDR), while others sought merely to reconstruct some semblance of a 'normal' life in what they had previously considered to be their homeland. But the experience of the Third Reich had left a lasting impact on the perceptions and culture of German-Jewish communities. The Holocaust was a defining element in attempts to construct any kind of identity – whether assimilationist or otherwise – in Germany, shaping the attitudes of second and third generations and constituting a focal point which had to be addressed, whatever the range of answers given.[11]

Under the conditions of state-ordained philo-semitism in the West, the sociocultural assimilation and easy intermingling of the pre-1933 period had been replaced by an acute, almost hyper-sensitivity to the issue of difference. A sharp separation was sustained between 'Germans' (in whose name terrible acts had been committed, but who had allegedly known nothing about it) and 'Jews' who remained 'other' – and reminded many non-Jewish Germans of their stigmatized status in the eyes of the wider world. A widely

[10] See the summaries of surveys in Werner Bergmann, 'Antisemitismus in öffentlichen Konflikten, 1949–94', and Werner Bergmann and Rainer Erb, 'Wie antisemitisch sind die Deutschen? Meinungsumfragen 1945–1994', in Wolfgang Benz (ed.), *Antisemitismus in Deutschland. Zur Aktualität eines Vorurteils* (Munich: dtv, 1995).

[11] On West Germany, see esp. Lynn Rapaport, *Jews in Germany after the Holocaust* (Cambridge: Cambridge University Press, 1997).

prevalent picture of 'Jews' was now often one of corpses, or Americans, or Israelis – not of those who had actually lived and been killed, whether Germans, Hungarians, Poles, or whoever (in all the varieties of pre-Holocaust European Jewish life). There was often little understanding or active memory of the fact that German 'Jews' plucked out from among their midst were also 'Germans'; there was, thus, an implicit continuity with a Nazi world view or conception of what the 'national community' was held to consist in. German Jews who were proud of their double identity, such as Michael Wolffsohn (who describes himself as a 'German-Jewish patriot'), are not only distinctive but also indicate, simply by the explicit discussion of the issue, its continuing sensitivity even half a century later.[12] Memories for these groups were clearly very different from those of their 'Aryan' compatriots.

Even many who lived through the Third Reich with less personal danger, but experienced a degree of rejection for whatever reason, still experienced difficulties with identity in German society after 1945. *Mischlinge*, those of mixed parentage (and often not practising Judaism) had a peculiarly ambiguous status. Neither members of the Jewish community, nor entirely secure among Germans who had swallowed the myth of 'Aryan' and 'non-Ayran', many suffered a sense of ill-ease, of not belonging. As one West German *Mischling* put it:

> You know, when one has another relationship to the Jewish religion and culture, it's probably less of a burden, but when one has none at all... My grandparents were already baptized, I grew up in an absolutely Christian home, and suddenly one is put in a caste to which one has no relation at all. That sticks to you for the rest of your life. Somehow idiotically.[13]

When one even begins to consider such issues, it becomes evident just how much 'memory' is not simply a question of intellectual

[12] Cf. e.g. Michael Wolfssohn, *Ewige Schuld? 40 Jahre deutsch-jüdische-israelische Beziehungen* (Munich: Piper, 1988), p. 8, where he describes himself as a 'German-Jewish patriot'.

[13] 'Frau Verena Groth' (not her real name) in Alison Owings, *Frauen: German Women Recall the Third Reich* (New Brunswick, NJ: Rutgers University Press, 1993), p. 113. Although these interviews were conducted in a rather naive manner, the material is often quite fascinating, revealing a very wide range of perceptions, from the committed right-wing nationalism of Frau Mundt, through the odd combination of humanitarianism, a desire to help and yet persistent racial categorizations evident in Frau von Lingen's testimony, to the ambivalent and schismatic identity of Frau Groth, the *Mischling* quoted here.

'pictures about the past', but is also very much about negotiating one's way – and one's identity – in relationships in the present. The tensions inevitably remain, on both sides; it is not easy for those who have been rejected from a social milieu to reintegrate as though nothing had happened – and even less so when the rejection was of the enormity of Nazi racialism.

'Jewishness' was for the most part (after the anti-semitism of the early 1950s, which was relatively muted in comparison with developments elsewhere in the Soviet bloc at this time) rather more suppressed as a domestic public issue in the GDR, although anti-Zionism, and anti-Israeli sentiments, remained a key strand in the GDR's official foreign policy. The sensitivities on a personal level were no less evident, although differently affected by the socio-political context. For one thing, 'Jews' were officially defined as a religious (rather than ethnic and cultural) community, and the proportion of religiously active Jews was a tiny and dwindling minority.[14] For another, as we have seen, despite certain privileges such as higher pensions, to define oneself as 'Jewish' was again to take on a very second-class status, this time as passive 'victim' of, rather than active 'resistance fighter' against, fascism. Thus for those who sought a more active political status as committed communists (or other active opponents of Hitler), the 'Jewish' element had to be downplayed. Although it was not a topic of repeated explicit public attention (as in the West), it was thus for many East Germans of Jewish descent very much alive on a more private level.

Let us take a couple of revealing examples from the early years in the GDR. The past was, inevitably, an explicitly discussed issue among children of Jewish survivors and returning emigrés. Irene Runge, for example, who was born and lived in the USA until the age of seven, and whose family then emigrated to the GDR in the McCarthy era, was among the Jews in the GDR interviewed by Robin Ostow in 1983–4. (All Ostow's interviews were conducted with a representative of the GDR state present; but they are revealing, nonetheless.) For all the essential, defining presence of the past for these Jewish survivors, it was not something which was explicitly discussed with their German contemporaries in the 1950s and 1960s. Irene Runge speaks of the way she was fully aware of the fact that her German schoolfriends had families and living relatives while she did not, but she never quite brought herself to confront the question out loud: 'they had pictures of their families: an uncle, brother or cousin in uniform, German uniform. But I was brought

[14] See esp. Robin Ostow, *Jews in Contemporary East Germany* (Basingstoke: Macmillan, 1989).

up to think of men in German uniforms as the enemy. They had relatives: they had their family around them, and we didn't have anybody...For us, our friends and comrades who also came back from emigration substituted for the extended family.'[15] With adults, too, awkward silences were the norm. In her interview, Runge repeats the official line that 'many of the real Nazis fled to the West', but concedes that 'maybe little Nazi functionaries stayed and rebuilt this country.' When asked how they reacted to Runge as a Jew, she replied: 'Well, there is guilt and repression. When they were children there were Jewish people; and then there were no Jewish people. When they heard I'm Jewish, they were shocked and didn't know how to behave. They didn't know what to ask me. It's something that's very complicated for them to deal with. For them being Jewish is associated with the distant past.'[16]

An older returnee, Clara Berliner, a committed Communist coming back to Berlin from Moscow, also betrays a degree of ambivalence about the extent and depth of East German *Vergangenheitsbewältigung* in the early years of the GDR:

> I really don't want to minimise this move: it was not at all easy. I was over forty, and my husband was over fifty and had lost his entire family except for his parents and brother – they all perished in Auschwitz. One naturally looked at everyone passing in the street and wondered what they were doing from 1933 to 1945. We knew that *theoretically* in the GDR the past had been overcome, but it was quite a while before one felt really integrated and at home.[17]

But Berliner very firmly emphasizes the 'thorough' way in which GDR schools discussed 'what happened under the fascists'. She identifies the issue as relating, not to 'Jewishness' (implicitly criticizing Ostow's focus), but to being a 'resistance fighter', again repeating the official historical perception, and ends with a ringing endorsement of the regime under which she chose to live: 'I think your readers should know that for us the problem is solved. As an anti-Fascist resistance fighter one has a social and political status in the German Democratic Republic that you can only dream of in other countries.'[18]

These topics could be pursued in far greater depth than is possible here. But these few examples must serve to raise a crucial point.

[15] Ibid., p. 45.
[16] Ibid., p. 50.
[17] Ibid., p. 86.
[18] Ibid., pp. 88–9.

What cannot be emphasized too strongly in this connection is that we should not over-homogenize 'East Germans' and 'West Germans'. Within each of these states, there were many different strands relating to different views, backgrounds and experiences. The war and the Holocaust were defining experiences not only for the generation that lived through them, but also for their children and grandchildren. The patterns of memory and historical consciousness – or at least, the nature of the challenges posed by one's relationship to the past – among perpetrators and their descendants are very different from those of survivors and their relatives.

Perpetrators – in the very broad sense of those who, in one way or another, actively participated in the machinery of mass murder – were not in the main notable by any public agonies of conscience, or indeed any public betrayal of personal memories of their past. Those who could not escape identification for the major roles they had played in the Third Reich tended to develop their own stories, often stereotyped and well-rehearsed versions of the past which could be presented in 'acceptable' forms in public.[19] Others preferred to keep quiet. Explicit 'memory' could have very real, and potentially adverse, implications for constructing a new life in the post-war present.[20]

The difficulties involved in grappling with memory – indeed, even allowing specific memories of particular incidents, or broader contexts of knowledge, to surface to consciousness – are evident also in the testimonies of the children of perpetrators. As one daughter of a man who had been in the SS later put it, even when there were stories about the past, they somehow evaded the issues and distorted the whole picture, in the process rendering it harmless. She writes as though directly to the father with whom she can (following his death) no longer communicate in person, and with whom she had failed to communicate despite a close and loving relationship in the past:

> You took the twelve years of Nazi dominion and dissolved them before me into separate incidents; then once you had simply removed the murder of the Jews from the whole picture, it all seemed to me more like an adventure than a systematically constructed

[19] For a particularly searching exploration of this theme with respect to one prominent individual, see Gitta Sereny, *Albert Speer: His Battle with the Truth* (Basingstoke: Macmillan, 1995). See also, e.g. Ulrich Herbert, *Best* (Bonn: Dietz Verlag, 1996).

[20] Cf. the discussion of denazification in ch. 3 above.

crime. In your stories, the suffering was taken out; the victims were missing, and along with them the perpetrators.[21]

Those children (or, in the case of Heydrich, a nephew) of prominent Nazis interviewed by Dan Bar-On in the 1980s reveal an extraordinary range of ways of coping, and varying degrees of explicit engagement with or repression of their parents' activities in the past.[22] Heydrich's nephew retained his name, but became an actor keen to perform pieces by Jews (Heine, Tucholsky); others preferred to retain anonymity and barely managed to confront the issue of their past, although the interviews suggest a tentative moving forwards in some cases. One converted to Judaism and became a Rabbi in Jerusalem; another became a Catholic priest; a third, whose Nazi father had committed suicide, had a son who also committed suicide. Many recount particular turning points, moments when they realized more acutely what had happened, or had to confront the past directly: often these turning points related to some moment when the past was presented in public, as in the war-crimes trials of the late 1950s and early 1960s, or at the time of the showing of the American television mini-series *Holocaust* in Germany in 1978. Many mention the total absence of any discussion of, or serious engagement with, the Nazi period at school, where it was not yet 'history'; neither in formal lessons, nor among one's friends, was it a topic of explicit debate.

The only general pattern to emerge, if one can call this a pattern, is one of intense psychological difficulty: difficulty in reconciling a real child's love for a lost father with what was known about what that father had actually done; difficulty in putting together childhood memories to construct a coherent story, which could be accepted by the post-1945 personality; difficulty in talking about these memories to an Israeli academic who could have been a compatriot, had his family not had to escape from Germany in the 1930s, but who could equally well have been one of their father's victims. What also comes out, movingly, are the ways in which both interviewer and interviewees move forwards in their understandings of themselves and each other in the process of these

---

[21] Irene Anhalt, 'Farewell to my Father', in Barbara Heimannsberg and Christoph Schmidt (eds), *The Collective Silence. German Identity and the Legacy of Shame* (San Francisco: Jossey-Bass, 1993; orig. German 1988), p. 45.

[22] See esp. Dan Bar-On, 'Holocaust Perpetrators and their Children' in Heimannsberg and Schmidt (eds), *The Collective Silence*; and Dan Bar-On, *Legacy of Silence: Encounters with Children of the Third Reich* (Cambridge, Mass.: Harvard University Press, 1989).

encounters, which serve not only to uncover but also to alter the patterns of memory and mutual understanding.

Not ashamed to be German? Historical consciousness in the GDR

How, more generally, did the kaleidoscope of personal memories and private stories intersect and interact with public representations of the past? The answer, as far as collective memories in the GDR are concerned, has to be a little complex: on the one hand, the narrative plots of the official tales, and the vocabulary in which they were phrased, do not in the main appear to have been so perfectly ingested and digested as to be generally reproduced as unquestionable truth; but on the other, the underlying moral of these tales, that one had little or nothing to be ashamed of, does appear to have achieved broad popular resonance. Hence, East Germans appear to have felt in the main no need to be 'ashamed to be German' (even if, at the same time, they did not swell with pride at being 'citizens of the GDR').

Public discourses about the past were, in both German states, deeply marked by officially ordained pieties and taboos, which often cut across private 'authentic' memories, traumas, and 'conversations' about the past on a family or local level. In the GDR, as we have repeatedly seen, an essentially simple message – the anti-fascist myth – was officially propagated through every possible avenue of education, socialization, propaganda. Needless to say, for the first generation of GDR citizens, this over-simplified view accorded very poorly with authentic experiences and memories. Perhaps the greatest dissonance was that between the myth of the Red Army as 'liberators', and the memories and tales of widespread rape and robbery.[23] But there were sufficiently compelling political reasons for conformity, both to prevailing political circumstances and to what amounted to a collectively exonerating myth. Any twinges of guilt, if such existed, were soon assuaged. (The SED was even popularly known as 'the big friend of the small Nazis', and many of the latter sought rapid refuge among the conformist ranks of the former.) There were powerful stabilizing factors, or at least reasons to keep fairly quiet and not rake over the ashes in private or in public.

[23] Cf. Norman Naimark, *The Russians in Germany* (Cambridge, Mass.: Harvard University Press, 1995), ch. 2.

Moreover, the Cold War context gave those who disliked the new dictatorship a perfect alibi: the GDR's overextension of the word 'fascism' to include the Federal Republic as heir to the Third Reich meant that being 'anti-antifascist' (which should logically mean being 'fascist') actually became, in a diffuse and ill-defined way, heroic resistance to yet another dictatorship. Thus anyone who was against the GDR must almost by definition be for democracy or for the West, irrespective of their attitudes towards the real Nazi past. This confusion was further complicated by the rather indiscriminate treatment of political enemies by the communist regimes in the GDR and the Soviet Union: those interned in camps after 1945 included not only former Nazis, but also Liberals, Social Democrats and Communists of the 'wrong' political persuasion, such that 'victims of Stalinism' became homogenized heroes or martyrs of the democratic cause irrespective of former backgrounds.[24]

The state itself, by presenting both the regime and the people in whose name it claimed to rule as the 'victors of history', drew a vicarious and early *Schlußstrich* as far as any real confrontation of the GDR's population with its history was concerned. This left its mark on the apparent lack of feelings of shame or guilt among the vast majority of the *Mitläufer* population.

Thus, in the first two decades or so of the GDR's history, there was no explicit or public 'working through the past'. The collusion of the older generation with the regime's official myth was not openly challenged. At the same time, the real anti-fascist credentials of many of the founding fathers of the GDR posed a substantial obstacle to any principled critique of their position. Christa Wolf, born in 1929, socialized under Nazism, a young adult in the founding years of the GDR, and – through all the phases of her ambiguous path through conformist supporter to democratic socialist critic and ex-*Staatsdichterin* (informally, official state poet) – a highly insightful observer of and participant in these processes, later described it thus:

A small group of antifascists, who ruled the country, at some indeterminate point, for pragmatic reasons, extended their victorious consciousness to the whole population. The 'victors of history' gave up the process of coming to terms with their real past, the past of the fellow-travellers, of those who were led astray, of those who had faith in the time of National Socialism. For the most part they told their children little or nothing about their own childhood and youth.

[24] This indiscriminate attack on a range of political enemies underlay some of the difficulties concerning the commemoration of 'victims of dictatorships', whether Nazi or communist, such as in Buchenwald after 1990.

Their underlying bad conscience rendered them ill-equipped to oppose the Stalinist structures and ways of thinking which for a long time constituted the litmus test for 'partisanship' and 'faithfulness to the party line'.[25]

This is of course but one, retrospective view by a particularly articulate participant who placed a great priority on the notion of 'subjective authenticity' (although cynical observers might point out that she was also an adept and experienced political animal with her own interests to bear in mind). But it is a view which is found repeatedly, in a wide range of sources.

Bärbel Bohley, for example, who was a far more outspoken critic of the SED regime in the 1980s, and one of the co-founders of the opposition group *Neues Forum*, makes surprisingly similar comments to those of the infinitely more conformist Christa Wolf. Bohley joined the GDR youth organizations, the Young Pioneers and FDJ (Free German Youth) voluntarily, and even, given the historical context, welcomed the building of the Wall in 1961. Bohley remembers growing up in the rubble and ruins of post-war Germany, with the evidence of the effects of war and mass migration all around her, and in particular remembers her own sense of mistrust of the older generation: what had they seen or done? In this context, she sympathized with the official view: 'It was easy enough then to pick up the key themes: We are the better Germany. We have cleared up. The Nazis are all in the West. That was for me believable. For me it was the better Germany.' Bohley continues by pointing out the continuity in the way the GDR system functioned, compared with the Third Reich: 'Society functioned, in a certain way, just like earlier. With fear and this double life.'[26]

All the evidence suggests a constrained silence, and an implicit collective agreement to accede to the new, officially ordained picture without further discussion. But tensions between former 're-sistance fighters' and their erstwhile oppressors seem to have persisted at an everyday level. A trade union report in early August 1961, for example, tells of someone whose father had been murdered by the Nazis and who had come to the GDR from the West. This (rather atypical) individual was threatened by his workmates in the following terms: 'He should get back to where he came from. He's a traitor to the German people, and if he doesn't go back, then

[25] Christa Wolf, '"Das haben wir nicht gelernt"' (Speech of 21 Oct. 1989), *Reden im Herbst* (Berlin: Aufbau Verlag, 1990), p. 96.

[26] 'Gespräch mit Bärbel Bohley', in Vera-Maria Baehr (ed.), *Wir denken erst seit Gorbatschow. Protokolle von Jugendlichen aus der DDR* (Recklinghausen: Georg Bitter Verlag, 1990), pp. 132, 133.

he'll have something coming to him.'[27] Similarly, acute tensions persisted at least through the 1950s between Christians who had belonged to the anti-Nazi Confessing Church and those who had been pro-Nazi German Christians. Such tensions not only would not easily fade away of their own accord, but they were even exploited by the SED for its own purposes in seeking to split the Churches.

The past seems also to have been a topic of informal conversation in the workplace, running along lines distinctly at odds with the regime's official views. There are indications that dissatisfaction with the present was expressed informally through comparisons with a Nazi past viewed in a remarkably positive light. Trade union (FDGB) records include reports on the ways, for example, in which older workers at the Großbaustelle Buna were talking about how much better things were in the old days, when youth was properly disciplined; in Bezirk Magdeburg, colleagues were recounting the tales of their wartime experiences in rosy terms; in the Kraftwerk Thälmann, youth were under the 'bad influence' of their seniors telling them that they would have had a much better deal under the Nazis.[28] And, for at least the first two decades of the GDR's existence, the records repeatedly document the use of swastikas as what seems to have been a popularly acceptable symbol of protest against the communist regime.

Habits of conformity to the demands of an intrusive regime were, however, relatively easily transposed from the Third Reich to the new conditions of required conformity in the GDR (although, when these directly affected personal interests, this was never quite as complete as previously perceived in the West). Most people soon learned to evince the politically desired responses to official opinion pollsters. In 1965, for example, on the occasion of the twentieth anniversary of the unconditional surrender of Germany, 90.7 per cent of GDR citizens who were questioned claimed that they perceived 8 May 1945 as a day of 'liberation of the German people from fascism'; only 6.1 per cent were prepared to admit that they considered it to be a day of defeat, while 3.2 per cent gave no answer.[29] Although the GDR pollsters comment with satisfaction on the apparent success of the 'numerous convincing materials published on this theme' in conjunction with the 8 May anniversary

[27] Zentralarchiv des FDGB, Bundesvorstand, 2677, 4 Aug. 1961. [Now in SAPMO-BArch.]

[28] FDGB, 2677, report of 14 March 1961.

[29] Heinz Niemann, *Meinungsforschung in der DDR. Die geheimen Berichte des Instituts für Meinungsforschung an das Politbüro der SED* (Cologne: Bund Verlag, 1993), Dok. I, fo. 31.

celebrations, the high rate of desired responses is more likely to indicate a population by now well versed in the art of public conformity, particularly when there were no personal costs for such compliance and some fear of negative consequences if one were caught stepping out of line.

In any event, the challenges and demands of 'coming to terms with the present' soon displaced any concern with a past that had officially already had a line drawn under it. For those too young to have experienced the Third Reich at first hand, the lack of alternative views and evidence allowed at least some aspects of the generally propagated picture to be internalized. Collective guilt was never a part of official GDR political culture, and, in the absence of continued public debate, private dissonances between myths and memories were at best muted and generationally specific. In any event the past was one problem the officially exonerated masses in the GDR did not have to face. If one looks, for example, at unrest in 1968 in the GDR, there is a strikingly high participation of young people in what muted and rapidly suppressed political protests there were.[30] But the issues were for the most part to do with the politics of the present: the Warsaw Pact invasion of Czechoslovakia and the suppression of Dubček's experiments with a more democratic socialism. If non-confrontation with an evaded past was a subdued aspect of the generational clashes here, it was not one which has left any massive sediment in the archival records which have been assessed so far.[31]

There were the first rumblings of a more honest public confrontation with the past in the 1970s and 1980s, evidenced for example in Christa Wolf's *Kindheitsmuster* (1976). In this extraordinary, semi-autobiographical act of conscious and active retrieval of the past, Wolf seeks to make connections across the divide of repression and self-alienation. The very first paragraph reads:

> The past is not dead; it has not even passed away. We separate it from ourselves and estrange ourselves.[32]

[30] Cf. M. Fulbrook, *Anatomy of a Dictatorship* (Oxford: Oxford University Press, 1995), ch. 7.

[31] There is, however, the suggestion that generational clashes were exacerbated by differences of attitude and behaviour between the 'HJ' and 'FDJ' generations'; cf. the as yet unpublished PhD research of Mark Fenemore at UCL on youth conformity and nonconformity in the GDR.

[32] Christa Wolf, *Kindheitsmuster* (Darmstadt: Luchterhand, 1979), p. 9. The English translation under the title 'A Model Childhood' is a little misleading: 'pattern of childhood' might be more appropriate.

The dilemma, for Wolf, is to 'remain without speech, or live in the third person'; by the end of her odyssey, returning with her husband, brother and daughter to the town, now in Poland, where she herself was a child, and working through the layers of memory and recollection, Wolf comes to some kind of resolution. The child (herself), whom she has addressed in the third person, the adult (herself) undertaking the journey, whom she has addressed throughout in the second person, now finally achieve some kind of reconciliation: on the last page of the book, she is finally able to say 'I', even if only to say – in answer to her own questions – 'I do not know'. The 'normalization' and incorporation of the repressed past into a continuity with current adult identity was an act of immense difficulty, and its presentation in public in the GDR was both partly camouflaged, and partly only possible in the conditions of (slightly) relaxed censorship in the early years of the Honecker era.[33]

There are other pale echoes, in the GDR of the late 1970s, of a desire to engage more explicitly with the past comparable to that exploding in West Germany at this time. An East German (non-religious, communist) Jewish singer, Jalda Rebling, speaks in one of Ostow's interviews of the impact of the showing of the American film series *Holocaust*, which, though screened on West German television, was of course watched by large numbers of East Germans.[34] Rebling comments: 'It was a very bad movie: that is, it emotionalised and commercialised the Holocaust without providing any historical analysis. It was a kind of Hollywood marketing of the Holocaust. But it had an enormous effect on people here... This was a time of new discussions among a new generation of Germans.'[35]

Interestingly, Rebling's interview indicates the rising to the surface of two alternative historical constructions, with the official line (which she reproduces) counterposed to a clearly prevalent if previously repressed and rather different view which implicitly assumes some kind of German collective guilt:

> People often approach me after concerts with all kinds of questions...They ...want to discuss the burden of guilt which the

[33] It is clearly impossible to do full justice to the complexities of Christa Wolf's engagement with both present and past in this context. There is by now a vast literature on Wolf's work and her politics, unleashed in part by the extraordinary controversy surrounding the public reception of her post-*Wende* novelette, *Was bleibt*, about a day under light Stasi surveillance and compounded by the later revelation that she herself had briefly informed for the Stasi while a student.

[34] Ostow, *Jews in Contemporary East Germany*.

[35] Ibid., pp. 65–6.

Germans brought on themselves. I think the idea of the guilt of a people is the wrong way to formulate the problem. There were also Fascists in other countries, and now there is a new Fascism. The central historical fact is rather the assembly line murder or extermination that took place, and it was not only of one people because we shouldn't forget that Gypsies, homosexuals, Communists and Social Democrats also perished in the camps. This was all part of a system, and the basic question is not one of the guilt or innocence of people, but of the necessity of understanding that kind of social order and precluding the possibility of its return.[36]

This official line of the Holocaust as part of a system, in which the roles could in principle be filled by anybody, had long been propagated in the GDR. But neither the message of cultural representations, nor the tales told in history books, had resolved the repressed issues for many East Germans.

Reactions to the showing of *Holocaust*, and discussions of appropriate ways of marking the anniversaries of *Kristallnacht* in 1978 and the outbreak of the war in 1979, even provoked the communist old guard of literati to lower their official masks and break long-standing taboos in private, very heated discussions. At meetings of the *Sektion Literatur und Sprachpflege* of the Akademie der Künste, from January to April 1979, there were extraordinary clashes over the issue of 'Jewishness', with very angry exchanges between authors including Stephan Hermlin, Alexander Abusch, Otto Gotsche and others.[37] Hermlin broke out in an emotional speech saying how he 'owed it to his father', who had been taken away by the Nazis on *Kristallnacht*, to say how delighted he was that *Holocaust* had finally raised the issue of Jewishness for open debate, and that it should no longer be a taboo subject in the GDR, politically inadmissible as 'reduction'. Hermlin and Abusch suddenly admitted to their sense of Jewish identity, which they felt had somehow been repressed, distorted, inadequately identified in the discussions of communist antifascism over many years; and Hermlin accused Gotsche very angrily of anti-semitism. Shades of a repressed past, in which the knowledge of real anti-semitism under the Nazis suddenly surfaced and broke through the state-ordained shibboleths about class struggle and communist solidarity, were clearly evident in this private breaking of taboos.

---

[36] Ibid., p. 67.
[37] Akademie der Künste, Archiv Signatur 897. I am extremely grateful to Jonathan Ross of King's College London for bringing the protocol of these meetings to my attention.

But this extraordinary surfacing of repressed feelings of difference and anger took place in a private meeting of GDR intellectuals, behind closed doors: it was not part of a more general public discussion of the past. Among ordinary members of the East German working class there appears to be little or no evidence of such explosions in relation to the past. The oral history interviews carried out by Lutz Niethammer, Dorothee Wierling and Alexander von Plato in the later 1980s suggest a lack of any real feelings of guilt or shame among the generation who were young adults during the war.[38] There is a relatively consistent separation of 'politics', or the evil deeds of the Nazis, from what the interviewee himself or herself did and thought.

It is difficult to convey briefly the richness of material in this fascinating book, but a few select examples will have to suffice here. 'Wolfgang Gröhner' saw politics only in terms of the framework for his own research projects and scientific expertise; despite the fact that he was employed on a key armaments project, he barely appears to have registered the war (merely an *'Ahnung'* from afar).[39] 'Herta Gunkel' expressed relief that she had not married a Jew whom she knew when young, thus having been saved from sharing his fate. She saw no connection between her own private world and the deportations which took place from Stettin, where she was living.[40] An extraordinary mixture of views and positions is revealed in the testimony of 'Ludwig Färber', who seemed to be able to make 'arrangements' with any political colour and any regime.[41] One of the most interesting testimonies is provided by virtually the sole 'genuine' former communist and antifascist resistance fighter encountered by this research team in their explorations of the complexities of East German memories. 'Ludwig Haber' was highly unusual in *not* having been a conformist member of the Hitler Youth or a Social Democrat, and in being willing to 'learn' the appropriate script of history as the SED wanted it presented; he was thus constrained into an uncomfortable reconfiguration and

---

[38] Lutz Niethammer, Dorothee Wierling and Alexander von Plato, *Die volkseigene Erfahrung* (Berlin: Rowohlt, 1991). This general point seems also to be confirmed by Wierling's current research on generational conflicts in the 1960s, in which the Nazi past seems to have played little or no role – Wierling, paper on 1968 delivered at a conference at Potsdam in Nov. 1998; see C. Kleßmann and H. Misselwitz (eds), *Geteilte Vergangenheit – eine Geschichte?* (Berlin: Chr. Links Verlag, 1999).

[39] 'Magnesium und andere Zeiten. Wolfgang Gröhner, Forschungsleiter, 81', ibid.

[40] 'Die Grenzen der Volkssolidarität. Herta Gunkel, Näherin, 80 Jahre', ibid.

[41] 'Seiltänzer mit Schulung. Ludwig Färber, Abteilungsleiter, 77 Jahre', ibid.

awkward representation of what was supposed to be his own life history for the purposes of political education as 'correctly' interpreted in the GDR.[42]

Comparing the results of these with similar oral history interviews carried out in the Ruhr area of West Germany, Alexander von Plato points out that there are key similarities, particularly with respect to the relative 'depoliticization' of memories of the Third Reich.[43] For very many Germans who were not designated by the Nazis as outcasts, the peacetime years were the 'good times', after the repeated experiences of upheaval, unemployment and hunger in the Weimar Republic. But there was a 'community of silence' when officially deprived of memories of the good times. These memories were subsequently recounted largely in terms of the parameters of private lives – getting married, having children, finding a steady job with a steady income, and not in terms of politics. There is much to suggest that the experiences of this generation led to a willingness to throw oneself into work and achievement, without wishing to be too closely attached to any particular political cause: this was, then, the *Aufbaugeneration*, the generation that helped to rebuild *both* the two German states after the war. Ulrich Herbert, reflecting on the same oral history material, comments on some of the similarities between the 1930s and the 1950s in this respect, between which the traumas of the 1940s serve as a 'negative counterpart' almost defining the 'normality' which preceded and followed the experience of total war.[44]

All the examples given so far were from people who had lived through the Third Reich, and who had their own, authentic, private memories – or were in a position to seek to retrieve some form of authentic memory, however overlain and distorted it may have been by subsequent learning experiences, compromises, accommodations to new forms of discourse about the past. What of the younger generation, those born into the GDR and socialized by these conformist elders?

---

[42] 'Widerwillige Geschichtsarbeit. Ludwig Haber, Professor für Philosophie, 73 Jahre', ibid.

[43] Alexander von Plato, 'The Hitler Youth Generation and its Role in the two Post-war German States', in Mark Roseman (ed.), *Generations in Conflict* (Cambridge: Cambridge University Press, 1995). One difference between East and West was that people in the GDR were more aware than their Western counterparts of the numbers of Soviet prisoners of war and communists who had been killed by the Nazis.

[44] Ulrich Herbert, 'Good Times, Bad Times: Memories of the Third Reich', in Richard Bessel (ed.), *Life in the Third Reich* (Oxford: Oxford University Press, 1987).

The evidence suggests that the absences in public debate were reflected in a less agonized approach to the past among younger generations of East Germans. A highly interesting survey of historical consciousness among 2,000 young people (some in high school, some apprentices) in 1988 was produced by the Leipzig Institute of Youth Research as a secret document for the purposes of refining and improving historical teaching.[45] In general, this survey showed that a smaller proportion of youngsters than the SED would have liked were interested in GDR and SED history or felt committed to the GDR as their fatherland. There had, however, been a dramatic increase in the percentage interested in the history of the Soviet Union between 1987 and 1988 (when, of course, revelations about the Stalinist period were becoming ever more interesting).[46] There was also a lively interest in the Third Reich, the division of Germany, and West German history. For many areas of history, there appeared to be '*Übersättigungserscheinungen*' (signs of having had more than enough of it). Moreover, the report writer identifies a degree of lack of trust of young people in relation to 'the official political and historical arguments and information' which 'acts as a sort of filter in the absorption of information relevant to ideology'.[47]

As far as the Third Reich is concerned, there are several remarkable features about the survey's findings, which include not only statistical data on multiple-choice questions, but also an appendix reproducing quotations from responses to open questions.

First, the young people surveyed appeared to have little or no sense of collective shame about the Nazi past. There was a sense of detachment, of distance; the Third Reich had nothing to do with them, they had not been alive at the time. From the SED point of view, this emotional detachment was regretted, since it indicated a failure of personal engagement in the continuing antifascist struggle in the present: a 'pragmatic, distanced and observational standpoint is predominant'.[48]

Secondly, their views on the Third Reich appear to have been more deeply affected by the tales that must have been told in their families than by the official pictures we have seen presented in the history books and public memorials. There was a remarkable willingness to make comments along the lines that the Third Reich

---

[45] 'Zum Geschichtsbewußtsein von Jugendlichen', by Dr Wilfried Schubarth, March 1989, *Zentralinstitut für Jugendforschung*, VVS I 138/2/89. I am very grateful to Mark Fenemore of UCL for bringing this document to my attention.

[46] Ibid., fo. 33.

[47] Ibid., fo. 32.

[48] Ibid., fo. 10.

must have had its good sides too, that people welcomed it for the return to full employment and so on – just the kinds of theme that came up in the memories of their parents and grandparents. There is virtually no use of stock phrases about 'false consciousness', 'exploitation of the working class', 'imperialist class interests' and so on. (The commentary is quite critical of the way in which the young people 'overstate' the role of Hitler and 'understate' the 'class character of fascism'.) The persecution of Jews is mentioned frequently, and on the whole rather dispassionately, with no attempt to explain it away in terms of something else.

Finally, there is a repeated empathy with those who joined the Nazi Party, often reinforced by comparisons with the sense of coercion about joining the SED and FDJ in the GDR (again, something the commentary did not like). The young people answering this survey clearly felt a degree of understanding for those who felt that, in order to make a life and career, some degree of conformity and membership in state organizations was required, whatever one felt inside. In answer to a question about how they would react if their 'Grandpa' (*Opa*) had been in the NSDAP, there was an overwhelmingly conciliatory, unbothered response. Several of the answers reveal just how real this question was: some of the respondents commented either that they had no grandfather (the war generation), or that indeed their own real-life grandparent had been in the Nazi party, but for good and understandable reasons; others put it in less personal terms, but with the same gist.

If the SED had been at pains to emphasize, in all its public proclamations, that ordinary people in the GDR had been the victims of Nazism, whatever real roles they had played under Hitler, then they had clearly scored a moderate and ambiguous success. By the late 1980s, young East Germans had not simply swallowed, uncritically, the official tales that were at some dissonance with the private stories told in the home; they appeared to have quite a multi-faceted, non-stereotyped, historical picture of the Third Reich; they were scarcely proud of being members of the 'antifascist state'; but, at the same time, they were not ashamed to be German.

Generational clashes within the GDR were, arguably, fought out more over issues to do with conformity in the present than with guilt relating to the past. In some cases, the symbols of the Nazi past were misappropriated, reused as signs of disaffection in the present: 'fascist' symbols could instantly indicate rejection of the 'antifascist state'. As the seventeen-year-old Sebastian Z. put it in an interview just after the 1989 revolution, describing the use of neo-Nazi slogans by his school classmates, irrespective of their participation in FDJ and other state activities: 'Many people in our class were of the view: better brown than red . . . The main thing was the defensive reaction (*Abwehrhaltung*) against the SED.'[49] Another seventeen-year old, Raoul H., makes a similar observation: while he and his classmates enjoyed the activities, the camaraderie, and singing the party-political songs in activities of the youth organization or on sports outings, gradually he became aware of the fact that many of his teachers did not appear really to believe what they were saying, and that they experienced tensions between their own views and pressures from above. Moreover, he and his classmates eventually felt 'surfeited' (*übersättigt*) with the emphasis on anti-fascism, with the consequence that many contemporaries adopted a stance of 'right-wing extremism' as just one form of protest against conformity.[50]

Dissonances between private historical pictures and the official antifascist myth were evident everywhere. It might have been comfortable for the first generation of former fellow-travellers to be told that they were, officially, 'victors of history', however little they believed in the other elements of the myth of 'liberation' from the fascist yoke of oppression. For later generations, a relative absence of inherited collective shame was often combined with a degree of understanding for the dilemmas faced by their parents and grandparents, and a distancing from the official tales told about the country's past.

Public pieties, private traumas: the West

West Germans might have taken note of Queen Gertrude's comment in Shakespeare's *Hamlet*: methinks the lady doth protest too much. A concomitant of the culture of public anguish in the West, with repeated ritual expressions of moral responsibility, was a degree of repressed resentment combined with an inadequate confrontation with private grief and trauma.

The experience of the war was a highly complex and multi-faceted one, involving as it did acts of intense brutality and cruelty, particularly for participants in Nazi crimes on the eastern front, but also experience of intense personal and human suffering, as bonds of love and friendship were severed by death. The latter experiences – the most searing private memories of war, for women, children and others remaining on the home front as well as for

---

[49] Sebastian Z. in Baehr (ed.), *Wir denken erst*, p. 32 (see n. 26 above).
[50] Ibid., p. 55.

serving soldiers who lost comrades and relatives - could not validly be introduced into the official conversations about the past. These private memories, private grief and mourning, could not easily be integrated into the official story of ritual guilt and mourning for those 'who had been murdered in the name of the German people', for which Germany must now take responsibility. Recent research suggests that, among older West Germans, memories of the war time period were highly fragmented, with key differences according to location and experience. They were, too, difficult to incorporate into a coherent story, and, in contrast to well-rehearsed tales of post-war reconstruction, were still acutely painful for many individuals. Domansky, for example, contrasts the ways in which personal experiences in the post-war period could easily be framed within the 'official grand narrative', with 'the gloss of a mythical new beginning that, through hard work, led to one's achievements as an individual and as a society'. By contrast, 'war memories were less encoded in safe narratives'.[51]

Whenever the sufferings of Germans themselves were raised, it was difficult for them to be respected as genuine without the retort that Germans had, after all, brought it upon themselves. Moreover, the official picture was always slightly at odds with private grief and mourning.[52] Nor was there any way of framing this mourning in an acceptable way. As Domansky points out: 'There did not seem to be any way of constructing post-World War II German society as a society indebted to the legacy of these dead. On the contrary, the legacy of the dead, forever tainted by the stain of National Socialism, had to be forgotten.'[53] She suggests a 'displacement' of mourning onto the loss of the GDR: commemorating 17 June as a 'national' holiday became an acceptable (democratic) focus of patriotic grief for the lost fatherland.

This antinomy led to the development of a number of 'historical pictures' (*Geschichtsbilder*) which partly overlapped, partly displaced each other. To provide a chronological account is hence to oversimplify, since these pictures of the past coexisted in uneasy confrontation or repressed silence, and reappeared in new variants with each new generational confrontation with the past. Developments in West German patterns of historical consciousness are

---

[51] Elizabeth Domansky, 'A Lost War. World War II in Postwar German Memory' in Alvin Rosenfeld (ed.), *Thinking about the Holocaust* (Bloomington and Indianapolis: Indiana University Press, 1997), p. 234, p. 235.

[52] The classic analysis of the Germans' supposed 'inability to mourn' was of course Alexander and Margarete Mitscherlich, *Die Unfähigkeit zu trauern* (Munich: Piper 1967).

[53] Domansky, 'Lost War', p. 243.

perhaps best seen in terms of a series of conversations, in which the discussion does move forward over time, but in which there are a variety of voices and a considerable degree of repetition of points of view. It is, at best, a confused conversation, in which what is left unsaid is often as important as what is expressed.

At the end of the war, many Germans had a world view which – even if they had lost their faith in Hitler as Führer – was deeply inscribed with Nazi concepts and patterns of thinking.[54] Let us take here the highly revealing example, brought to our attention by the research of Susanne zur Nieden, of unpublished private diaries. Written for no audience, with no outside pressure to conform to any speech rules or prescribed emotions, nor intended as *post hoc* self-justification, written purely as a private conversation with oneself, these diaries provide an intriguing insight into how people conceptualized the world at the time.[55] Zur Nieden's most striking findings are the strength of Nazi military and ideological propaganda revealed in these private outpourings, and the almost total personal identification of the women whose diaries she studied with the fate of the regime and of 'Germanhood' (*Deutschtum*). May 1945 is perceived and recorded in these private diaries 'as tragedy and great injustice... [A]ny feeling of liberation or joy that the war is finally over is rarely to be found... The bitter complaints indicate the extent to which the identity of many women was dependent on an idealized notion of Germanness.'[56] The diaries of the women studied by zur Nieden are in the main characterized by a sense of self-pity at the frightful things being done to Germans, with little or no evidence of their own involvement in or responsibility for Nazism or the war.

There is revealed in these diaries an almost total incapacity to think of any future beyond Nazism, and a determination to fight to the last for the fatherland, rather than go down to defeat under the Russians – or even the Americans. The extent to which not only Nazi ideas, but also commitment to more long-standing, traditional Prussian nationalist world views, were imprinted onto the mind of even an impressionable young woman with a social democratic and

---

[54] On the loss of faith in Hitler in the closing years of the war, see particularly Ian Kershaw, *The Hitler Myth* (Oxford: Oxford University Press, 1987).
[55] See Susanne zur Nieden, '"Ach, ich möchte... eine tapfere deutsche Frau werden". Tagebücher als Quellen zur Erforschung des Nationalsozialismus', in Berliner Geschichtswerkstatt (ed.), *Alltagskultur, Subjektivität und Geschichte. Zur Theorie und Praxis von Alltagsgeschichte* (Münster: Westfälisches Dampfboot Verlag, 1994).
[56] Ibid., p. 183.

somewhat dissident father, is revealed in diary extracts such as the following (dated 2 January 1944):

> All well and good, but what will become of Germany, my sacred, national, Prussian Germany? We will be a colony of America, the economy will recover with American gold, the apartment houses will be rebuilt.
>
> But we will forever have an American occupation, the German army will be completely dissolved, everything which has hitherto made my heart glow will be at an end. The Prussian tradition, the German soldiers of Frederick the Great and the Soldier King, the German, Prussian officer – all, all will be finished. They will take from us every shred of national honour, they will dissolve the sacred German Empire. What use is it to me then that the economy recovers? We will be vassals of America. Isn't it better then to die? Because a Prussian and a German cannot live without honour.[57]

But, as it turned out, the presciently foreseen economic miracle transformed West Germans' perceptions of their past, such that few would wish later to have died for the sake of 'German honour' and Prussian military traditions. Even the writer of this particular diary entry, who did not read her diary notebook scribbles again until handing them over for zur Nieden's research, confessed that she was quite amazed 'what nonsense she had scribbled down at the time'.[58] It raises the interesting question of the changing parameters, the changing concepts within which even private remembering takes place.

During the 1950s, around half of all Germans questioned in opinion polls still believed that, had it not been for the war, Hitler would have been one of the greatest German statesmen ever. For example, a survey by the Allensbach Institute for Demoscopy (*Institut für Demoskopie*) asked the following question: 'Everything that was built up from 1933 to 1939 and a lot more was destroyed by the war. Would you say that, had it not been for the war, Hitler would have been one of the greatest statesmen ever?' In May 1955, ten years after the end of the war, nearly half (48 per cent) answered in the affirmative; a further 14 per cent professed not to know. Only just over a third (36 per cent) at this time gave a clearly negative response (2 per cent gave 'other answers').[59]

---

[57] Ingrid Hammer and Susanne zur Nieden (eds), *Sehr selten habe ich geweint. Briefe und Tagebücher aus dem Zweiten Weltkrieg von Menschen aus Berlin* (Zürich: Schweizer Verlagshaus, 1992), p. 289.

[58] Ibid., p. 316.

[59] E. Noelle and Erich Peter Neumann, *Jahrbuch der Öffentlichen Meinung 1947–1955*, vol. 1 (Allensbach: Verlag für Demoskopie, 1956), p. 277.

By the early 1960s, the neuralgic character of the history/identity issue was becoming apparent in surveys of schoolchildren. A study of pupils in the upper forms of *Gymnasien* (the equivalent of British selective secondary or 'grammar' schools) revealed widespread ambivalence: for example, only between one-third and a half of those surveyed believed that Nazism was really as bad as it was currently being painted.[60] This study had the advantage (unlike most demoscopic surveys) of eliciting qualitative data, with highly intriguing statements from the children given in support of their answers to quantifiable multiple-choice questions.[61] Between one-quarter and one-third were at best ambivalent, or even positively agreed with, the statement that 'the Jews are our misfortune', often for reasons to do with the shadow of guilt. Thus, the 'Jewish question' had led Hitler down the wrong tracks, which 'virtually forces us to see ourselves as criminals and to lose our self-respect'; '[D]eep guilt is attached to the German people (*Volk*) today. Our image in the eyes of the whole world has been defiled'; 'If the Jews had not existed, then it would not have come to the extermination and to Germany's bad name'; 'The NS-regime's hatred of the Jews developed because of their existence – and this in turn led to the total collapse of Germany.'[62] There was an overwhelming sense of ambivalence about patriotism: many had highly positive feelings about their *Vaterland* and *Volk*, but felt that patriotism had become uncomfortable, was seen as old-fashioned, as laughable.[63] Just under 90 per cent wished that the histories of other peoples would be presented in as critical a light as German history.[64]

The kinds of images coming up in these comments by school-children in the early 1960s were clearly widely prevalent among their parents. Although the prevailing picture was already being challenged in public in the 1950s, by articulate left-liberal intellectuals and political writers at the time – Heinrich Böll, Günter Grass[65] – it never disappeared entirely, and, as we have seen,

[60] Rudolf Raasch, *Zeitgeschichte und Nationalbewußtsein* (Berlin: Hermann Luchterhand Verlag, 1964), p. 92.

[61] The phrasing of many questions also sheds interesting light on the perceptions of those carrying out the survey. For example, the typically passive tense of the Adenauer period is repeated in the statement: 'It depresses me that crimes were committed in the name of the German people' (ibid., p. 299) – with which, incidentally, between 69.6% and 80.3% agreed.

[62] Ibid., pp. 106, 125. Other comments about the Jews were straightforwardly racist.

[63] Ibid., pp. 197ff, 213ff.

[64] Ibid., p. 298.

[65] See e.g. Heinrich Böll's *Billiard um halb Zehn*, and Günter Grass's *Cat and Mouse* and *Tin Drum*.

echoes of it could still be heard in some of the public debates and political controversies of the 1980s, where it was resurrected and rehabilitated in certain conservative quarters. But as far as the younger generation was concerned, this kind of picture soon changed dramatically.

An explosion of challenges occurred as a part of the generational clashes that were prevalent throughout the western world in the later 1960s, encapsulated in the notion of '1968' as a phenomenon. Transnational youth culture was characterized by a range of general themes – 'flower power', 'make love not war', opposition to American military involvement in Vietnam, and a democratized youth culture (expressed not least in the kind of popular music epitomized by the Beatles) which challenged traditional authority in everything from hair length to intellectual expertise. This phenomenon was diverse and many-stranded, with varying degrees of real political impact in places as disparate as Paris and Prague. But, in the aftermath of the Eichmann and Auschwitz trials, with the massive public spotlight on Germany's past, youth revolt was refracted through a particular prism in Germany. Again and again in the later 1960s, young West Germans confronted and challenged members of their parents' generation about what they had done, or failed to do, in the Third Reich.

A generational conversation began that, in some quarters, ended in confontation: a generalized denunciation of 'fascism' came to include the whole of 'bourgeois materialism' and post-war *spießbürgerlich* (petty bourgeois in a derogatory sense) and amnesiac culture. This led, among a small minority of activists, into the far-left extremism of the 1970s. In one fashionable western neo-Marxist interpretation, Nazism was again set in the context of 'fascism' and hence capitalism: for some left-wing extremists, condemnation of the past intrinsically had also to entail massive and indiscriminatory condemnation of the present. Even for those who adopted less extreme interpretations, collective pictures of – or failures to remember – the past were inextricably linked with critiques of the present. After 1968, the Third Reich could no longer be excluded as a focal point of discussions of German identity in the West.

If the 1950s and 1960s had been characterized by a combination of public piety and private silence, the 1970s witnessed a dramatic expansion of public concern with the past in West Germany. From films such as Fest's *Hitler* or Syberberg's *Hitler* through to the screening of the American television series *Holocaust*, or the story of *The Nasty Girl* (a schoolgirl uncovering the murky past of ordinary citizens in her home town of Passau), or the efforts of 'barefoot historians' and 'historians of everyday life' to resurrect and celebrate traces of the past from the suppressed oblivion of post-war normality, public and popular confrontations were all-pervading.[66] There is no doubt that many of these phenomena were dramatic means of vividly re-portraying the issues to new generations, or bringing back to the forefront of attention perceptions and feelings which had lain dormant for an older generation; and some new themes and issues genuinely arose in the process. *Holocaust*, for example, for all its sentimentality, did at least invite Germans to empathize with the family of victims who were not only Jews but Germans, and educated middle-class Germans at that.[67] But none of these succeeded in 'overcoming the past': there was what might be called an intrinsically self-contradictory cultural feeding frenzy, an orgy of public engagement with an 'unresolved past' that seemed – like pulling the dressing off and scratching a wound to see how well it was healing, or tearing up a plant by its roots to see how well it was growing – only to exacerbate an obsession.

But the obsessions were not all in the direction of public confessions of guilt and shame at being German. Edgar Reitz's lengthy four-part film *Heimat* (1984), set in the Hunsrück, sought to bridge the yawning divide between the realities of a repressed past and the identities of the present.[68] *Heimat* provides an acceptable past for Germans; it barely adumbrates the Holocaust, and then in hushed whispers, in a small huddle of the initiated, in the local dialect (but also in the slightly problematic presence of a nine-year old child):

---

[66] On film, see esp. Anton Kaes, *From Hitler to Heimat: The Return of History as Film* (Cambridge, Mass.: Harvard University Press, 1989); Eric Santner, *Stranded Objects: Mourning, Memory and Film in Postwar Germany* (Ithaca, NY, and London: Cornell University Press, 1993); see also Erica Carter, 'Culture, History and National Identity in the two Germanies since 1945', in M. Fulbrook (ed.), *German History since 1800* (London: Arnold, 1997).

[67] Moishe Postone even gives the film *Holocaust* a pivotal role as breaking the 'collective somnambulism' in which a majority of West Germans had been able to 'sleepwalk' through the Cold War, the economic miracle, even the politics of the 1960s and new generational clashes about the past. Moishe Postone, 'After the Holocaust: History and Identity in West Germany' in Kathy Harms, Lutz Reuter and Volker Dürr (eds), *Coping with the Past. Germany and Austria after 1945* (Madison, Wis.: University of Wisconsin Press, 1990). See also the discussion in *New German Critique*, 19 (winter 1980), 20 (spring/summer 1980) and 21 (fall 1980); and Peter Märtesheimer and Ivo Frenzel (eds), *Im Kreuzfeuer: Der Fernsehfilm Holocaust. Eine Nation ist betroffen* (Frankfurt: Fischer Taschenbuch Verlag, 1979).

[68] For an interesting attempt to locate *Heimat* in the context of changing longer-term meanings of the concept of *Heimat*, see Alon Confino, 'Edgar Reitz's *Heimat* and German Nationhood: Film, Memory and Understandings of the Past', *German History*, 16, 2 (1998), pp. 185–208.

Wilfried: The Final Solution is being carried through radically and mercilessly. I'm not allowed to say this to you – but amongst ourselves, we're all in the know. All of them, up the chimney!
Pauline: Wilfried, I don't understand. What do you mean: up the chimney?
Wilfried: Pauline – the Jews, I mean.
Pauline: Oh, come off it.
Wilfried: Look, in front of the kiddies, I can't explain in detail.
(*To the officer*)
My comrades are suffering greatly in relation to this matter, as you can well imagine... a very unpleasant task.
Robertchen: Who goes up the chimney?
Pauline: Come on, keep quiet, Robertchen![69]

In this brief scene, amidst the sixteen-hour overview of *German* experience from 1918 to the 1980s, we have nevertheless a reaffirmation of the myth of essential innocence: whispered rumours of far-away things, utterly remote from everyday life and reality, and, even when hinted at, rapidly suppressed in front of the children.

What was perhaps most characteristic of the engagement with the past in 1980s West Germany was the overt clash of competing memories. Another epic, Claude Lanzmann's film *Shoah*, evoked very different memories. Lanzmann was a Frenchman who spent years doggedly pursuing minute but highly specific traces of the past through persistent questioning of a range of witnesses, perpetrators, bystanders, survivors of the Holocaust.[70] Through his painstaking efforts to reconstruct every detail, his persistent questioning of even the slowest and most reluctant witnesses, his lingering shots of the landscapes of the past, Lanzmann built up an extraordinarily compelling documentation of the facets of memory in the late 1970s and 1980s. Some of these memories were those of the perpetrators, often unaware that they were being filmed. *SS-Unterscharführer* Franz Suchomel from Treblinka, for example, describes the way 'The smell was infernal... It stank horribly for miles around. You could smell it everywhere... More people kept coming, always more, whom we hadn't the facilities to kill. The gas chambers couldn't handle the load... The Jews had to wait their turn for a day, two days, three days.'[71] Other voices were those of

[69] Edgar Reitz and Peter Steinbach, *Heimat: eine deutsche Chronik*, Screenplay (Nördlingen: Greno, 1985), pp. 298–9.
[70] See the text of the interviews in C. Lanzmann, *Shoah* (New York: Pantheon Books, 1985).
[71] Ibid., p. 55.

the victims, providing horrific eyewitness testimonies, and, in the case of Auschwitz survivor Filip Müller, the nearest one is ever likely to get to an account of what it was like to die in a gas chamber:

> How they tumbled out of the gas chamber! I saw that several times. That was the toughest thing to take. You could never get used to that. It was impossible.
>
> You see, once the gas was poured in, it worked like this: it rose from the ground upwards. And in the terrible struggle that followed – because it was a struggle – the lights were switched off in the gas chambers. It was dark, no one could see, so the strongest people tried to climb higher. Because they probably realized that the higher they got, the more air there was. They could breathe better. That caused the struggle. Secondly, most people tried to push their way to the door. It was psychological: they knew where the door was; maybe they could force their way out. It was instinctive, a death struggle. Which is why children and weaker people, and the aged, always wound up at the bottom. The strongest were on top. Because in the death struggle, a father didn't realize his son lay beneath him . . .
>
> [When the doors were opened] People fell out like blocks of stone, like rocks falling out of a truck. But near the Zyklon B gas, there was a void. There was no one where the gas crystals went in. An empty space. Probably the victims realized that the gas worked strongest there.[72]

The effects of this massive renewed confrontation with the recent past were variable. Some people were simply fed up with too much confrontation with the past; the desire to be a 'normal nation', interpreted as one that no longer needed to be obsessed with its history, was widespread, not only among conservative nationalists of an older generation but also among considerable numbers of young people. Others were concerned to fight tenaciously against any signs of allowing the past to fade from public consciousness.

In the 1980s some West Germans still could not make connections between their personal sufferings and what Hitler had perpetrated. Much of the public interest in the *Historikerstreit* arose from the widespread recognition of personal experience evoked by Hillgruber's plea for empathy with the experiences of soldiers on the eastern front and embattled communities forced eventually to flee their homelands. This was, it seemed, at last a recognition of what so many Germans had felt for so long but never thought it was

---

[72] Ibid., pp. 124–5.

permissible to articulate. Counterposed to these rumblings of barely suppressed self-pity were often the shrill tones of those who over-reacted in some sort of emotional frenzy of public shame, as though repeating often enough phrases such as 'ashamed to be German' would in some way provide absolution. Somewhere in between came the highly principled tone of much West German engagement with issues such as environmentalism, the Third World, racism, peace. Much of this presented highly laudable counterpoints to some of revisionist currents which were now more audible, although on occasion those over-conscious of the burdens and legacies of German history could barely distinguish between political responsibility and the effectively irresponsible impotence of some forms of moral high ground. The breaking of taboos in the 1980s, combined with a widespread interest in exploring the nature of everyday life, experience and popular memory, revealed just what a maelstrom of often mutually incompatible prejudices and assumptions lay below the orderly surface and the public rituals of West German political commemorations.

Because of the prevalence in public debate of the issue of 'coming to terms with the past', and because of the high public profile of intellectual debate in the media (television debates, highbrow weeklies), it is easy to overlook the continuation of quiet under-currents of older views.[73] Yet, for all the increasing complexity and sophistication of available historical pictures, debates often still revolved around questions which had more to do with contemporary politics and personal emotions than historical accuracy. The suppression of emotions and the sensitivities and taboos of the early period repeatedly stamped their mark even on later debates. The disjuncture between the officially permissible and the taboo led for many individuals into a suppression of their true feelings, and a failure to think through clearly the real connections. Because certain subjects simply could not be discussed, implicit assumptions about causality remained unchallenged. There were also signs of new (minority) political currents harking back to the past, both in a resurrection of neo-Nazi violence and in the rise of new far-right parties. It was not pre-eminently the older generation who lent support to the neo-Nazi movements of the 1980s; even when led by members of an older generation (as in the case of Franz Schön-huber, a former member of the SS and founder of the *Republikaner*) these were in the main supported by disaffected young males

[73] See esp. the 'Letters from Germans' repr. in Primo Levi, *The Drowned and the Saved*, for startling evidence of certain confused and self-exonerating historical pictures among some of even his well-meaning readers.

(primarily in the 18–25 age group). The growth of right-wing political parties in the Federal Republic in the 1980s posed an electoral challenge to the mainstream conservatives, to which the defensive response (in the attempt not to lose the populist vote to the far right) was a public sanctioning of views which were no longer officially taboo. Many older Germans who had difficulties with certain pieties about the past breathed sighs of relief at the rightward, more nationalist drift of German conservatism under Chancellor Kohl, and felt that the time might be ripe for reappropriating the past, for being allowed, at last, not to have to be ashamed to be German. It was this popular chord with which the right-wing historians and their chancellor struck such resonance – and to which they were in part responding, in order to expand their pool of voters on the right.

Divided memories and historical consciousness

In September 1990, when the by now perennial question was posed as to whether Hitler would have been one of the greatest statesmen ever if the war had not been lost, two-thirds (67 per cent) of West Germans were now quite sure that he would not; only just over a quarter (26 per cent; depending on how one looks at it, as many as a quarter) thought he would. The percentage still admiring Hitler was highest among FDP supporters (35 per cent) and lowest among supporters of the Greens (6 per cent).[74] There had clearly been some shifts in historical perception since half the West German population had agreed with this statement in the 1950s.

But, if historical consciousness was fractured across different political and generational groups within one state, it was even more fractured across the German/German divide. The historical pictures of residents of the 'five new *Länder*' (ex-GDR) and West Germany were in some respects similar, but forty years of different exposure to historical material and conditions of debate had left remarkably strong traces. In answer to the question 'Is there something specific in our history, which particularly distinguishes us from other countries' and, if so, 'what for you is the distinctive feature of our history…?' there were dramatically different answers in East and West. In January 1989 (before the collapse of the Wall) and again in August 1992 (two years after unification) over half (52 per cent) of West Germans were stably of the view that

[74] Elisabeth Noelle-Neumann and Renate Köcher (eds), *Allensbacher Jahrbuch der Demoskopie, 1984–1992*, vol. 9 (Munich: K. G. Saur, 1993), p. 375.

the Third Reich, Nazism, Hitler, were the key and specific features of German history which rendered it different from all others. When East Germans were polled on this question in December 1990 (shortly after unification) only 5 per cent thought that the Third Reich complex was of such importance; by contrast over a third (36 per cent) mentioned the Wall, the fact that Germany was a divided land (an issue mentioned by only 11 per cent of Westerners in both polls). These percentages had shifted significantly two years later, in August 1992, but were still nowhere near the West German perceptions: a mere 11 per cent of East Germans now weighted the Third Reich more strongly, and the Wall had slipped slightly to 30 per cent.[75] It was quite clear that, whereas West Germans continued to be obsessed with an unresolved past, East Germans had suffered more immediate problems with a divided present.

For a majority of people, 'historical consciousness' was more likely acquired through the interplay between commemorations and creative representations on the one hand, and private conversations with family and friends on the other, than through the writings of professional historians, although these too helped to shape as well as reflect broader controversies. Together, the combinations and interconnections form the inchoate shapes of 'collective memory' – which, in its selectivity, involves also collective forgetting. As Hartman has put it:

> forgetting on a collective scale can itself assume the guise of memory, that is, of a religious or collective type of remembrance ... It constructs, that is, a highly selective story, focused on what is basic for the community and turning away from everything else. The collective memory, in the process of making sense of history, shapes a gradually formalized agreement to transmit the meaning of intensely shared events in a way that does not have to be individually struggled for. Canonical interpretation takes over, ceremonies develop, monuments are built. An event is given a memory place (*Lieu de Mémoire*) in the form of a statue, museum, or concentration camp site, an annually repeated day. The repetition involves public rituals that merge individual sorrow or joy with communally prescribed forms of observance.[76]

But this is not necessarily simple and easily effected: what is particularly striking in the German case is the multiplicity of contested 'collective memories'.

[75] Ibid., p. 385.
[76] Geoffrey Hartman, 'Introduction: Darkness Visible', in Hartman (ed.), *Holocaust Remembrance: The Shapes of Memory* (Oxford: Basil Blackwell, 1994), pp. 15–16.

Even those memories which became crystallized in ritually pre-scribed forms and repetitions were not necessarily uncontentious and generally accepted. Across both sides of the Iron Curtain, there were different fractures, different dissonances between public and private, between memories of victims and perpetrators, between collaborators and conformists, between parents and children.[77] There could be no easy 'collective memory' in Germany after the Holocaust. At most, what one can conclude from a survey of these complex fractures is that, first of all, the past formed no easy basis for the construction of national identity in the present; but that, while in the West it appeared an inescapable focal point around which all debates must revolve, in the East it tended to slide away – or be actively repressed – into a less emotionally invested distance, while identity was rather defined by the present.

[77] A highly interesting and relevant piece of work in this context is Gabriele Rosenthal (ed.), *The Holocaust in Three Generations: Families of Victims and Perpetrators of the Nazi Regime* (London: Cassell, 1998), based on interviews with families from East Germany, West Germany and Israel. Unfortunately this book appeared too recently for me to take it into account in the above discussion.

7
Citizenship and Fatherland

Given the curious combination of perpetual penance and a sense of superiority, of constant self-consciousness in the eyes of each other and the world, the Germans on both sides of the Wall had a very strong sense of *who* they were: who was included, who excluded. Defining the nation was a great deal less problematic than giving it a value, a meaning.

In the West, ultimately, bestowing value on the new identity was in an oddly positive/negative sense along the lines of 'the burden of our history bestows on us the task of being the most morally aware and upright nation, the most committed to peace on earth' (etc.). The absorption in constant confessions of guilt, the state of permanent penance, almost prevented West Germans from admitting anyone else to their community of the agonized soul. This emotional aspect consolidated the legal and constitutional enshrinement of the essentially ethnic definition of what it was to be German: Hitler's ethnically pure *Volksgemeinschaft* lived on, rueing the acts of its forebears but unable to escape the character of the definition bestowed upon it. Yet, increasingly with the passage of time, West Germans began to feel uncomfortable with both the 'perpetual penance' and the 'ethnic German *Volksgemeinschaft*' elements. By the 1980s it is clear that increasing numbers – of both older and younger Germans, but for different reasons – sought to shake themselves free from this ambivalent legacy of inherited guilt. In the process, the *sense* of national community began to diverge from the constitutionally enshrined and politically stipulated definition of 'Germans' as a community of ethnic descent irrespective of political boundaries.

Untroubled by such institutionalized guilt, the East Germans were able, officially at least, to alter their definition of who could be included in the national community. But, given the constant obsession in the GDR with its affluent twin in the West (on the part of rulers and ruled alike), the official redefinition never caught on. Memories of war and imposed division were reinforced by the constant presence of the Wall; a sense of the wider German nation was sustained by the very fact of unwilling imprisonment.

This chapter will look, first, at political definitions of and entitlement to citizenship – legal membership of the national community – in the two states; then at changing popular conceptions of the nation through the forty years of division – which at first seemed so temporary, so provisional and reversible, and towards the end appeared to be an immutable fact of life for the long-term foreseeable future.

Citizenship and the nation in the Federal Republic

Perhaps one of the most curious, ironic legacies of the Nazi dictatorship was the retention in West Germany of an essentially ethnic, or at least blood right, definition of 'German'. The concept of a German 'race' – however uncomfortable the explicit use of this term may be – was enshrined in the German citizenship laws of the Federal Republic. Although, following reunification, some amendments to the citizenship laws relaxed and diluted the criteria for application for German citizenship, there was still a distinctively ethno-cultural bias to the underlying assumptions. Dual nationality was not permitted, deterring many potential applicants and underlining the presumed exclusivity of German identity; and the standards applied encouraged *assimilation* – that is, seeking to become similar – rather than the *integration* of members of a multi-cultural community capable of celebrating diversity and difference.

We need first to consider briefly the historical background to post-1945 German conceptions of citizenship. There was a wide range of constructions of 'German-ness' preceding the twentieth century, with different strands intertwining in different proportions and degrees. Some were to prove historically more tenacious than others. Even the most ethnic versions of German identity included elements of culture and, particularly, language. The linguistic and cultural elements predate the ethnic elements in the weight attached to them.

In the late medieval/early modern 'Holy Roman Empire of the German Nation' (note the very terminology), the myth of common descent was involved at the level of the German 'tribes' or *Stämme*, while an overarching 'German-ness' was presumed to have more to do with the German language than with any presumed model of close kinship. Cultural conceptions of German identity flourished particularly in the late eighteenth and early nineteenth centuries, before modern political nationalism was of any significance. In the post-Napoleonic German Confederation of the nineteenth century, there were a variety of criteria, meanings and functions of 'citizenship' for different purposes at different local and state levels. Even when the principle of descent was prioritized (as for entitlement to poor relief within a particular locality), this was not based in a concept of ethnicity.[1] Imperial Germany, dubbed by John Breuilly 'the first German nation state', was not ethnically or culturally homogeneous.[2] There were many 'non-German' citizens of the Second Reich, such as French in Alsace-Lorraine, Danes in Schleswig, and Poles in the state of Prussia; there were also many 'ethnic Germans' living beyond the bounds of the Reich – including the ten million or so German inhabitants of Austria-Hungary who had been excluded in Bismarck's 'small German' creation. The year 1871 had, in essence, marked less a 'unification of Germans into a nation state' (despite the representations of nationalist historians at the time and later) than a form of hegemonic expansion of Prussia, which consolidated its political position while allowing a great deal of regional leeway and variety. Citizenship in the Reich was initially determined by citizenship in one of the constituent states of the Reich, which, as codified in the North German Confederation and then in the new Empire, came to prioritize the principle of *jus sanguinis* ('blood right', or rights based in descent) over *jus soli* (rights derived from 'soil' or place).

The 1913 Citizenship Law both amended and made uniform the diverse arrangements obtaining across the constituent states of Imperial Germany.[3] It had distinctly ethno-cultural overtones, particularly in some of the more extreme nationalist assumptions lying behind support for it in some quarters. Nevertheless, it did not directly entail an explicitly ethnic conception of citizenship, but

[1] See, for a particularly clear and interesting analysis, John Breuilly, 'Sovereignty, Citizenship and Nationality: Reflections on the Case of Germany', in Malcolm Anderson and Eberhard Bort (eds), *The Frontiers of Europe* (London: Pinter, 1998).

[2] For an excellent brief analysis of the unification of Germany in 1871, see John Breuilly, *The Formation of the First German Nation-State, 1800–1871* (Basingstoke: Macmillan, 1996).

[3] See John Breuilly, 'The National Idea in Modern German History', in M. Fulbrook (ed.), *German History since 1800* (Arnold, 1997).

rather embodied the principle of descent, or *jus sanguinis*. This privileged the descendants of non-resident German emigrants (the so-called *Auslandsdeutsche*), while there were massive barriers against the naturalization of descendants of immigrants (who would have benefited from *jus soli*), who were deemed to be inferior 'foreigners of the people', *Volksfremde*. As Brubaker has put it, 'the 1913 law severed citizenship from residence and defined the citizenry more consistently as a community of descent'.[4] Part of the intention was the protection, preservation and expansion of *Deutschtum*, which was held to be slightly separate from citizenship as such (there were, after all, considerable numbers of *Reichspolen* ('Reich Poles'), often deemed to be at least rather inferior citizens if not actually outright *Reichsfeinde* (enemies of the Reich)). Among the conservative nationalists who opposed any naturalization of immigrants and their descendants, there was an extraordinarily deep-rooted, widespread, and absolute opposition to the notion of *jus soli*, citizenship by virtue of place of birth (whether through attribution or rights to naturalization) in order to prevent any further ethnic diversity. In these circles, whose views were ultimately successfully enshrined in law, blood was in principle deemed to be more powerful in determining political loyalties than any education or socialization could possibly be (in contrast to the situation in neighbouring France, where in principle it was possible to *become* French).[5]

After the defeat of Germany in the First World War, and the territorial revisions of the Versailles settlement, both the reduced German state and the concept of German citizenship became more homogenously ethnic in character; the principle of descent remained, but it was the ethnic Germans in the newly created 'Polish corridor' who now felt displaced. An ethnic, and now stridently nationalist, sense of identity was of course massively exacerbated in Hitler's conception of an ethnically homogenous 'national community' or *Volksgemeinschaft*. With the Nuremberg Laws of 1935, German Jews (defined by the Nazis as those who had three or four Jewish grandparents, or as those who had two Jewish grandparents and also practised Judaism) lost full German citizenship, which became explicitly racist in character. From the stigmatization of Jews as second-class citizens, it was an alarmingly small

---

[4] Rogers Brubaker, *Citizenship and Nationhood in France and Germany* (Cambridge, Mass.; Harvard University Press, 1992), p. 115.

[5] See Brubaker, *Citizenship*; and, for comparisons between citizenship entitlement in Britain, France, Germany and Italy, see David Cesarani and Mary Fulbrook (eds), *Citizenship, Nationality and Migration in Europe* (London: Routledge, 1996).

step to complete physical annihilation in the ultimate attempt epitomized by Auschwitz to create an 'ethnically pure' racial state.

The Federal Republic of Germany of course totally repudiated the racist elements of Nazi citizenship. But, because of the loss of territories after 1945 which the Federal Republic refused to recognize as final (the Oder–Neisse border with Poland was only finally – and belatedly – confirmed by Chancellor Kohl in 1990), the principle of *ethnic* descent was, if anything, strengthened. Article 116 of West Germany's Basic Law (*Grundgesetz*) bestowed automatic rights of citizenship and residence in West Germany on those who were, or were the spouses or descendants of, citizens of Germany in the boundaries as of 31 December 1937 (that is, prior to the territorial expansion which began with the annexation of Austria in 1938). It also permitted former German citizens, and their descendants, who had lost their citizenship between 30 January 1933 and 8 May 1945 for political, racial or religious reasons, to apply for a resumption of citizenship ('*sind auf Antrag wieder einzubürgern*') – clearly not quite such an automatic matter. As many critics have pointed out, the principle of descent requires proof of descent; which might be easier for the grandchild of a German SS-officer at Auschwitz whose family papers had survived than for a grandchild of one of his German Jewish victims whose family and possessions had been annihilated. Moreover, *Volksdeutsche* from Russia, Poland and elsewhere in eastern Europe, who had held German citizenship for generations, had a right to resettle in West Germany, even if they had never set foot on West German soil and barely spoke any form of recognizable German language, while second- and third-generation 'immigrants' with a German education and upbringing and fluent German as a first language found it extremely hard, indeed virtually impossible, to gain German citizenship.[6] What had been primarily a community of descent with 'ethno-cultural' overtones in Imperial Germany had, in the Federal Republic, become more purely 'ethnic' in conception.

Yet this was a state which was in most other respects officially, and explicitly, 'post-national'. Here lies one of the deep internal antinomies of post-war official West German political culture. It faced in two directions at once: while – for the time being – nationalism had been totally and utterly discredited and any nationalist sentiment was virtually taboo, at the same time the Federal Republic was officially committed to the reunification of 'Germans',

---

[6] Virtually impossible in practice, owing to the very exacting and specific set of criteria which had to be met before a case for naturalization could be considered, although not absolutely impossible in principle.

understood as an ethnic community of descent, on German soil. This ethnic definition was, almost paradoxically, there precisely to uphold liberal-democratic values more conventionally associated with non-ethnic concepts of citizenship as willed participation in a particular democratic form of political community. The Federal Republic defined itself as a community of political freedom and democracy, in which all 'Germans' should be entitled to live: thus, there had to be a means to recognize the citizenship rights of those who found themselves on soil occupied by different political ideologies and regimes. The Preamble of the West German Basic Law committed 'the whole German people' to work for the 'preservation of its national unity as a state' and 'to complete the unity and freedom of Germany in free self-determination'. West Germany was therefore constitutionally opposed to the recognition of any separate East German citizenship. The Preamble indeed explicitly claimed to speak for all Germans, including 'those Germans who were prevented from participating in this process'.[7]

The mainstream and predominant, largely unexamined assumption among articulate West Germans playing leading roles in the construction of public political culture was that there simply existed a German people defined by a combination of homogenous ethnicity and common culture. One or another of these elements might attain greater weight, but the simple existence of a nation in some way bound together was an essentially unexamined basic assumption to be found almost across the entire political spectrum.[8]

Take, for example, the 'Reports on the State of the Nation' delivered to the West German parliament by two rather different politicians, Chancellor Kiesinger (CDU) in 1968, and Chancellor Brandt (SPD) in 1970. Kiesinger defines the German nation thus:

> Our fellow countrymen (*Landsleute*) are Germans like ourselves, among whom many are also from quite other regions of Germany and from German areas of colonization outside the old Reich borders. Wherever people from the two parts of Germany meet up with each other, without being under any political constraint, it becomes

[7] Extracts from the Basic Law in V. Gransow and K. Jarausch (eds), *Die deutsche Vereinigung* (Cologne: Verlag Wissenschaft und Politik, 1991), pp. 29–30.

[8] This was for the most part far from being racist in import, although it should be noted that such a background consensus about the very existence of a clearly definable *Volk* must prove a helpful precondition for movements on the further right.

evident that people of one language, one history, one culture, feel they belong together...Even the SED regime had to recognize the fact that the Germans perceive themselves as one nation.[9]

In Brandt's view:

> In the concept of the nation historical reality and political will are united. The nation embraces and signifies more than common language and culture, than state and social order. The nation is founded on a continuing feeling of belonging together of the people of a *Volk*. No one can deny that, in this sense, there is, and will continue to be, a German nation, for as far ahead as we can imagine.[10]

These were of course formal statements issued by succeeding Chancellors of the Federal Republic in a highly important public forum at a time of delicate negotiations and shifts in the relations between the two German states.[11] They both give due emphasis to the subjective element – the sense of community, of belonging together – but seem to accord this a certain objective basis in reality. (Note, for example, Brandt's tautological slippage into the use of the word '*Volk*'.) Precisely because of the political division, the concept of a nation was officially kept alive more tenaciously than it might otherwise have been. This prevailing assumption (which was enshrined in the citizenship entitlement outlined above) was highly exclusive: however well-meaning successive governments may (or may not) have been towards 'immigrant' communities (including third-generation descendents born and bred in Germany), the notion of dual nationality appeared in some sense to be an inadmissible contradiction in terms.

A very delicate line had to be trodden here. The SPD was seeking through recognition of political division to preserve human contacts between East and West, predicated on a view of an all-German nation whose interests it was trying to serve. Desire for political unity was by no means ever a sole prerogative of the right (and sometimes the CDU needed to be reminded that it was a conservative Chancellor, Konrad Adenauer, who had chosen to embark on the path of western integration at the expense of national unity in

---

[9] Kurt-Georg Kiesinger, 'Der erste Bericht zur Lage der Nation', 11 March 1968, repr. in F. J. Schmitt (ed.), *Im deutschen Bundestag. Deutschland und Ostpolitik* (Bonn: C. Bertelsmann Verlag, 1973), vol. 2, p. 116.

[10] Willy Brandt, 'Der dritte Bericht zur Lage der Nation', 14 Jan. 1970, ibid., p. 281.

[11] The outcome of Brandt's views, as we know, was the post-*Ostpolitik* concept of 'two German states within one German nation'.

the 1950s).[12] This was accompanied by rejection of more radical forms of nationalism seeking to revise, for example, post-war political boundaries.

Although mainstream political views of the nation and *Ostpolitik* converged after the intense political battles of the early 1970s were over, conservative conceptions of the nation remained a little volatile with respect to the right-wing fringes in a way that was perceived as potentially dangerous on the left. Gestures were repeatedly made by the CDU/CSU to the constituencies of refugee communities (not only in the early decades of the Federal Republic, but continuing even in conservative 'Sunday speeches' to groups such as the 'Silesian expellees' in the 1980s), to persisting *Stammtisch* (pub regular) nationalists, and, in the 1980s with the formation of new right-wing parties (the *Republikaner* and the *Deutsche Volksunion*), to potential defectors on the right whose votes were crucial to margins of electoral victory for the CDU/CSU in some *Länder*.

Many left-liberals, however, came to reject an essentially mono-ethnic construction of German identity, and sought to construct 'post-national' forms of identification. If it was no longer possible to be proud of one's nation, and if indeed the very concept of nation had to be rejected because of a potentially resurgent aggressive nationalism, then in what could one anchor one's faith, to what could one feel a sense of commitment and loyalty? Certainly not to what left-liberals denigrated as 'DM-nationalism': pride in the Federal Republic because of its economic success. The answer, for philosopher Jürgen Habermas and others, was the constitution of the Federal Republic. It was possible to be a 'constitutional patriot', proud of the way in which the post-war Republic had succeeded in ensuring a lasting combination of both democracy and stability, for the first time in Germany's turbulent history. This achievement should be recognized, and citizens of the Federal Republic had a right to be proud of it – as citizens, defined in terms not of ethnicity but of shared commitment to the political values and norms of democracy. It was in this sense, too, that intellectuals such as Jürgen Kocka could greet and celebrate the achievement of 'national' unity after 1990, interpreted as a vindication, not of the ethnic nation, but rather of the values of liberal democracy and civil society.[13]

Of some interest in this connection, however, is the continued strong belief in the German nation as an enduring entity, even

---

[12] On left-wing views of the nation, see e.g. Peter Brandt and Herbert Ammon (eds), *Die Linke und die nationale Frage* (Hamburg: Rowohlt, 1981).

[13] Cf. the essays in Jürgen Kocka, *Vereinigungskrise. Zur Geschichte der Gegenwart* (Göttingen: Vandenhoeck and Ruprecht, 1995).

among left-wingers who were firmly opposed to the possibility of reunification as a nation state. Let us take a few moments to consider, as an important if somewhat eccentric example, the curious views of that notable critical intellectual Günter Grass. From the debates over recognition of the GDR in the late 1960s through to the debates over possible unification of the two German states in 1990, Grass's position was consistent: because of Auschwitz, Germany should never be more than a cultural nation, perhaps a loose confederation, but not a unified nation state.[14] 'The Germans' could, in view of their history, not be trusted with political power.

In 1967 he put it thus: 'Here is my thesis:... our *fundamental disposition* indicates that we are not suited to forming a nation-state.'[15] In 1990, essentially the same argument was made:

> A unified German state existed, in varying sizes, for no more than seventy-five years... The crime of genocide, summed up in the image of Auschwitz, inexcusable from whatever angle you view it, weighs on the conscience of this unified state... That place of terror, that permanent wound, makes a future unified German state impossible. And if such a state is nevertheless insisted upon, it will be doomed to failure.[16]

Also written in 1990:

> We have every reason to fear ourselves as a unit. Nothing, no sense of nationhood, however idyllically coloured, and no assurance of late-born benevolence can modify or dispel the experience that we the criminals, with our victims, had as a unified Germany. We cannot get around Auschwitz. And no matter how greatly we want to, we should not attempt to get around it, because Auschwitz belongs to us, is a permanent stigma of our history – and a positive gain! It has finally made possible this insight: finally we know ourselves.[17]

It is evident in these and other writings that Grass assumes 'the Germans' to have an enduring character as a 'nation' which does not and cannot permit them to have political power in the form of a united state. It is a form of what one might call an inverted nationalism, an anti-nationalist nationalism, an essentialist view predicated on a deep belief in the reality of a German national identity

[14] See the selection of essays translated into English and repr. in Günter Grass, *Two States – One Nation? The Case against German Reunification* (London: Secker and Warburg, 1990).

[15] Grass, 'The Communicating Plural' (1967), ibid., p. 72; italics added.

[16] Grass, 'Short Speech by a Rootless Cosmopolitan' (1990), ibid., pp. 5–6.

[17] Grass, 'Writing after Auschwitz' (1990), ibid., p. 123.

over generations. Leaving aside the very genuine anguish Grass experienced over the Nazi past, what do we really see here? An absurdly emotional, irrational view; one that is deeply a-historical, in not even considering the contingency of political developments and not entertaining the possibility of cultural change; and one that is almost offensive in its suggestion that obsessive German navel-gazing has been in some way assisted by the 'stigma' of Auschwitz as a 'positive gain'.

The would-be socialist nation in the GDR

The GDR of course inherited the same legacy of German citizenship assumptions prior to 1945. The 1949 constitution of the newly founded GDR was in essence compatible with that of the Federal Republic (although of course the political realities of the time were already very different). The 1949 constitution said nothing about the communist character of the new German Democratic Republic, and, like the West German constitution, claimed to be able to speak for all Germans. It spoke rather more vaguely than the West German version (which specifically enumerated the *Länder* that had agreed the Basic Law), of 'the German people' having 'given themselves this constitution'. It stated laconically and ambiguously that 'Germany is an indivisible democratic Republic, composed of German states' which 'determines all matters which are essential for the existence and development of the German people as a whole ... There is only one German citizenship'.[18]

The construction of the Berlin Wall in 1961 put something of an abrupt and concrete end to hopes of reunification in the immediate future. Moreover, the political rethinking that was to culminate in the *Ostpolitik* of the early 1970s was evident already in the 1960s. The 1963 Programme and Statute of the SED, for example, was already beginning to differentiate between a bourgeois and a socialist nation, although still adhering to the view that reunification would take place on the basis of the whole German nation entering a socialist phase:

> The German nation is divided into two mutually hostile states, rooted in diametrically opposite social conditions. In no way has the German nation thereby ceased to exist, but it finds itself, when

[18] Extract from the 1949 GDR constitution repr. in C. C. Schweitzer et al., *Politics and Government in the Federal Republic of Germany: Basic Documents* (Leamington Spa: Berg, 1984), p. 378.

viewed in historical perspective, in the transitional stage towards a socialist nation, a stage which will be concluded when the social conditions of existence of the nation are reformed in the whole of Germany.[19]

It was a relatively small step, in the late 1960s with the new overtures from the West for jettisoning the Hallstein doctrine and recognizing the status quo, to articulating the view that the GDR would become a socialist nation on its own. The separation of a 'bourgeois' and a 'socialist' nation was supported by apparatchiks such as Kurt Hager, Hermann Axen and Albert Norden; and although there were considerable political shoals to be navigated along the way, not only with the transition from Ulbricht to Honecker, but also in respect of West German domestic politics, the constitutional jettisoning of notions of an all-German nation in 1974 (on which more in a moment) marked merely the end point of a longer process of rethinking.

The East German concept of citizenship was clarified in the 1967 Law on Citizenship. It claimed that citizenship of the GDR

> came into existence, in accordance with international law, upon establishment of the German Democratic Republic... The citizenship of the German Democratic Republic is membership of its residents in the first peace-loving, democratic and socialist German state, in which the working class exercises political power in alliance with the farmers' cooperative class, the socialist intelligentsia and other labouring people.

Entitlement was based on having been a German national at the time of the establishment of the GDR, or through descent, or through birth within the GDR, or through naturalization. It could be withdrawn 'for serious violation of civil duties' (for example, by flight from the GDR).[20]

This concept of citizenship continued to emphasize the principle of descent, but already made explicit comments about the political form in which citizenship was to be enjoyed (if that is the right word for many people in this context). The new constitution of 1968, in contrast to the 1949 version, made the political character of the regime quite explicit; the preamble stated that 'the people of the GDR... have given themselves this socialist constitution.'[21]

---

[19] Quoted in Werner Weidenfeld, *Die Frage nach der Einheit der deutschen Nation* (Munich and Vienna: Günter Olzog Verlag, 1981), p. 94.
[20] Schweitzer et al. *Basic Documents*, pp. 379–80.
[21] Ibid., p. 378.

There was, however, no real change with respect to the issue of German-ness. According to the 1968 constitution, the GDR was 'a socialist state of the German nation', and it was 'imperialism under the leadership of the USA in conjunction with West German monopoly capitalist circles' that had divided Germany 'in order to build up West Germany as a basis of imperialism and the struggle against socialism, in contradiction to the vital interests of the nation'. The GDR was now constitutionally committed to 'overcoming the division of Germany which had been imposed on the German nation by imperialism' and to 'the step-by-step rapprochement of the two German states up to their unification on the basis of democracy and socialism'.[22]

This commitment did not last long. No sooner had the various treaties which constituted *Ostpolitik* been signed, culminating in the ambiguous formulations of the Basic Treaty between the two German states of December 1972, than the GDR gave itself yet another constitution, effectively renouncing all previous sentiments of German national unity.[23] The constitution of 7 October 1974 no longer referred to *'das deutsche Volk'* (the German people), but rather *'das Volk der Deutschen Demokratischen Republik'* (the people of the GDR); the GDR was now defined as 'a socialist state of workers and peasants'. From then on, officially, there was a fundamental dissonance between the West German commitment to an ethnic conception of German nationhood transcending state frontiers, and the East German reformulation of the concept of nation in terms of politics and class rather than ethnic descent.

If one examines the East German theoretical reformulation, however, it appears not a little ambiguous. In an article in *Neues Deutschland* in February 1975, two leading GDR theoreticians sought to add the required air of scientific verisimilitude to the new Party line.[24] They did this by definitional fiat, seeking to legislate for an absolute distinction between 'nation' and 'nationality': 'The nation therefore always includes economic, social, political, ideological and ethnic factors in a dialectical unity', although the decisive factor is 'the social, class-relevant aspect'. 'Nationality' is, by contrast, defined more narrowly as the 'total complex of

---

[22] Gransow and Jarausch, *Die deutsche Vereinigung*, pp. 40–1.

[23] For the text of the Basic Treaty, see ibid., pp. 43–5.

[24] Alfred Kosing and Walter Schmidt, 'Nation und Nationalität in der DDR', *Neues Deutschland*, 15 Feb. 1975, repr. in *Deutschland Archiv*, 8/11 (Nov. 1975), pp. 1221–8. Cf. also Hermann Axen, *Zur Entwicklung der sozialistischen Nation in der DDR* (Berlin, 1973).

ethnic characteristics, traits and features of a population'.[25] Later, 'nation' is effectively simply equated with 'state', as when it is pointed out that many capitalist 'nations' (used simply to refer to currently existing states) contain within them several 'nationalities'.[26] Meanwhile, 'nationality' is defined as both historical heritage and social reality:

> The vast majority of citizens of the GDR are by nationality German, in terms of their descent, their language, their life styles, their traditions – in short their ethnic characteristics. The socialist nation in the GDR is of German nationality. At the same time there are citizens in the GDR of other nationalities, above all the relatively significant groups of citizens of Sorbian nationality.[27]

There is a certain underlying essentialism evident here: a firm belief in the reality of a persisting ethnic-cultural group, the Germans, now simply redefined as 'nationality' rather than 'nation', which, meanwhile, has been redefined to mean, essentially, 'citizenship'.

The problem for the SED theorists was, of course, that – as we shall see in a moment – many of their citizens did not accept this reformulation. Nor did the West German government. The Federal Republic of Germany explicitly stated that the Basic Treaty did not affect its position on German citizenship, nor its commitment to the reunification of all Germans in peace and freedom. The Basic Treaty itself included a phrase recognizing fundamental disagreements in principle: it was concluded 'without prejudice to the differing views of the Federal Republic of Germany and the German Democratic Republic on questions of principle, including the national question'. The extent of this disagreement was clarified in a letter from the West German government to the GDR government of 21 December 1972, stipulating that 'this Treaty does not conflict with the political aim of the Federal Republic of Germany to work for a state of peace in Europe in which the German nation will regain its unity through free self-determination'.[28] And it was this position which made it possible for hundreds of thousands of East Germans to stream westwards with the opening of the Austrian–Hungarian border in the summer and the collapse of the Berlin Wall in November 1989; it was this commitment which permitted, eventually – and so unexpectedly – the fulfilment of at least that part of the constitution on 3 October 1990.

[25] *Deutschland Archiv*, 8/11, p. 1224.
[26] Ibid., p. 1226.
[27] Ibid., p. 1227.
[28] Schweitzer et al., *Basic Documents*, pp. 383, 384.

The German nation: alive and well in the GDR?

Within this constitutional, legal and political framework, what one might call 'live' (and often unexamined) conceptions of the nation diverged markedly. Broadly speaking one can summarize the general lines of development as follows. In the West, while official lip-service was paid to the concept of one German nation in two German states, as time went by more and more people lost interest in and a sense of community with their alleged brethren in the East. Different underlying presuppositions about the bases of the 'nation' became evident in political clashes: 'ethnic' and 'homogeneous cultural' versions were challenged by those seeking instead a 'post-national' form of 'constitutional patriotism', while many West Germans simply evaded the question by emphasizing instead the less problematic poles of regional and European foci of identity. Conversely, in the GDR, despite the official determination to construct a quite new sense of a separate GDR nation in the 1970s and 1980s, and despite the emergence of more critical forms of a kind of counter-GDR identity, at the same time a popular sense of an all-German identity remained widely prevalent. If it was not an immediate or sole cause of the collapse of the East European communist system in 1989, it was nevertheless an underlying strand which was readily available and could be appropriated in the changed circumstances of 1989–90.

If one examines both the results of sociological opinion polls in the GDR, and the less systematic but no less illuminating insights from archival sources (particularly local party and trade union reports), one sees very clearly the retention of a strong sense of all-German identity among the East German population. This was, however, simultaneously tempered by a recognition of current political realities, and a real sense of GDR-specific identity in a manner not intended by the regime.

In the GDR in the 1950s, the overwhelming assumption was that political division was a purely temporary state of affairs, and the issue of reunification was very high on the immediate political agenda. There were strong reactions against remilitarization, for example, expressed in comments such as 'we do not want Germans to be shooting Germans'.[29] After the erection of the Wall, many East Germans recognized the realities of the present and did not wish to step out of line in public. Reactions to the building of the Wall are

[29] FDGB, Bundesvorstand, 2672, Information no. 4, 20 Jan. 1956.

also more complex than might initially be thought.[30] However, the private reactions which have been caught in the records provide very strong indications of a sense of a nation which has been divided, with even the regime's own functionaries having difficulties in defending the erection of this euphemistically termed 'anti-fascist protection Wall', but suggesting that the end ultimately justified the means.[31] Discussion of the 'National Document' in 1962 similarly indicated widespread difficulties with the official line: comments are reported such as 'Why does Walter Ulbricht say that the two German states are hostile to one another?' and 'The unitary German state may have been split, but not the nation'.[32] 'Unclear and negative conceptions' were to be found even among functionaries, who were criticized for failing to realize that the 'militarists and fascists, who are again in power in West Germany' constitute 'the greatest danger for peace and the nation'. Nor do workers and peasants appear to have been entirely convinced that 'it is the task of all who work to use their productivity in the battle for the enhanced strength and security of the GDR, in order that the GDR may fulfil its historic mission'.[33] The situation does not appear to have improved greatly even among young people, who could not be expected to have much memory of an undivided Germany, in 1964: 'In some discussions, particularly among young people, a lack of clarity is revealed concerning the national question, the class character of the two German states, and the readiness to defend itself of the GDR.'[34]

Public conformity was, however, an important transitional step for a population most of whom still remembered Germany before division. Many of the answers given to opinion poll questions from the 1960s onwards are, hence, entirely in the direction desired and expected by the regime. In an opinion poll carried out in preparation for the introduction of the new constitution in 1968, for example, 80.4 per cent agreed with the sentiments of the overtly leading question, which left nothing to chance:

Article 8 of the draft Constitution states the following: 'The German Democratic Republic and its citizens are striving, furthermore, to

[30] Cf. the recent research by Mark Allinson on popular opinion in Thuringia (UCL PhD, 1997 forthcoming with Manchester University Press), and Patrick Major's forthcoming work.

[31] Cf. M. Falbrook, *Anatomy of a Dictatorship* (Oxford: Oxford University Press, 1995), pp. 69–72, 190–3.

[32] FDGB Bundesvorstand, 2678, 15. Information, 19 April 1962.

[33] Ibid., 16. Information, 2 June 1962.

[34] FDGB Bundesvorstand, 2680, 20 Jan. 1964.

overcome the division of Germany which has been forcibly imposed by imperialism, and are seeking for a step-by-step rapprochement of the two German states culminating in their unification on the basis of democracy and socialism.' Is that also in accord with your views?[35]

It would be a brave soul indeed who dared to transgress the line of the answers obviously solicited here. But in some questions the desired line was less immediately apparent, and at least the general pattern of the – clearly still to some extent guarded – answers quite revealing.

The following question in this same survey, for example, posed the question: 'If, among your circle of friends or work colleagues, there is a discussion about whether you see the German Democratic Republic or the whole of Germany as your fatherland, what is the majority view?' Despite the clear clues provided by the previous question, a staggering (and to the GDR researchers alarming) 59.9 per cent replied that 'the whole of Germany is my fatherland'; a mere 37.2 per cent gave the (in this case) 'politically correct' answer that it was the GDR.[36] Although there were marginal improvements, from the SED's point of view, in the percentages replying to the same question in subsequent surveys, there was still deep concern among party researchers. As the commentary on the results of a survey one month later put it:

> From these results one must conclude
> that knowledge about the GDR's historic mission – the model of Germany's future – is not clearly enough developed among the population,
> that the concept of fatherland requires more precise elaboration,
> that, in our agitational activities, it is necessary to explain more frequently and forcibly why for the citizens of our country only the GDR can be the fatherland.[37]

The new constitution obviously did not achieve instant changes in East German consciousness. The same concerns are evident in party reports from the Leipzig region to Walter Ulbricht on the occasion of Willi Brandt's meeting with Willi Stoph in Erfurt in

---

[35] Heinz Niemann, *Meinungsforschung in der DDR. Die geheimen Berichte des Instituts für Meinungsforschung an das Politbüro der SED* (Cologne: Bund Verlag, 1993), Doc. IX (28.2.1968), Q. 9 (no pagination in repr. documents section).

[36] Ibid., Q. 10, p. 13 of Dok. IX.

[37] Ibid., p. 6 of Dok. X (19.3.1968).

1970: 'There was however...among all strata of the population evidence of inappropriate class attitudes with respect to the evaluation of the Erfurt meeting. This is shown in particular in the following: The necessity and significance of the international legal recognition of the GDR as the basic precondition of the securing of peace is not as yet fully appreciated.'[38] Similar 'misconceptions and hesitations' (*Unklarheiten und Schwankungen*) are evident, a year later, in the report from the SED First Secretary in Potsdam to Ulbricht: 'Great lack of clarity was revealed...about the class character of the concept of the fatherland. While 42.3 per cent expressed their conviction that they viewed the GDR as their fatherland, 40.2 per cent explained that the whole of Germany was their fatherland, even if it was divided.'[39]

Interestingly, however, generational shifts were already apparent. In the March 1968 survey, as many as two-thirds (66.7 per cent) of those under the age of twenty were prepared to say that they saw the GDR as their fatherland.[40] A steep learning curve with respect to desired answers about the GDR is also apparent: monthly repetitions of the question elicited ever-better results, from the SED's point of view. Nevertheless, not only the specific party reports from Leipzig and Potsdam just mentioned, but also a more general survey covering the period 1971 to 1974 had to admit that: 'The fact that there are such strong variations in the evaluation of the Federal Republic's official policies shows that, among a large proportion of the population, there is insufficient clarity about the class character of Bonn's politics.'[41]

A report on popular responses to the 1972 Basic Treaty between the GDR and the FRG is also very revealing. Despite being mostly extremely positive (the 'beautification' – *Verschönerung* – of reporting, telling the regime what it wanted to hear, had already set in), there are some rather hard-hitting points: 'In discussions and expressions of opinion it becomes clear that the Brandt–Scheel government's policies are not being properly evaluated from a class standpoint.' The primary concern of most people is the possible 'relaxation of travel conditions': it is notable that 'judgements

---

[38] 'Aus dem Bericht des 1. Sekretärs der Bezirksleitung Leipzig der SED, Paul Fröhlich, an Walter Ulbricht von 30. März 1970', repr. in Gerhard Naumann and Eckhard Trümpler (eds), *Der Flop mit der DDR-Nation 1971* (Berlin: Dietz Verlag, 1991), p. 172.

[39] 'Aus dem Bericht des 1. Sekretärs der Bezirksleitung Potsdam der SED, Werner Wittig, an Walter Ulbricht von 31. März 1971', repr. ibid., p. 218.

[40] Niemann, *Meinungsforschung*, p. 12 of Dok. X.

[41] Ibid., p. 13 of Dok. XIV, 'Über die Entwicklung von Meinungen der DDR-Bürger zu einigen Grundfragen unserer Politik (Zeitraum 1971–1974)'.

of the treaty are primarily based in personal and family considerations.' Many citizens do not have a 'full appreciation' of why they
cannot travel freely to the West. There are even difficulties among
the 'leading cadres', many of whom had renounced their positions
because they did not wish to be affected by the related increased
security measures.[42]

It is hardly surprising that 'confusions' continued to exist in the
population, even after the constitutional changes of 1974. Erich
Honecker himself did not do much to help clarify the official line
when he reiterated the new theoretical distinction between 'citizenship of the GDR' and 'German nationality':

> This distinction is decisive. Our socialist state is called German
> Democratic Republic, because the vast majority of its citizens are,
> by nationality, German. There is therefore absolutely no reason for
> any confusion when filling up forms... The answer to this sort of
> question runs quite simply, and without any ambiguity: citizenship –
> GDR, nationality – German. That's the way it is.[43]

Whether one wished to refer to an essentially ethnic-cultural concept of 'German' as 'nation' (wrong answer) or as 'nationality'
(right answer) probably seemed of little relevance to most East
Germans who were not too interested in the niceties of communist
theoretical hair-splitting.

Moreover, the indigenous Sorb community was also officially
treated as in some respects a separate 'nation', and much emphasis
was laid on the way in which the regime fostered Sorb institutions,
language and culture, even though in practice its social and economic policies tended to undermine the conditions for the continuation of a viable Sorb community.[44] And, despite avowals about
'international socialism', or the international solidarity of the working class, foreign workers in the GDR were kept in segregated
hostels, well separated from the local population, whose attitudes
often evinced a degree of racism rooted in a quite traditional ethnic
conception of the nation.[45]

[42] FDGB Bundesvorstand, 2688, 16 Nov. 1972.
[43] Erich Honecker, speech to the Central Committee of the SED, 12 Dec.
1974, printed in *Neues Deutschland*, 13 Dec. 1974, and repr. in Peter Brandt and
Herbert Ammon (eds), *Die Linke und die nationale Frage* (Hamburg: Rowohlt,
1981), p. 325.
[44] Cf. e.g. Peter Barker, 'The Sorbian Minority in the GDR before and after
the *Wende*', *GDR Monitor*, 24 (spring 1991), pp. 21–37; M. Krüger-Potratz,
'*Anderssein gab es nicht*' (Münster: Waxmann Verlag, 1991).
[45] As one report put it: 'From the standpoint of proletarian internationalism,
our workers show great reservations in respect of the Algerian workers.

For all these complexities, in the course of the 1970s and early 1980s increasing numbers of younger people did perceive the GDR as their country, however much they may have disapproved of particular aspects of life in the GDR. In the aftermath of the collapse of East German communism, it is sometimes forgotten that, in the 1980s, as many as one in five of the adult population were members of the ruling SED. This was a state that was carried as much by conformity and accommodation as by repression. Concepts such as 'GDR-citizen', 'the non-socialist foreign countries' and so on became part of the everyday speech of young people in the GDR, however disaffected they may have been. In retrospect, the middle years of the GDR constituted some sort of 'golden age', in which there was a degree of political stabilization and acceptance of the status quo, even though there is as yet no firm agreement over the exact period-ization of this golden age.[46] International recognition, apparent improvements on the consumer front, dramatic sporting successes, simple habituation, all played some role here. Even those who were most strongly critical of the regime in the 1980s were, for the most part, deeply committed to some form of reformed socialism, paying due respect to issues of peace, the environment, human rights, which might be realizable in a continuing GDR.

On the other hand, the perception of an alternative in the West remained very real. Connections with western relatives remained highly important, as a source of western goods and currency, and as a contact to the outside world. When asked in March 1990 whether they had relatives or friends in the West, 84 per cent of East Germans said yes, and only 16 per cent said no. When a year earlier, in January 1989, West Germans had been asked the same question about whether they had relatives or friends in the East, only 32 per cent had replied in the affirmative, and 68 per cent had said they had no such personal contacts.[47] West Germany obviously continued to have great personal salience for East Germans, in a way that was not echoed among the majority of West German relatives and friends. And while the official, militaristic 'friend/

Nationalist tendencies are displayed in the international attitude of many of our colleagues', FDGB 5414, 12 Dec. 1975. Cf. also my article 'Germany for the Germans?' in D. Cesarani and M. Fulbrook (eds), *Citizenship, Nationality and Migration in Europe* (London: Routledge, 1996).

[46] Cf. e.g. the survey on 'the best years in the GDR' in Elisabeth Noelle-Neumann and Renate Köcher (eds), *Allensbacher Jahrbuch der Demoskopie 1984–1992*, vol. 9 (Munich: K. G. Saur, 1993), p. 388, where there are clear majorities for the 1960s and 1970s, with a sharp drop for positive perceptions of the 1980s (scoring, remarkably, even lower than the 1950s).

[47] Elisabeth Noelle-Neumann, ibid., p. 411.

foe mentality' never fully caught on in the GDR, a strong strand of anti-communism in the West allowed suspicions of the GDR regime at least to draw down the shutters on a state in which they were not very interested.

The direct salience of West Germany for a majority of East Germans was to some degree even fostered by a state that was deeply paranoid about western competition and potential undermining, constantly determined to 'overtake' the West or prove itself to be superior in material as well as ideological respects, and yet at the same time was increasingly economically dependent on the West. It was perhaps the culmination of Erich Honecker's career to be received in state in the Federal Republic in 1987, and to return to his native region in the Saarland. The tense and asymmetrically symbiotic relationship between the two states, in which the East was constantly focusing on, competing with, and yet also dependent on the West, ensured that all-German commonalities could never be forgotten in the GDR.

Contested concepts of the nation in the West

Meanwhile, in the West both the interest in unification and the conception of fatherland appeared to be waning. Generational shifts were very striking. In an opinion poll of January 1976, carried out by the Allensbach Institute for Demoscopy, for example, West Germans were asked whether they 'greatly wished' for reunification, or whether it was not very important to them. The overall results reveal 61 per cent 'greatly wishing' for reunification, with 36 per cent thinking it not so important. But the gradient with respect to age was quite dramatic: only 44 per cent of those less than thirty years of age were very keen on reunification, in contrast to 77 per cent of those aged sixty and over.[48] (The corresponding figures were 57 per cent of the 30–44 age group, and 65 per cent of the 45–59 age group.) Similarly, younger West Germans were increasingly finding problems with the emotive word 'fatherland'. On being asked whether it had 'good resonance' or 'no longer had any place in the present day and age', 65 per cent of those aged under thirty thought it no longer appropriate, and only 32 per cent felt it had a good resonance. Those aged over sixty had diametrically opposed views: 67 per cent thought the word had positive associations, and only 30 per cent felt it no longer appropriate.[49]

[48] Weidenfeld, *Frage nach der Einheit*, p. 47.
[49] Ibid., p. 49.

In the 1980s national pride was lower in West Germany than anywhere else in western Europe, and West Germans scored abysmally in comparison with their American counterparts. While a remarkable 79 per cent of US citizens declared themselves to be 'extremely proud' to be American, 66 per cent of citizens of the Republic of Ireland, and 55 per cent of the British enjoyed similar sentiments, a mere 21 per cent of West Germans were able to take such pride in their nation.[50] If one takes the other end of this spectrum, those who admitted to being 'not very proud', 'not at all proud', or 'undecided', one finds the complementary side of the picture: a mere 4 per cent of Americans, 9 per cent of Irish, and 14 per cent of British professed such difficulties with national pride, in contrast to 41 per cent of West Germans.

On the other hand, among West Germans there were viable alternatives. Both regional identities and a sense of being 'good Europeans' provided a degree of alibi and compensation for being 'ashamed to be German'. These proved to be useful and acceptable escape routes from identification with a problematic fatherland.[51]

Regional identities had always been strong – or relatively easily constructed and propagated – among the diversity of lands in central Europe which, over the centuries, had coalesced or regrouped in one or another more inclusive political form, from the loose framework of the Holy Roman Empire through the German Confederation to the Second Empire and into the changing state forms and political boundaries of the turbulent twentieth century. The construction of 'regional' identities is in principle little different from that of 'national' identities: a story is told about a common past, certain values and features are emphasized and sung from on high, common rituals and symbols serve to forge a visible community, common institutions and experience shape similarities of behaviour, expression and outlook. After the Napoleonic reshaping of German states, for example, many German rulers of the nineteenth century engaged in processes of regional identity building: Bavaria under King Ludwig II is a prime case in point.

[50] These and the following figures in this paragraph are taken from Elisabeth Noelle-Neumann and Renate Köcher, *Die verletzte Nation. Über den Versuch der Deutschen, ihren Charakter zu ändern* (Stuttgart: Deutsche Verlags-Anstalt, 2nd edn, 1987), p. 50.

[51] See e.g. Werner Weidenfeld and Karl-Rudolf Korte, *Die Deutschen: Profil einer Nation* (Stuttgart: Klett-Cotta, 1991), pt 3, 'Region, Nation und Europa', for useful empirical evidence on the multi-layered consciousness of West Germans in the 1980s (although the notion that being a 'Bundesbürger' did not fully satisfy an alleged need for identity is a little more contentious).

'Regional' identities do not have a 'real essence', any more than 'national' identities; under certain conditions they appear more or less salient, more or less usable (and, indeed, more or less capable of being drawn upon as the basis for 'national' identities, should inter-state power politics work in their favour, as was the case with Prussia).

Regions certainly proved to be a prime basis of identity for many Germans in the Federal Republic. A retreat into regional identities and alibis appeared almost as soon as the war was over. The first issue of the newly licensed *Süddeutsche Zeitung*, published on 6 October 1945, for example, made a ringing declaration for a new sense of regional and European identity among Bavarians:

> The 'Süddeutsche Zeitung' will take succour from the south German, and in particular the Bavarian, sense of historical consciousness. Rejecting an arid, un-Germanic centralism, it will represent a power-ful federalism connected to all the best traditions. Fighting against all Prussian-militaristic tendencies, it will cultivate those religious and cultural forces which are precisely at home in Bavaria and which Germany once had to thank for respect and sympathy in the world. It will be open as a voice of freedom in the present for all those young forces who want to participate in the spiritual and cultural transfor-mation of Europe.[52]

With this, the self-appointed journalistic medium for a new identity disassociated itself from the 'Prussian-militaristic' tendencies which had, implicitly, been responsible for the Nazi regime.

Meanwhile, of course, the 'Prussian militarists' were equally dis-claiming any responsibility for Hitler. Hitler was, after all, simply what President Hindenburg had called a 'Bohemian corporal', an Austrian who had little in common with 'real' Prussian/German values. Prussian militarism had been usurped and misled by Hitler; the true German military traditions in which one could take pride were represented, not by the SS, but by the Wehrmacht, which had (on this view) sought merely to defend Germany's honour, and by the men of the July Plot, who had valiantly sought to save the fatherland from total defeat.

Regional identities did not even need to define themselves against Hitler; they simply existed, as a focus for a sense of belong-ing, of attachment, of sense of *Heimat*, at a time when being 'Ger-man' had too many unpleasant connotations. The Rhineland, the Hunsrück, the Hansestadt Hamburg, the Black Forest – or wherever

---

[52] *Süddeutsche Zeitung*, 1, 6 Oct. 1945.

- took the place of a dismembered and discredited 'Germany'. Moreover, the federal political structure of the Federal Republic served to reinforce and provide institutional underpinnings for regional differences, particularly in the spheres of education and culture. Regionalism was a political and social reality in everyday life.

At the other end of the spectrum, whatever the other bases of post-war West European integration, a professed commitment to 'Europe' took on alibi functions for many West Germans. The distant origins of the European Union (notably the European Coal and Steel Community) lay partly in Allied post-war attempts to contain potential German might. But very soon Germans adopted the European cause as their own: being the most in favour of closer European cooperation, leading towards economic and eventually perhaps political integration, was a key theme in Germany from the 1950s to 1989. The shift in tone in the 1990s was to some extent based in the undeniably greater economic problems experienced by united Germany, which posed unexpected obstacles to meeting strict targets for monetary integration. But it was also very evident, even before the scale of the costs of unification became apparent, that enthusiasm for a united Europe was waning in at least some quarters (and quite vociferously among, for example, Bavarian right-wing circles) in the context of a united German state. In answer to the question 'Are you proud to be a European?', the number responding 'absolutely' (*unbedingt*) dropped from 26 per cent in 1989 to 12 per cent in 1991, and the number responding 'on the whole' (*überwiegend*) dropped from 47 per cent to 41 per cent.[53]

A distinctive combination thus stamped its mark on West German national identity for forty years: escape into regionalism on the one hand, Euro-enthusiasm on the other. And, in between, there were clashes between opposing conceptions of any 'German' identity, from the mono-ethnic/cultural, to the 'post-national' or constitutional versions. It was, in short, an essentially contested term: not even the criteria of definition were shared, as debates over expanding the bases of German citizenship or allowing dual nationality revealed.[54] Resistance to easing citizenship applications on the part of even third-generation 'guest-workers' (*Gastarbeiter*) revealed just how deep-seated the ethnic assumptions were, even at a time when constitutional commitment to reunification seemed to be

[53] Noelle-Neumann and Köcher (eds), *Allensbacher Jahrbuch*, vol. 9, p. 1011.
[54] See e.g. Karen Schönwälder, 'Migration, Refugees and Ethnic Plurality as Issues of Public and Political Debates in (West) Germany', in Cesarani and Fulbrook, *Citizenship, Nationality and Migration*.

fading as a matter of practical aspiration. While racist conceptions on the far right were strenuously opposed not only by left-liberal 'post-nationalists', but also by many in the centre ground who still retained live distinctions between 'foreigners' and 'Germans' (but believed that the latter had a historically imposed duty to be nice, rather than nasty, to the former), it was clear that there was no uncontested, generally accepted sense of what constituted the nation in West Germany.

Thus the concept of the nation diverged in a variety of ways in the two German states. Constitutionally, the definitions of citizenship entitlement were mutually incompatible and politically inflammatory. Popular assumptions began to diverge from official versions. The notion of what the nation itself consisted in was itself politically variable and contested. And these developments were hardly hovering in thin air, isolated in some ethereal sphere of constitutional amendments, political negotiations and intellectual deliberations. Over forty years, the two societies of East and West were diverging in ways that made experienced collective identities very different on each side of the Iron Curtain. While politicians and intellectuals agonized on the unity or otherwise of the German nation, the people were getting on with real life; and the realities of identification formed the basis of new patterns of identity and belonging, which might, if left long enough, have formed the basis of new forms of (proto-national?) identity in each case.

8
Friends, Foes and *Volk*

Identity is neither simply a matter of discourse, of cultural construction; nor is it an essence persisting over generations. Constructions of collective identity change, with changes in experienced realities.

This is important. 'Ordinary Germans' are, for example, not – as on some views – always 'essentially' anti-semitic, even if anti-semitism is allegedly 'latent' for long periods of time.[1] Nor are 'ordinary Germans', or 'post-national Germans', or 'citizens of the GDR', simply what they are told to be, what on certain constructions they 'ought' to be or become. Purely cultural or political or intellectual constructions and propagations of identity will not resonate without an appropriate basis of experience. What 'being German' consists in is neither a persisting essence, nor a moral prescription, but rather a set of cultural, social and political patterns that are historically malleable and situationally variable.

The division of Germany into two very different states after 1945 provides a remarkable historical laboratory for exploring the degrees of mutability of 'identity' in different circumstances. The emerging differences between what became labelled *Wessis* and *Ossis* in the aftermath of the *Wende* show just how variable and malleable are the patterns of behaviour, orientation and

---

[1] This is the thrust of Daniel Goldhagen's argument with respect to German history for several centuries preceding the Holocaust: Daniel Jonah Goldhagen, *Hitler's Willing Executioners: Ordinary Germans and the Holocaust* (New York: Knopf, 1996). However, Goldhagen then starkly and illogically contradicts his previous theoretical stance by suggesting that all has changed since 1945, and that the curse of centuries has somehow, miraculously, been lifted.

self-perception that together form the bundle of attributes often deemed to constitute a 'national identity'.

The imagined community: communications, culture and identity

One of the most influential contributions to debates over national identity is Benedict Anderson's concept of 'imagined community'.[2] This approach, while a major advance for theories of national identity, needs both extension and qualification. First, the character of communications has changed dramatically since the period of the emergence of 'nations' which formed the prime focus of Anderson's work; and secondly, there are more experiential and institutional aspects to the 'imagined community'. Nevertheless, a few words are in order here about the 'imagined communities' of East and West Germans.

It is clear that communications and the map of the 'perceived world' are crucially important in the construction of a sense of identity. What are designated or perceived as centres, peripheries, the dark or blank or empty areas, familiar territories and danger spots? What parts of the map are salient, easily coloured in, full of detail and knowledge? What boundaries are taken for granted, 'the way the world is', and which are seen as alien, imposed, 'unnatural'?

One of the most important facets of this question is of course travel. Until the twentieth century, very few people in Europe – apart from royalty, and diplomatic, professional and trading groups – travelled very far at all from their immediate localities and regions. Emigration or immigration for economic or political reasons was a matter of major personal and family relocation, often permanent: the pattern of movement then remained relatively circumscribed. With the growth of railways, and the invention of the motor car, movements back and forth across Europe (finishing school, the Grand Tour, the Cure, and so on) began to increase among the more affluent classes. But it was only with the massive population movements unleashed by two world wars that most of the 'common people' expanded their geographic horizons.

At the end of the twentieth century, matters are very different. There has been a now taken-for-granted, but only a short time ago almost unforeseeable, explosion of rapid communications: cheaper

[2] Benedict Anderson, *Imagined Communities* (London: Verso, 1983, rev. edn, 1991).

flights and competition among airlines making international air travel a mass phenomenon; global satellite and cable television channels making 'national' arenas of popular culture and mass media almost outdated; the mobile telephone, fax machines and e-mail facilitating personal bombardment by instant communication almost anywhere, anytime. This explosion of communications has a history, however, and the history of the parameters of the 'well-trodden world' was a little different in East and West Germany.

In West Germany in the 1950s, road communications were still relatively poor (although Hitler's programme of autobahn-building obviously had advantages not only for military mobilization but also for post-war civilian life, once any sort of normality was re-established). Many villages in remote areas, such as Upper Bavaria, were still connected only with un-metalled roads. It was not until the 1960s that road and railway construction meant a rapid and effective communications network across the Federal Republic. With the 'economic miracle' and the dramatic rise in consumer spending, cars soon became an almost universal commodity. Higher wages, shorter working weeks and longer holiday entitlements soon meant that West Germans were among the most cosmopolitan of West Europeans.

In principle, West Germans could – particularly with the easing of travel restrictions after *Ostpolitik* – also travel to eastern European countries. But with their lower standards of living, lower standards of comfort, and compulsory currency exchanges, there was little incentive to do so if one had no personal reason. The perceived universe of home, for West Germans, was the West.

In a sense, the converse was true, although on a vastly reduced scale, for East Germans. Holidays were taken, in the main, through organized groups (such as the FDJ for young people, or, more generally, the trade union organization, the FDGB) within the GDR, at domestic resorts such as the Baltic coast or in the mountainous regions of the southern GDR. If one was fortunate, one might participate in organized tours to other eastern European states or even the Soviet Union, though such tours were strictly controlled and supervised to ensure there were not too many opportunities for uncontrolled interaction with other visitors (particularly visitors from the West). Applications could be made for visas for non-organized private or family holidays abroad: the popularity of Hungary as a destination was apparent when droves of East Germans left through Hungary for Austria in the summer of 1989. The main point, however, to be noted about all of this is the essential state control of all travel. East Germans were dependent on organizational sponsorship for transport and accommodation, and for state approval of visa applications: the opaque capriciousness of an unknown functionary could foil all plans for exploration of pastures new, while stepping out of line politically in however small but suspicious a manner could mean even being turned off a train to a concert in East Berlin and sent back home. The boundaries of the permissible, explorable universe were very firmly set by the state – and this of course, most clearly, in the hideous length of that conglomeration of *Sperrgebiet*, no-man's-land, minefields, tank tracks, watchtowers, concrete blocks and barbed wire which constituted the 'inner-German border' or, in its Berlin variant, the Wall. Only the politically reliable *Reisekader* ('travel cadres') who were deemed to be effective ambassadors for the GDR (with appropriate minders in tow), or pensioners who constituted an economic burden on the state, could easily obtain visas to travel to the West – as well as those few dissident spirits who were ultimately selected for a one-way ticket.

Hence, although the realities of travel were eastern-orientated, state-controlled, and radically restricted, the mental horizons inevitably roamed across to the forbidden land on the other side. A yearning for seeing the beyond meant that it could not be ignored in the way of affluent, unrestricted westerners who had no interest in spending time in the east.

Not able to travel west in reality, many East Germans nevertheless participated avidly in western culture through the air waves. In the 1950s, East Germans were dependent on western radio reports for news of what was 'really going on' in their country. The RIAS station in West Berlin played a modest role, for example, in broadcasting the demands of demonstrators who had downed tools on 16 June 1953, and their decision to call a general strike for 17 June. But it was still relatively easy for East German authorities to control the access of western reporters to news, particularly if incidents were rapidly suppressed. For example, reports of an attempt at a repeat of 17 June in Magdeburg in 1956 were rapidly squashed, and the unrest failed to spread. The role of rumour was possibly far more important at this time: and rumours in the 1950s ran in all manner of often mutually contradictory directions.

When television ownership first began to be widespread, in the 1960s, the East German regime attempted desperately to prevent its population from having access to western broadcasts. It was much easier to control the import of western newspapers, journals and books (the printed media which required physical transportation). In the 1970s, the SED gave up in a losing battle, and, with the 'opening towards the West' consequent on *Ostpolitik*, watching western television was no longer banned. In the course of the 1970s and 1980s, with television ownership growing rapidly, a sense of 'cultural community' with the West remained very much alive, for all except, perhaps, those forlorn souls in the so-called *Tal der Ahnungslosen* ('the valley of those without a clue'), the residents of the south-eastern area of the GDR where reception of western stations was technically impossible.

The effects of the general availability of western television ran in several directions. On the one hand, of course, the East German population were exceptionally well-informed (among Soviet bloc states) about the real conditions in their own country. Even if western reporters could not necessarily have as much access to information as they might have liked, they nevertheless could carry far more informative reports on the realities of life and politics in the GDR than the GDR's own media ever carried. The GDR population was also able to watch documentaries and news reports about the rest of the world, about history and politics (and indeed entirely non-political programmes) that to some extent counteracted the impact of the GDR's own propaganda. Some of this was clearly of importance in raising questions, issues, alternative points of view (as we have seen when noting the interest in the American television series *Holocaust*, above).

On the other hand, however, under the prevailing political conditions of the 1970s and most of the 1980s, this impact was limited. It takes a fairly active engagement with any subject, and discussion among a group, for alternative views and issues really to make much of an impact on consciousness, let alone have implications for action in the real world. Under conditions in which the GDR looked as if it would last forever, the odd programme on unofficial peace initiatives, environmentalists and human rights dissenters, or a Wolf Biermann concert, was not sufficient for most GDR citizens to risk their own lives, careers, futures, or the prospects for their children.

It was of course a very different matter when conditions changed dramatically with the growing holes in the Iron Curtain in the summer of 1989. And when, in the autumn of 1989, people could see with their own eyes demonstrations marching peacefully through Leipzig and other cities, without major bloodshed, then western television reporting of the 'gentle revolution' certainly played a role in giving others the courage to come out and join the demonstrators on the streets. In the meantime, of course, over the preceding decades, it had helped to keep alive the residual sense of all-German identity that could be drawn on in the changed rhetoric of street politics after 9 November, when 'Wir sind das

Volk' (we are the people) changed into 'Wir sind ein Volk' (we are one people).

The importance of western television in the GDR thus needs to be very carefully qualified. The other side of the story is simpler. Few westerners without a professional interest in the GDR would have wished to spend much time watching GDR television or reading the boringly repetitive success stories of over-production, health and welfare for all, sporting success and the like which passed as 'news' in East German newspapers and magazines. The 'imagined community' sustained by the media in the West was very much western-oriented: from dubbed Hollywood movies to French and Italian cinema, West Germans participated in broader western cultural developments and had little knowledge of or interest in the East.

There was too a degree of genuine 'Sovietization' of East German culture in ways that have not always been adequately appreciated. As Norman Naimark has brilliantly shown, even from the very earliest days of the Soviet occupation there was an interaction between German and Soviet culture that was more than superficial imposition.[3] This continued through the activities, for example, of the German–Soviet Friendship Society, and East Germans learned Russian as their second language in schools (reportedly rather more willingly in the Gorbachev era of *glasnost*). The central European location of Germany had always meant a degree of ambivalent cultural oscillation between East and West. The older German antinomy between *Kultur* and *Zivilisation*, prevalent among German intellectuals at the turn of the century, involved a degree of superciliousness about the alleged superficiality of western pragmatism, empiricism, and the like, in contrast to the supposed 'depth' of German culture. A fascination with Russian culture in the nineteenth century was sustained even through the rejection of Bolshevism from the 1920s onwards. Given this longer background, it is not difficult to see points at which the cultural interaction of East Germans and Russians, even under the changed political circumstances of the GDR, was not without some intrinsic authenticity.

Although it may sound a little paradoxical, the westernization or 'Americanization' of West Germany from the early post-war years onwards constituted perhaps a more radical break with the central European cultural heritage. But from the films of the 1950s, through the changed culture of trade unions, management and industrial

---

[3] Norman Naimark, *The Russians in Germany* (Cambridge, Mass.: Harvard University Press, 1996).

relations, to the proliferation of McDonalds drive-thru's [*sic!*], the impact of America on West German culture, in the broadest sense, cannot be overlooked.

That there were reactions against Americanization and America cannot be denied. These came from the most diverse political quarters: on the one hand, those of the older generation who adopted a relatively traditional position of cultural disdain, on the other, most forcefully in the 1960s, those who found that the political saviour and protector of 'freedom and democracy' had feet of clay when it came to the use of napalm in Vietnam. In the late 1970s and 1980s, the West German peace movement demonstrated very emphatically against the American decision to station Cruise Missiles in Germany, and anti-Americanism was to be found across from the far left to the far right of the political spectrum, although for very different reasons at each end. Yet at the same time, in many respects, the Federal Republic was a thoroughly Americanized society, reflected in the cosmopolitanism and almost perfect command of the English language of its professional and business classes. It was indeed a measure of the degree of that Americanization that so many could come out in social movements and citizens' initiatives, protesting against aspects of government politics. Student protests in the late 1960s had, after all, been as prevalent in Berkeley as in Berlin; there was more to 'Americanization' than slavish adoption of or simple subservience to official state policy.

What do these brief and general reflections on large and complex topics lead us to conclude about the 'imagined community'? The answer is asymmetrical. The 'imagined community' for West Germans was, increasingly, the western world: region within West Germany, western Europe, the 'western world' in the larger sense of the sphere of American influence. The area behind the Iron Curtain was, for most West Germans, one of the blank spots on the map, about which they had little curiosity. For most East Germans, the area of familiarity was the other side; but there remained an intense interest in things western, a great desire to be able to participate in western culture (from the Rock'n'Roll crazes of the 1950s, through Beatles, Blues and Blue Jeans in the 1960s, to the Rock concerts of the 1980s) and to be able to travel to the West. Two of the most telling slogans of the 1989 revolution, which appeared well before 'We are one people', were 'Visa-free to Hawaii' *(Visa-frei nach Hawaii)* and 'Bike ride through the whole of Europe, but not as an old grandfather' *(Radtour durch ganz Europa, aber nicht als alter Opa).*

Friends and foes: communities of common fate and common destiny

National identity is not only a question of an 'imagined community': it is also, crucially, a community of common experience, of sense of common fate and destiny.

There are several aspects to this. First, modes of interpersonal behaviour, and indeed the very construction of individual 'personality', are to some extent influenced by sociopolitical circumstances which elicit, shape and reward certain types of behaviour and not others. A sense of similarity, of 'being like' or 'sharing characteristics with' other people with whom one identifies, can be expressed in a wide variety of ways, from hairstyles and clothing fashions to tastes in music, career and lifestyle aspirations, to understanding 'in-jokes' not accessible to those 'not in the know', or not party to the secrets and subversive moments of 'our' community. There is, too, what might be called the 'banal nationalism of everyday life': the sense of being 'at home' in certain surroundings, certain ways of life, and finding others alien, different, 'foreign'. Finally, there is the question of the construction of difference, and most crucially, of enmity: who is the common foe?

It is quite obvious that, over forty years, the very different political and socioeconomic structures and developments in the two German states had a crucial impact on society.[4] Patterns of property ownership and class structures were radically different; levels of income and expenditure diverged markedly; political circumstances and constraints, and the conditions for public debate and civil society, were almost diametrically opposed. Although West German regional disparities never entirely disapppeared (with marked contrasts, for example, between Rhinelanders and Bavar-

---

[4] While there has for some time been an interesting literature on many aspects of West German social history, covering a wide range of topics from Americanization to the integration of refugees, the social history of the GDR is only just beginning to be developed. See for selected examples: R. Bessel and R. Jessen (eds), *Die Grenzen der Diktatur* (Göttingen: Vandenhoeck and Ruprecht, 1996); Hartmut Kaelble, Jürgen Kocka and Hartmut Zwahr (eds), *Sozialgeschichte der DDR* (Stuttgart: Klett-Cotta, 1994); C. Kleßmann and G. Wagner (eds), *Das gespaltene Land: Leben in Deutschland 1945 bis 1990* (Munich: C. H. Beck, 1993); Jürgen Kocka, *Historische DDR-Forschung* (Berlin: Akademie Verlag, 1993); and the brief overview and discussion in M. Fulbrook, 'Ossis and Wessis: The Creation of two German Societies' in M. Fulbrook (ed.), *German History since 1800* (London: Arnold, 1997).

ians, Swabians and Frisians), the growing contrasts between East and West outweighed all variations within either state.

What were the implications for characteristic modes of interpersonal behaviour? Let us take just a couple of – necessarily brief – examples. Everything in the GDR was organized on a 'collective' basis, and rationalized on the premise of the 'collective good'. The role of the individual was very markedly demoted in both theory and practice. Theoretically, the entire Marxist-Leninist outlook was rooted in a belief in classes as the actors of history: individuals who disagreed with what was supposedly in the best long-term interests of their class might be suffering from 'false consciousness', which it was the task of the vanguard (Leninist) party to dispel. Any individual who resisted the process of enlightenment through 'criticism and self-criticism', and who thus impeded the onward march of history according to the scientific laws of Marxism-Leninism, was in some way to be rendered ineffectual, silenced, exiled: there was no space for any one who dared, at least in public, to 'think differently'.

This had several consequences in practice. Social and political life was always organized on the basis of 'collectives', which were to foster (and police) a sense of collective identity. Life as a member of a collective started from an extraordinarily early age. The very comprehensive child care system of the GDR, which enabled the vast majority of mothers of young children to continue working with barely a break, ensured that the predominant experience of the very small was, almost right from the start, an experience of living as part of a group, with all the constraints and pressures to conform that that entailed. (One East German psychotherapist has even criticized the alleged long-term effects of forcible potty training in organized rows of harangued toddlers.[5]) In schools, conformity rather than originality was rewarded: one had to learn to repeat the received wisdom, not to query or debate. Leisure time was strictly controlled: the state was paranoid about what young people might get up to if left to themselves, outside the control of the official youth organizations. The same was true even after GDR citizens had successfully reached adulthood. Conscription and military service reinforced the already learned habits of obedience and discipline. (Although it was possible to do alternative service as 'construction soldiers' (*Bausoldaten*), this had heavy consequences in terms of blocking off most future career paths, leaving virtually

[5] H.-J. Maaz, *Der Gefühlsstau. Ein Psychogramm der DDR* (Berlin: Argon, 1991).

only theology and the church as avenues for those with an intellectual inclination.)

In employment, the collective was equally important, although not always in the intended manner. In a planned and centrally controlled economy, with guaranteed jobs and no fear of unemployment, there was little incentive for individual competitiveness – hence the absence of what East Germans later denigrated in the West as the 'elbow society'. The state itself tried to foster a combination of collective spirit with a degree of competition, attempting through such mechanisms to raise productivity (as in the activist Hennecke movement, or the various competitions between brigades and factories for the overfulfilment of production plans). These official campaigns were only partially successful, since a variety of (often counter-productive) means were found to circumvent the rules of the game (setting unrealistically low targets which could easily be overfulfilled, using up stocks, failing to allocate appropriate funds for investment or renewal of outdated equipment and so on).[6] Moreover, the state-run monopoly trade union organization, the FDGB, was not widely seen as a real avenue for the expression of workers' interests. But a version of collective spirit nevertheless was persistently, doggedly present, partly in opposition to state policies. The records of unofficial work stoppages in the the GDR reveal a high level of genuine solidarity among workers and a sense of fairness in relation to wage rates and work loads, with workers prepared to risk penalties for walking off the job in protest about perceived unfair treatment of colleagues.

The ambivalent sense of collective spirit was also evident in the sphere of leisure. Any organized activity, from outdoor sports through to high culture, could only be undertaken within the context of a state-run leisure organization. But even the much vaunted retreat into the privacy of the 'niche society', a notion first popularized by Günter Gaus, had a collective element to it.[7] The so-called double-track life (*Zweigleisigkeit*) practised by so many people in the GDR – conformity in public, authenticity in private – was based on a kind of widely shared complicity in unspoken modes of survival, accommodation, indeed simultaneous participation in and critique of the sociopolitical structures of the GDR.

Recent approaches to the social history of the GDR have begun to stress much more the ways in which people – in all manner of social roles – reached forms of accommodation with the situation in which

---

[6] See e.g. Jeffrey Kopstein, *The Politics of Economic Decline in East Germany 1945–1989* (Chapel Hill, NC: University of North Carolina Press, 1997).

[7] Günter Gaus, *Wo Deutschland liegt* (Munich: dtv, 1986; orig. 1983).

they found themselves. The theoretical opposition between 'repressive regime' and 'repressed society' is hard to find in practice, where textures of social experience are in the main more multifaceted and complex than black-and-white versions of 'totalitarian dictatorship' would have us believe.[8]

The extraordinary prevalence of political jokes in the GDR, as previously in the Third Reich, was a characteristic feature of life under a dictatorship. It was a gentle way of letting off steam, of making fun of a state which it was recognized one could do little to change. Jokes such as 'Über Spanien lacht nur die Sonne: über die DDR lacht die ganze Welt' brilliantly undermined the GDR's claims to being the epitome of all that was wonderful in the world.[9] Similarly, the official world view was gently mocked in jokes such as the 'Good Socialist Work Mottoes', including: 'We are always ahead! If we are at the back, then the back is ahead'; 'We don't actually know the Plan, but we'll produce double it!'; 'No one is completely useless – he can always serve as a bad example!' – and so on. The sheer difficulty of translating these jokes into English, in which the connotations of official slogans are lost, indicates the extent to which they were deeply embedded in a historically very specific political context. For many the DDR stood for 'Der Doofe Rest' (those dumb enough to have been left behind).[10]

Socioeconomic and political conditions in West Germany were markedly different. Again, only a few salient facets can be briefly

[8] See e.g. Alf Lüdtke and Peter Becker (eds), *Akten. Eingaben. Schaufenster. Die DDR und ihre Texte. Erkundungen zu Herrschaft und Alltag* (Berlin: Akademie Verlag, 1997); Corey Ross, 'Constructing Socialism at the Grassroots' (UCL PhD thesis, 1998). It has to be said, however, that debates over interpretations of the social history of the GDR are likely to run along lines comparable to the debates over *Alltagsgeschichte* ('the history of everyday life') in the Third Reich. There are diametrically opposed views in principle over whether one should adopt a postmodernist approach to the reconstruction of disparate 'mosaic stones' or seek to achieve – or construct – a synthesis of the whole in which patterns of willing participation, grumbling accommodation and self-preservation in everyday life may be cast in a very different light. Clearly these issues cannot be explored in further detail here.

[9] This linguistically only works properly in German. The literal translation is: 'Only the sun shines over [– laughs about] Spain; the whole world laughs about the GDR.'

[10] One final one on the GDR's way of dealing with problems: A complains to B that he suffers terribly from bed-wetting. B suggests psychotherapy to deal with the problem. After six weeks they meet again and B asks A whether the problem has now been solved. 'Yes', replies A. 'So you've stopped the bed-wetting?' asks B. 'No' replies A, 'but now, instead of being ashamed, I'm really proud of it!' For these and other GDR jokes, see e.g. Reinhard Wagner (ed.), *DDR-Witze* (Berlin: Dietz Verlag, 1994).

adumbrated here. A great deal of research has been carried out, for example, on the ways in which a more democratic form of political culture began to emerge in West Germany in the late 1950s and 1960s, arising from the virtuous combination of new institutional and constitutional structures and the much-vaunted 'economic miracle'. An affluent and individualistic lifestyle became the prevailing norm (even if only at the level of aspiration) for most people. Competitiveness, originality, initiative were rewarded in education and employment. Mobility and enterprise were important for achievement. Of course there were wide variations, with competing models of society and behaviour: the student movements of the 1960s, the citizens' initiatives of the 1970s, the peace and environmentalist movements of the 1980s, presented often highly pointed political challenges, counter-currents against a tide of perceived selfishness and materialism. It would be ridiculous to overgeneralize. But it is important to emphasize the central point that the very roles people came to play, their aspirations and expectations, were integrally affected both by divergent patterns of economic development and by the general character of their social and political surroundings.

Hence, for example, whereas in West Germany it was assumed on the whole that women would cease to engage in paid employment when they had young children, it became taken for granted that GDR women would work, and have careers (even if there remained gender biases and inequalities of achievement), whether or not they had family obligations. Although the domestic division of labour proved remarkably resistant to state intervention and proactive change, one can still discern very significant shifts in gender relations in the GDR. The historical construction of gender roles, underpinned by institutional and cultural conditions (educational and training opportunities, popular images and prevailing assumptions, availability or otherwise of childcare facilities), provides a very clear illustration of the malleability of social roles.[11]

Even the languages began to diverge. There is a well-worn joke about the British and the Americans: 'English is the common language which divides us'.[12] The two Germanies only had forty years

[11] Cf. e.g. the overview and summary in Ute Frevert, 'Gender in German History', in M. Fulbrook (ed.), *German History since 1800*.

[12] As any one who has participated in transatlantic communication is well aware, there are a number or words and phrases which are simply used differently on either side of the 'pond'. The habit of saying 'elevator' instead of 'lift', 'apartment' instead of 'flat', or 'I'll call you' instead of 'I'll ring you', is quickly acquired by expatriate Britons; it may take a little longer to feel quite

for their language to diverge, and the grammar perhaps remained more similar than the 'English' of several hundred years' divergence. There were of course specific terms which differed, and terms the meaning of which required explanation to those living on the other side of the Wall. The Americanization of business German in the West was particularly striking, with a liberal sprinkling of words such as 'Boss', 'Manager', 'Computer', 'Output'. The converse in the GDR was, perhaps, the proliferation of organizational acronyms (DSF, FDJ, FDGB and so on) and the use of terms for GDR-specific institutions which were non-existent in the West (the HO, Intershop, Exquisit and, not least of course, Stasi), reflecting a different social and political world.

All of this leads into the question of what might be called the collective identities of everyday life, of communities of common fate. In answering questions such as 'Who is like us? Who is different?', West and East Germans would begin to give very different answers – even at the level of outward and visible signs of identity and belonging, such as fashions and tastes in clothing, lifestyles, music and food. There is also the deep-rooted issue of a sense of place, of 'feeling at home', of what one feels nostalgia for (the smells of certain sorts of cooking, of pine trees, or Trabi fumes and brown coal dust); the sense of familiarity with particular transport systems or feeling 'lost' or 'trapped'; of knowing 'how the system works', and how to attain one's ends and goals within a particular set of structures.

Last, but certainly not least in the context of this analysis, is the issue of common destiny. There is nothing like a sense of adversity (of 'being in the same boat') for forging a strong sense of collective identity. A sense of common identity is forged most forcibly under conditions of external, existential threat. ('We all hang together, or we'll hang separately.')

The construction of a friend/foe mentality was central to the GDR. As far as the communist leadership was concerned, the 'capitalist-imperialist' class enemy in the West was very real; from its very inception, the GDR was intrinsically locked in an existential battle for survival. But the official mentality was hard to transpose to all sections of society, despite the immense efforts devoted to this task. From kindergarten to retirement, East Germans were exhorted to view the capitalist west as an existential threat, the epitome of all evil against which a permanent state of readiness for military defence was essential. The nature and means through which this

---

comfortable substituting 'pants' for 'trousers', and few British would even begin to try to re-acquire the seventeenth-century construction 'I had gotten'.

militarization was put into practice changed in details over forty years: the formal creation of the National People's Army or NVA (out of already existing troops) in 1956, the introduction of conscription in 1962, the introduction of military education as a compulsory subject in schools in 1978, were all part of a wider penumbra of socialization into a friend/foe mentality. The misleadingly entitled *Gesellschaft für Sport und Technik* (Society for Sport and Technology), offering as it did superior sporting and camping facilities, was one means of sucking young people into paramilitary training; the adverse consequences for future career prospects if one sought to do alternative military service as a 'construction soldier' (*Bausoldat*) was a more negative mechanism for minimising the proportion who escaped the official militarization programme. Everywhere, propaganda beamed the message that the West was the real enemy of freedom, peace, humanity itself. This was particularly the case when the stationing of nuclear missiles in Europe became an issue from the late 1970s and in the new 'mini Cold War' of the Reagan era in the 1980s. The official state peace movement was premised on the view that NATO missiles were uniquely evil, in contrast to the Warsaw Pact missiles' function of protecting peace.

But the message, prevalent throughout every aspect of GDR education, institutional structures, ideology, was not effective. To be all-pervasive does not ensure success. The West, far from being perceived as the ultimate threat to humanity, remained alluring to large numbers of GDR citizens. Tante Amalie in Hamburg did not suddenly acquire the role of devil incarnate. The official friend/foe mentality propagated by the SED did not lodge itself in the hearts and minds of the DDR-Bürger.

The situation in West Germany was perhaps a little less clear cut. Anti-communism was a sufficiently deep-rooted ideology for it to achieve widespread resonance in the 1950s. A clear distinction was made between what was perceived as the illegitimate regime in the 'Zone' (since the GDR was not officially recognized) and the innocent people. Nevertheless, the Adenauer government was prepared to give up the pursuit of unity in favour of western integration, as its responses to the Stalin notes of 1952, and the June uprising of 1953, clearly showed. Although perhaps less virulently in later decades, and with a softening or crumbling not only on the left, but also among left-liberal parts of the political spectrum, anti-communism remained a background assumption throughout the forty years of division. *Ostpolitik* clearly marked a change of perspective, in that Brandt sought to recognize political realities and improve human contacts and conditions by acknowledging the status quo; and in this sense there was a softening of the friend/foe imagery. Moreover, as indicated in the previous chapter, the Germans in the East became less and less salient for West Germans – if they were not relatives or personal friends, they were more likely simply to be non-persons than foes.

The notion of an enemy is usually predicated on a cause: it entails a definition of values which are to be defended or propagated. The values of anti-communism were clearly very widely shared in the West, but the enmity was directed solely (and not even always) at the regime which embodied the communist ideal; it was not directed against the people. And as far as most East Germans were concerned, the anti-capitalist values of their regime did not constitute a basis for enmity against the West: they were, on the contrary, subverted by the SED's own appropriation of materialist standards in its bid to outdo the West on its own consumerist ground. A sometimes cyclical, sometimes more regular emphasis on consumer satisfaction (in the Ulbricht era, often only briefly sustained in the wake of popular unrest) and on competing with the West tended to undermine official attempts to render capitalism unattractive. It was, ironically, only a tiny minority who in the 1980s criticized the regime from the principled viewpoint of anti-materialism (with its emphasis on environmentalism, peace, human rights); and it was this tiny minority which provided the leaven for the unrest of autumn 1989 which was to challenge the regime for reforms from within and yet precipitate its total collapse and disappearance.

One *Volk*? The mobilization of national sentiments in 1989–1990

The highly intrusive, demanding political regime of the GDR forged a very real sense of 'GDR identity' among its citizens, who were bounded by it in an almost too literal, physical sense. This was not exactly the identity of proud 'GDR-citizens' demanded by the rulers, but something verging on what was later called (referring to east German identity after unification) a *'Trotzidentität'* – a 'despite-identity', an oppositional identity. This was not uniform, by any means: degrees of support, unthinking conformity, passivity, withdrawal, resistance and opposition varied widely within the GDR, and there were many strands in GDR political culture. A collective identity as GDR citizens who were prepared to enunciate their own views became most evident, among a highly visible minority, in the breathtaking weeks of autumn 1989 when hundreds of thousands found the courage to come out on the streets and proclaim that *they* were the people, and that they were no longer prepared to allow the SED to speak in the name of the *Volk*. And West Germans arguably became most aware of their collective identity when they realized that their poor relations over the Wall, who began flocking to them in droves once the Wall was opened, were barely recognizable as even distant cousins. When the Wall came down in reality, it remained in people's heads – or so the saying soon went. Hence the notions of *Wessis* and *Ossis* emerged as means to encapsulate the new proto-national identities that had surreptitiously been emerging beneath the notice of public pronouncements on the official unity of the nation. But in the meantime, for a few brief moments in the late autumn of 1989, the Germans on both sides were prepared – happily in the East, uneasily in the West – to appeal to the notion of being one *Volk*.

The GDR did not collapse because of a nationalist quest for reunification. The quest for reunification arose as a result, not a cause, of the collapse of communist rule in the GDR. But both the rhetoric of, and the constitutional and political commitment to, national unity were potent political weapons in the radically changed circumstances after the fall of the Wall. Because East Germans were not ashamed to be German, the notion of national identity was available for widespread popular mobilization at a time of regime implosion. And because the West German leadership was constitutionally committed to reunification, it was a rhetoric which could – with some sensitivity and degree of taboo still evident on the left – be appropriated by the CDU in the person of the 'unification Chancellor', Helmut Kohl. A diagonal alliance of East German *Volk* and West German conservative leadership seized and elaborated on a nationalist rhetoric which was not so easily available in other quarters.

This is to put the situation rather starkly. On balance the above statements are true, although obviously the historical realities – as always – are a little more complex. Let us briefly look at the role of beliefs in, and desire for, 'national unity' in the initial process of unification.

The GDR was an increasingly unstable state in the later 1980s, for a variety of reasons to do with both international and domestic factors. Internationally, both the world economic situation and the political situation within the Soviet bloc were of vital importance. Domestically, the growth of small, politically active reforming groups within the GDR in the 1980s coincided with increasing unrest within the SED about the leadership's policies.

Following the oil crises of 1973 and 1979, and the general economic recession of the 1980s, the East German economy plunged into an unsustainable spiral of increasing international indebtedness. The ageing leadership around Honecker proved unwilling even to acknowledge the scale of the GDR's mounting economic problems, let alone take action to deal effectively with them. Problems which might have been contained if action had been taken in the mid-or late 1970s, or even as late as the early 1980s, became ever more insurmountable by the closing years of the GDR's existence. Honecker simply refused to abandon his commitment to the proclaimed 'unity of economic and social policy' which he had announced shortly after becoming SED leader in 1971; and his continued commitment both to massive consumer subsidies on the one hand, and investment in the hopelessly uncompetitive microchip industries on the other, spelled economic disaster. On the other hand, abandoning consumer satisfaction in favour of balancing the economic books might have spelled earlier political disaster. It was a no-win situation.

The accession of Mikhail Gorbachev to power in the Soviet Union in 1985 changed the international political context of economic decline. The Soviet leader, facing comparable domestic economic problems on a far larger scale at home, initiated processes of reform, restructuring, and more open discussion which were anathema to the East German leadership but which gave considerable hope to those at lower levels of the political hierarchy in the GDR who were aware of the general parameters of economic and environmental disaster facing their country. Gorbachev's political tones also struck chords with those yearning for a more open and democratic form of socialism within the GDR. Most importantly in terms of practical impact was the Soviet decision to renounce previous policies of intervention in the domestic affairs of East European states. This permitted processes of political change in neighbouring states, particularly Poland and Hungary. The decision of Hungary to loosen border controls with Austria, starting in May 1989 and confirmed in September 1989, was the immediate precipitant of the regime crisis in the GDR, as a flood of refugees sought to flee west through the now porous Iron Curtain in the summer of 1989.

This regime crisis, now becoming acute although of fairly long gestation, provided the occasion for the mobilization of unrest from below.[13] Those who wished to remain in their homeland but who were increasingly frustrated by Honecker's incapacity to engage with ideas of reform slowly gathered the courage to participate in

---

[13] I have discussed the growth of political activism in the 1980s, and the role of dissenting groups in 1989, in far greater detail in M. Fulbrook, *Anatomy of a Dictatorship: Inside the GDR, 1949–1989* (Oxford: Oxford University Press, 1995). This is a brief summary for the purposes of the argument subsequently developed in this chapter.

public demonstrations. From early September to early October, leaving the sanctuary of the churches and taking to the streets to demonstrate in favour of reform was a highly risky matter. When Gorbachev made it clear, during his visit on the occasion of the GDR's fortieth anniversary on 7 October, that the Soviet Union would not come to the defence of the East German leadership or assist in the suppression of dissent by force (as it had done in 1953), the East German authorities had to change their repressive tactics. On 9 October the planned massive use of force to suppress the Monday Leipzig demonstration was called off at the last minute. In mid-October a leadership coup ousted Erich Honecker (formally he retired on grounds of ill health) and installed Egon Krenz. For the following three weeks, a pretence was made at steering a new, reformist course, although behind this lay a grim determination to try to cling onto power. But the attempt failed in the debacle of 9 November, when the Berlin Wall was opened without proper advance preparation and coordination with the border guards. After that, the snowball towards national unity started rolling.

What was the role of a belief in national unity before and after 9 November? Before 9 November, it was a potent force with respect to the *possibility* of fleeing to seek a better life in the West. Those who abandoned the GDR in the summer of 1989 were able to take advantage of automatic citizenship rights in the Federal Republic, in a way that was not open to the citizens of other eastern bloc states. Arguably, it was citizenship entitlement and the prospect of an improved material and political situation, rather than any more ethereal belief in the unity of the nation, which motivated people to leave for the West prior to the opening of the Wall. Furthermore, those who were committed to staying behind – those who came out on the streets in September bearing banners with the slogan 'Wir bleiben hier!' (We are staying here) – wanted neither to leave, nor to destroy, the GDR, but rather to reform it.

However, under the radically altered circumstances after 9 November, the situation was very different. Chancellor Helmut Kohl, caught unawares while on a trip to Poland by the unexpected turn of events, hastily rushed back to the scene of world history in Berlin on 10 November. Standing at the Wall, he proclaimed 'Wir sind doch ein Volk' ('we are one people, after all' – note the linguistic hint, the little word 'doch' betraying a glimmer of doubt about the degree to which this assertion had previously been genuinely held). By the following Monday, the slogans at the Leipzig demonstrations had begun to include, among the multifarious and often humorous banners, new tones of nationalism: the doubly defiant

'Wir sind das Volk' (we are the people) had become 'Wir sind ein Volk' (we are one people).

This did not make the earlier events of autumn 1989 a movement for national reunification. But the fall of the Wall genuinely unleashed a tidal wave of joy, even euphoria, particularly among Berliners. The heady atmosphere and excitement in Berlin was remarkable, and deeply rooted in the long-time front-line situation of Berlin as a divided and, in its western half, beleaguered city. The Wall had snaked like an ugly scar through the city, creating an unnatural and brittle liveliness in the unique circumstances of the West (whose ageing population was swelled by the ranks of young couples tempted to settle with large housing loans, and young men enticed by the avoidance of military service), and a constant provocation to both rulers and ruled alike in the infinitely drabber streets of the East. Moreover, there had long been a very strong sense of Berlin identity, rooted in Berlinese dialect and history, captured and encapsulated in many and varied cultural representations, from the renowned Weimar culture to the cartoons with their Berlinese captions of the artist Heinrich Zille. The victory of liberty and humanity over the hated Wall was a genuine source of real celebration in Berlin.

It was of course greeted and celebrated elsewhere too: the sense of euphoria was to some degree infectious, and the general issues and principles at stake were almost universally lauded in West Germany, although with less fervour and engagement in some quarters. It is important to note here, however, that at this point no one seriously thought that, within less than a year, the GDR would have been absorbed into an enlarged Federal Republic. Even when, on 28 November – nearly three weeks after the fall of the Wall – Helmut Kohl brought out his Ten Point Plan, this arch mover of unification was only contemplating a loose confederation moving gradually towards closer cooperation over a period of ten years or so.

Unification on 3 October 1990 came about because of the subsequent pattern of events. The government of the GDR crumbled as the SED renounced its now unsustainable claim to power and was replaced by an interim coalition. With the opening of the inner-German border, the trickle of refugees turned into a steady stream heading westwards in search of a better life. The economy of the GDR, already in decline, went into a tail-spin. Pressures on housing, social benefits, and employment opportunites in West Germany grew to such an extent that the West German government became fearful of a domestic political backlash. Meanwhile, the international 'window of opportunity' had to be seized if the agreement of the Soviet Union to a renunciation of its claims on East Germany, and an orderly withdrawal of its troops, were to be negotiated. In the context of mounting crises, the promise of a one-to-one currency conversion ensured the conservative Alliance for Germany (backed by the West German CDU) a significant victory – in essence, a vote for speedy unification – in the first democratic elections to be held in the GDR in March 1990. With the (entirely predictable) dramatic rise in unemployment and chaotic economic circumstances that were a direct result of currency unification in the summer of 1990, the fragile East German coalition government collapsed and unification was brought forward to the first possible moment following the completion of international negotiations and approvals.

The narrative just presented, however briefly and baldly, has implied that it was economic and political collapse which made unification the only viable prospect – both for East and West Germany. Constitutional commitment to this had to be combined with appropriate international politics. But it should be noted that the political will to unification, on specific terms, was powered by the leadership of the West German CDU. A majority of East Germans had, in democratic elections, expressed a desire for unification; a national rhetoric was available, without any penumbra of sensitivities and taboos, to a population that was not ashamed to be German. Many West Germans, by contrast, evinced a markedly higher degree of unease about the concept of an ethnic German *Volk*; but they were constitutionally committed to unification without the need for any further democratic consultation. A significant minority had doubts about both the speed and the details of unification; many Social Democrats, for example, would have preferred a coming together to form a new state under Article 146 of the Constitution, rather than the more rapid incorporation of newly recreated *Länder* under Article 23. As we have seen above, the self-appointed voice of Germany's conscience, Günter Grass, went so far as to argue that after Auschwitz unification should not even be contemplated. Even so, Kohl's role as 'Unification Chancellor' – and the weakness of the opposition – ensured the CDU/CSU government (in coalition with the FDP) a renewed victory in the first all-German general election of December 1990.

The rhetoric of national unity was clearly an important factor in this victory. The opposition SPD failed to strike the right chord: it only adopted the wailing tones of warning, rather than combining these with a sense of celebration that was clearly widely yearned for, at least among the middle ground of voters (as well as in those conservative quarters which would never have voted for the SPD in any event). But the popularity of the notion of unity, in advance and in the abstract, began to wane as the new social and economic realities began to bite.

Telling new tales: 'overcoming the past' after 1990

These realities hit hardest in what were now termed the 'five new Länder' – eastern Germany.[14] With the new currency terms, East German industry was unable to hold its own in face of western competition, while at the same time losing its traditional soft currency Soviet bloc markets. Rising unemployment rapidly followed. At the same time, the collapse of the social infrastructure, and in particular the loss of subsidized child care, hit women particularly hard. Unemployment among women rose disproportionately. In the first two years after unification, the birth rate dropped by one-half, a demographic blip normally only seen in times of total war. This collective expression of cumulative private decisions born out of a degree of personal despair and uncertainty about the future provides an extraordinary indicator of social distress. And in the following years the persistent strength of the successor party to the SED, the reformed Party of Democratic Socialism (PDS), as a protest party seeking to represent the interests and anxieties of easterners provided a similar measure of a degree of resentment at the character of unified Germany.[15]

With the invasion of *'besser-Wessis'*, the economy of the five new *Länder* was radically restructured, the professions were weeded for politically suspect individuals, and well-paid westerners (with salaries incremented by what was known as 'jungle money' for their labours in the wilderness) took over a range of positions of power and authority. In regional politics, local administration, higher education and throughout business and professional life, a radical 'restructuring' took place that, in some cases, seemed geared to

[14] For reflections on a range of aspects, see e.g. M. Mertes, S. Muller and H. A. Winkler (eds), *In Search of Germany* (New Brunswick, NJ: Transaction Books), 1996; repr. of special issue, 'Germany in Transition', of *Daedalus*, 123 1 (winter 1994); Jürgen Kocka, *Vereinigungskrise* (Göttingen: Vandenhoeck and Ruprecht, 1995); Jonathan Osmond (ed.), *German Reunification: A Reference Guide and Commentary* (Harlow: Longman, 1992).

[15] Consider e.g. the strength of the protest vote in the *Land* election in Saxony-Anhalt in April 1998, when the right-wing DVU and the left-wing PDS together claimed one in three of the votes cast (32%); and the strong showing of the PDS in the general election of September 1998, when it entered the Bundestag with over 5% of the national vote.

ensuring that no one could ever accuse the Germans again about being half-hearted in 'overcoming a dictatorship'.

Under these conditions, a very strong sense of East German collective identity began to be evident. In 1991 well over one-third of East Germans emphasized a GDR-identity rather than an all-German identity. When asked whether they felt themselves primarily to be 'German' or 'East German', or to have primarily a regional identity, East Germans split with 37 per cent professing an 'all-German' identity, 37 per cent considering themselves to be East German, and 21 per cent having a regional identity (5 per cent were undecided). The corresponding figures for West Germans were a revealing 57 per cent as all-German; 15 per cent as primarily West German; 19 per cent as primarily regional; and 9 per cent undecided.[16] Similar research reveals extraordinary mutual misperceptions and stereotypes of one another on the part of easterners (*Ossis*) and westerners (*Wessis*).[17] Interestingly, some research suggests that those most likely to have a strong sense of East German identity were predominantly young, highly educated people (it could be suggested containing a disproportionate percentage of those who had done well, or been conformist, under the previous system) who were not primarily the social losers in the unification process. They were perhaps informed to some extent by a 'post-material' rejection of some of the impositions from the West. This phenomenon has been caught in the notion of a '*Trotzidentität*'.[18] Meanwhile, many articulate Westerners seemed more self-assured of their role as those who had successfully made the transition into good democrats.

In the new circumstances of the 1990s, the concept of the nation and the character of the divided past began to be viewed in a new light. The debates began to place interpretations of both GDR history, and the history of the Third Reich, into new contexts.

In the immediate aftermath of the end of the GDR, a very black-and-white picture of the GDR rapidly replaced the more nuanced views which had been widely prevalent in the previous two decades. For example, the dramatic attack on Stasi informers, as though this were the means to expunging all evil, was based in a newly resurgent understanding of the nature of the East German

[16] Elisabeth Noelle-Neumann and Renate Köcher (eds.), *Allensbacher Jahrbuch der Demoskopie 1984–1992*, vol. 9 (Munich: K. G. Saur, 1993), p. 396.

[17] Ibid., p. 497.

[18] See e.g. Thomas Gensicke, 'Vom Staatsbewußtsein zur Oppositions-Ideologie. DDR-Identität im vereinten Deutschland', in Axel Knoblich, Antonio Peter and Erik Natter (eds), *Auf dem Weg zu einer gesamtdeutschen Identität?* (Cologne: Verlag Wissenschaft und Politik, 1993).

dictatorship as one based almost solely on repression and force, essentially resurrecting Cold War views. In the 1950s and early 1960s, the GDR (or 'the Zone', as many still insisted on calling it) had been dismissed as a totalitarian dictatorship imposed by the Communists on an unwilling populace; but more differentiated analyses began already with the pioneering work of Peter Christian Ludz in the mid-1960s. Throughout the 1970s and 1980s western scholars, such as Hartmut Zimmermann, Dietrich Staritz, Gert Joachim Glaeßner, Hermann Weber, Ilse Spittmann and others were beginning to explore some of the complexities of the East German political structure and the ways in which state and society interacted.[19] Although this research was of necessity based on a relatively limited array of published sources, it was characterized by a real determination not just to denounce the GDR (although political and moral judgements were often implicit and sometimes quite explicit in western approaches to '*Systemvergleich*'), but also to understand it in shades of grey, exploring patterns of change and development.[20] Some scholars adopted approaches (such as the more widely applicable 'convergence theory' popular among American political scientists in the 1960s) which tended to stress similarities based in common technocratic tendencies in industrial and bureaucratic societies, irrespective of differences in political systems. Others sought to keep lines of communication open and to engage in a dialogue which would have been closed off if the goal were simply denunciation.

After the *Wende*, the political emphasis of the intellectual landscape changed. The concept of totalitarianism, which had for long lain dormant, stirring only occasionally in quarters dismissed as too right-wing to be taken seriously by most academics, now enjoyed an extraordinary resurrection. The impetus for this resurrection came from widely diverse sources. On the one hand, there was the very understandable sense of emotional outrage felt by victims of former communist regimes, who wanted to express their anger through the use of an analytic concept emphasizing oppression and injustice. On the other hand, there were those in the West who felt

[19] It should be noted that Staritz was later revealed to have informed to the Stasi. Many of the western scholars who wrote on the GDR had personal, and often bitter, experiences of communist politics; for example, Karl Wilhelm Fricke, Hermann Weber, and – for the early occupation period – Wolfgang Leonhard (who left for America rather than West Germany).

[20] For a fuller survey of pre-1989 approaches, cf. M. Fulbrook, *The Two Germanies 1945–1990: Problems of Interpretation* (London: Macmillan, 1992) and the revised and updated version under the title *Interpretations of the Two Germanies* (Macmillan, 1999).

a sense of vindication and superiority, and who similarly wanted to employ a term which highlighted the use of repression and force as the key explanatory factor in any account of political stability and change.[21]

The new historical picture which was presented was one of heroes, villains, and victims: of an evil gang of criminals at the top oppressing an innocent people below, challenged only by a few resourceful heroes of the opposition.[22] Curiously, although the archives were now open, providing rich materials for the construction of a far more differentiated picture than was previously available, they were at first rapidly plundered simply in order to pad out and prop up preconceived views based essentially in a desire to effect a political and moral demolition job. In a classic work of this character, the East German writers Armin Mitter and Stefan Wolle reproduced lengthy (and highly interesting) quotations from the archives in pursuit, essentially, of a sustained denunciation of the GDR.[23] From the West, scholars such as Jochen Staadte, Klaus Schroeder and Jens Hacker repudiated previous scholarship on the GDR as essentially having been taken in by Honecker's propaganda and been subservient to left-liberal political interests in the period of *Ostpolitik*.[24] They too presented a much starker picture of the East German dictatorship resting principally on repression and force – what Mitter and Wolle termed, somewhat abruptly, as 'resting on Soviet bayonets'.

This picture of a dictatorship held together solely by suppression and force was not universally accepted. Very soon, alternative perspectives were being put forward from a range of viewpoints. Clearly some were directly rooted in very obvious political interests. For example, the memoir literature of former pillars of the regime, from Honecker himself through his short-lived successors Egon Krenz and Hans Modrow, and other Politburo members such as Günter Schabowski, was – however fascinating – essentially geared to demonstrating high-mindedness of purpose

---

[21] I have discussed this at greater length in M. Fulbrook, 'The Limits of Totalitarianism: God, State and Society in the GDR', *Transactions of the Royal Historical Society*, 6th ser., 7 (1997).

[22] Cf. M. Fulbrook, 'Reckoning with the Past: Heroes, Victims and Villains in the History of the GDR', in P. Monteath and R. Alter (eds), *Rewriting the German Past* (Atlantic Highlands, NJ: Humanities Press, 1997).

[23] Armin Mitter and Stefan Wolle, *Untergang auf Raten* (Munich: C. Bertelsmann Verlag, 1993).

[24] Jens Hacker, *Deutsche Irrtümer* (Frankfurt am Main: Ullstein, 1992); Klaus Schroeder (ed.), *Geschichte und Transformation des SED-Staates* (Berlin: Akademie Verlag, 1994).

and humanity of objectives deflected in face of adverse conditions. Similarly, the responses of the party of Democratic Socialism (PDS) to the (essentially West) German Parliament's official inquiry (*Enquetekommission*) into the character of the dictatorship were on the whole characterized by a degree of self-serving sympathy with certain aspects of the past. On the other side of the erstwhile political fence, the memoirs of former victims and opponents of the regime were equally partial (in a variety of directions), with intense controversies over specific issues such as the complicity of the Protestant churches in sustaining the dictatorship through its compromises and links with the Stasi.[25]

More generally, there were often very bitter debates about even the issue of who should be 'allowed' to write GDR history. The *Unabhängige Historiker-Verband* (Independent League of Historians) was founded already in January 1990, in reaction against the SED-dominated historical profession of the GDR, which was seen as simply the servant of the repressive state.[26] Members of this grouping, which failed to gain a serious institutional foothold in the new western-dominated research landscape, launched extraordinarily scathing attacks on particular individuals and institutions (such as Jürgen Kocka and the *Forschungsschwerpunkt Zeithistorische Studien* in Potsdam), in their bitterness at what they felt was a double rejection in both the old and the new regimes.

Nevertheless, within this highly charged atmosphere and acutely politicized context, more nuanced and analytical approaches were being developed particularly by historians coming from a social history perspective. Works by both East and West German historians who were prepared to use the new archival material to explore beyond the apparatus of power and repression and delve into the realms of everyday life soon revealed that relations between 'state' and 'society' were a lot more complex than the 'totalitarian' model would have one believe.[27]

All of these 'historical pictures' (*Geschichtsbilder*) can in one way or another be seen to be contributing to new debates on 'overcoming the past' in Germany. Debates flourished on modes of that by

[25] Cf. Fulbrook, 'Reckoning with the Past', and M. Fulbrook, 'Aufarbeitung der DDR-Geschichte und "Innere Einheit" – Ein Widerspruch?', in C. Kleßmann and H. Misselwitz (eds), *Geteilte Vergangenheit – eine Geschichte?* (Berlin: Chr. Links Verlag, 1999).

[26] See esp. Rainer Eckert, Ilko-Sascha Kowalzcuk and Isolde Stark (eds), *Hure oder Muse? Klio in der DDR. Dokumente und Materialien des Unabhängigen Historiker-Verbandes* (Berlin: Berliner Debatte, 1994).

[27] See e.g. Bessel and Jessen, *Grenzen der Diktatur*; Kaelbe, Kocka and Zwahr, *Sozialgeschichte der DDR* (n. 4 above).

now traditional pastime, *Vergangenheitsbewältigung*, often with quite interesting and insightful contributions as people sought, once again, to make sense of radical historical ruptures in politics and consciousness.[28] Some scholars started to look at the post-1945 restructuring in a new light, not always with uncontentious conclusions.[29] Even among the moderate centre, there were new tones of more or less quiet or strident triumphalism at the apparent historical vindication of the nation.[30] On the right, there were on occasion some quite extraordinary effusions of hot air.[31]

Although left-liberal historians continued to argue against any explicit appeal for a *Schlußstrich* with respect to the Third Reich, this did at first appear to have been coming about through the rethinking of GDR and German history after 1990. For, from most perspectives across the political and theoretical spectrum, the 1989 revolution was interpreted as in some way a *Nachholrevolution*, a 'catching up' of the East with a delayed trajectory from dictatorship to democracy that had already successfully been accomplished in the West. And many West Germans – not only the conservatives who had supported Helmut Kohl, but also many Social Democrats and Greens – came, almost grudgingly on occasion, to the view that the Federal Republic had in some sense come to maturity; that the democratic constitution had in some way actually proved itself as a viable vehicle which it was quite right to extend to the East.[32] Thus Habermas's notion of 'constitutional patriotism' seemed to have found a firmer anchor. (From a conservative perspective, of course, the same result could be arrived at more quickly: 1989 was simply the vindication of the West, the victory of capitalism over communism.) For a few years after the sudden, unexpected, dramatic turn of historical events in 1989–90, it did appear as if the Nazi past would finally become distant history, displaced by the post-war period as the new *Sonderweg* on Germany's road to modernity.

[28] See e.g. Klaus Suhl (ed.), *Vergangenheitsbewältigung 1945–1989. Ein unmöglicher Vergleich?* (Berlin: Brandenburgische Landeszentrale für politische Bildung, 1994).

[29] Cf. e.g. Christa Hoffmann, *Stunden Null? Vergangenheitsbewältigung in Deutschland 1945 und 1989* (Bonn: Bouvier, 1992).

[30] Cf. Stefan Berger, *The Search for Normality* (Oxford: Berghahn, 1997), for a detailed account of (and perhaps an overly sensitive reaction to) these trends.

[31] Cf. e.g. the emotional ramblings in Hellmut Diwald, *Deutschland einig Vaterland* (Frankfurt am Main: Ullstein, 1990). This is, however, mild by comparison with, for example, the extreme revisionist and anti-semitic views presented in Georg Franz-Willing, *Vergangenheitsbewältigung. Bundesrepublikanischer Nationalmasochismus* (Coburg: Nation Europa-Verlag, 1992) who seems to have little, if any, regard for any notion of historical evidence.

[32] For a clear statement of this view, see esp. Kocka, *Vereinigungskrise*.

But not so. The debates over the Third Reich and the more general issue of recasting German history in the service of a new patriotism were simply transmogrified. The past still continued to be very much a matter of the present, of contemporary politics in united Germany.

For example, the long-standing debate about designing and constructing a new German Historical Museum by the Reichstag in West Berlin was transformed by the takeover of the former East German Museum of German History in the Zeughaus on Unter den Linden in (former East) Berlin, to house the new German Historical Museum. The old communist success stories and tendentious displays were removed to present a more multi faceted perspective on German history in a new display, with a series of temporary exhibitions and ambitious long-term plans.[33] Despite the greater openness and pluralism of approach in the new Museum, the Holocaust was still set apart – physically as well as metaphorically – from the long sweep of German history. Unlike any other period or topic, it had its own room which was not a through-way to the next exhibit. Here one could – quite appropriately – engage in private, undisturbed meditation and reflection. But this emotional 'setting apart' was accompanied by an abdication of the historical duty of explanation. Just as in many West German historical accounts over the previous forty years, the Holocaust was treated as being on a unique plane, somehow 'above' or 'outside of' the normal level of historical debate, where only emotional contemplation, and not historical explanation, was possible. It seemed, in the physical treatment of this topic in this museum, as if virtually nothing had changed with respect to 'overcoming the past' or the 'normalization' (in Martin Brozsat's sense) of German history.

Meanwhile, the obsessive concern with guilt and shame continued unabated, as in the stormy debates over the plans for a 'Holocaust Memorial' in Berlin. Chat-show hostess Lea Rosh, who had adopted a Jewish name to indicate empathy, became particularly obsessed with this project.[34] The intensity of the discussions around how to memorialize, what physical shape to give to the symbolization of the past, were focused around the competition for architectural designs. What was lost from these German debates

---

[33] See the rather self-serving account by the Museum's first Director, Christoph Stölzl, 'Museum Turned Upside Down', in Hermann Glaser (ed.), *What Remains – What Lies Ahead: Cultural Upheaval in East Germany* (Bonn: Inter Nationes, 1996), pp. 151–4.

[34] See e.g. Jane Kramer, 'The Politics of Memory', *New Yorker*, 14 Aug. 1995, pp. 48–65.

was any sense that such obsession with memorial culture, rather than sober pedagogy, might be counter-productive. A straightforward museum, seeking not only to explain the steps leading, historically, down the path to Auschwitz, but also representing the range and diversity of Jewish life across Europe before its near-extinction, might well have served the cause of genuine historical memory better. An outsider might be forgiven for thinking, on occasion, that much of the *Angst* and anguish devoted to memorialization was more geared towards making the angst-ridden individuals feel better than to educating anyone else about what had been lost and why.

Similarly, the reception of Daniel Goldhagen's book, *Hitler's Willing Executioners: Ordinary Germans and the Holocaust*, on his highly successful media tour in Germany in the summer of 1996 was very revealing. Although shredded by many professional historians, Goldhagen's thesis clearly struck a widely popular chord with lay members of his audiences.[35] It played both on their desire to wallow in a degree of public guilt on behalf of their forebears, and at the same time vindicated their sense that, since 1945, they had made a clean and final break with the past, and had become radically different, allegedly no longer plagued by the centuries' old curse of 'eliminationist anti-semitism'. Few would be either sufficiently well-informed or theoretically acute to identify the problems in Goldhagen's wider argument; most latched on, instead, to the emotive style and the dramatic presentation of what are undoubtedly heart-rending details.

The examples of German concern with a past that still refused to become history, even more than half a century had passed, could easily be multiplied. Neuralgic locations were everywhere, from Christo's wrapping of the Reichstag to debates over what to do with the Wall. The travelling exhibition organized by the Hamburg Institute for Social Research on the crimes of the Wehrmacht (*Vernichtungskrieg. Verbrechen der Wehrmacht*), for example, raised such political hackles that massive demonstrations and counter-demonstrations had to be dealt with by police force when it was shown in Munich in 1997.[36] Although there are shifts in the character of the debates, it was quite clear that interpretations of history and identity in Germany continued to be a matter of massive public interest and engagement.

[35] For early reviews, see Julius Schoeps (ed.), *Ein Volk von Mördern?* (Hamburg: Hoffmann and Campe, 1996).
[36] See the very insightful review by Eve Rosenhaft, 'Facing up to the Past – Again? "Crimes of the Wehrmacht"', *Debatte*, 5/1 (May 1997), pp. 105–18.

The debates continue. An outsider could be forgiven for sometimes wondering whether there is not a degree of obsession in this collective indulgence in national navel-gazing. As the twentieth century ends and a new millennium begins, the enlarged German state is a very different entity from what it was over half a century earlier. It is embedded in a very different world and European context, both economically and politically. The mobility of labour, and the internationalization of culture, are posing serious challenges to any conception of the nation as a homogenous ethnic and cultural entity. Changes in patterns of values, in the character of the political system, and in prevailing political cultures have made citizens of Germany today very different from their (real or assumed) ancestors. Engagement with the admittedly fascinating course of German history should finally be wrenched away from emotionalized engagement with national identity building. Let us turn, then, finally, to the wider implications of this study.

9

The Nation as Legacy and Destiny

There is no such thing as an ordinary nation. 'National identity' is not a set of enduring characteristics, to be defined, listed, celebrated or denigrated; and the pursuit of an 'acceptable', or a 'positive', national identity is the pursuit of the holy grail, the search for the pot of gold at the end of the rainbow.

It is only when a variety of factors combine, under particular historical circumstances, that a sense of national identity will be widely shared and accepted (even deeply felt). One might hazard the generalization that only extremely rarely (if ever) do a majority of members of a given community share a deep-rooted and essentially unproblematic belief in their collective identity as a 'nation'. Moreover, for the most part it is not even an issue for most people (and perhaps is only salient when in a situation of challenge or difference). 'Nations' are merely one of the many ways humans have devised, in different historical circumstances, to endow large numbers of people with certain collective identities.[1]

If national identity is not an essence, but rather a set of processes, what are the factors involved? These have to do both with aesthetic representations, and with experienced and reinterpreted realities, in the present; and they have to connect the collective entity as defined in the present with both a presumed collective past and some vision of a common fate and a common future, to suggest some enduring and binding elements of common legacy and com-

[1] I recall my own amazement (and difficulty in replying), when another passenger waiting on a railway station, in an isolated rural part of India in 1972, engaged in conversation and asked me two questions predicated on a quite different world view: 'To which caste do you belong?' and 'How does it feel to be a member of the British Raj?'

mon destiny. Let us briefly review the peculiarities of the German case in the light of these broader ruminations.

Legacy

A 'nation' is formed in part through a belief in its common, collective past: in tales of creation, in stories of battles fought and victories wrought, of bitter defeats and returns to fight another day, of national heroes and martyrs who played a role in the struggle to bring the nation to its current moment in the present. The national history may be presented, anthropomorphically, as a tale of birth, youth, maturity and destiny; of the path towards redemption. Myths of common ancestry (Adam and Eve, Romulus and Remus) often form a part of these tales, but are not essential; the 'American dream', the 'frontier mentality', the heroic struggles of settlers and colonialists against the adversities of nature and indigenous peoples (!), may be quite enough without any pretence at shared genetic heritage.

Yet the myth of the common past was peculiarly problematic in Germany after 1945. The general issues are clear. When the past seems utterly discredited, when all roads seem to lead to Hitler, or fail adequately to oppose him, in what can a nation take pride? And when the nation splits into two, and each opposes and abhors the other, how can they distinctively reclaim and reinterpret a common heritage?

What we have seen is a complex story of dissonance and dissembling. East Germans were led to believe that they had collectively been the 'innocent victims' of the Nazi system which many of them had once sustained; they had then become the 'victors' of history, 'liberated' by the Russians in whose camps many had in fact suffered, at whose hands their relatives had fallen, and by whom their womenfolk had been raped. Many West Germans had to subordinate their private grief at loss of relatives and friends, and their own distress and suffering in a period of massive upheaval, to the officially acknowledged greater grief and suffering of the victims and survivors of the murderous policies of the Nazis. Public penance and official philo-semitism were accompanied by the repression of private mourning and surviving anti-semitism. 'Working through the past' was complicated and overlain by pressures for conformity to the new rules of political culture, and by processes of 'surviving the present'. Under different circumstances in East and West, only certain aspects could be expressed, only certain emotions and activities could be openly admitted to.

Many of those who lived through the Third Reich were only too glad to have the chance to forget it, to turn to building a better future. In the 1950s, the predominant concern in both East and West was not 'coming to terms with the past', but rather laying the foundations for the future – and ensuring the best possible personal situation within that future. Yet even as the future appeared to be becoming more secure, the parameters of division more permanent, a new generation was coming to maturity that would explode any easy suppression or redesignation of the past. In the 1960s there were cataclysmic debates between generations in the West, and a more muted set of generational and political opposi-tions in the East. The past would certainly not pass away; but nor, it turned out, would dramatic confrontation necessarily shed more light than heat. In effect, in many quarters emotion took precedence over reason.

In the end some of the positions adopted were self-defeating. East Germans were continuously, repeatedly, exposed to a series of state-supported myths which were central to the official legitimiza-tion of the communist regime. A variety of subordinate myths constituted what was essentially the key, founding myth of the 'antifascist legacy' of the GDR: the myth of innocence on the part of workers and peasants; the myth of antifascist heroes – but vir-tually no victims; the myth of 'liberation' by the Red Army; and the myth that all the villains were in the West. But these officially sanctioned and propagated pictures of and stories about the past failed fully to influence, shape, and resonate with popular percep-tions and memories. There were striking dissonances, particularly in the first two decades or so, between official views on the one hand, and real experiences and private memories on the other. Yet at the same time the incentives for collusion with and participation in the official stories about the past were relatively great, and many succumbed to the various temptations (and pressures) to support the official line(s). In the later years of the GDR, while a minority viewed any official version with a high degree of scepticism, a relatively large proportion of the East German population was both young enough, and sufficiently lacking in historical curiosity and exposure to articulate alternative points of view, to accept at least the moral message, if not the narrative details, of the official historical picture.

In West Germany, there were also crucial changes over time. Many West Germans came to believe that it was quite impossible, indeed impermissible, to be proud to be German. The concomitant of the pre-1945 *Sonderweg* thesis – that Germany had trodden a special path down the road to modernity – was a new, left-liberal version of a post-1945 *Sonderweg* – that Germans had uniquely to be ashamed of their nation. At the same time, many younger West Germans were simply fed up with what seemed to be a national obsession with the past. They were tired of having the Holocaust apparently 'rammed down their throats' all the time; they simply wanted to be allowed to be 'normal', unburdened by the immense legacies of their national past. In the 1960s and after, the explosion of cataclysmic debates about 'overcoming the past' provoked a variety of reactions. These ranged from an incorporation of a ritualized confession of guilt into West German official political culture (inherited already from the early days of the Adenauer government), through a desire to be rid of all debate about the past, to 'normalize' German history and be allowed to get on with the present and future in peace, to a quite opposite and impassioned determination to keep memories alive. While the ritualized professions of guilt and responsibility in the West had their counterpart in the GDR's official insistence on innocence, West Germans could never hope to sustain the same degree of basic ignorance as their GDR contemporaries. Yet the sheer scale of West German *Vergangenheitsbewältigung* may well have been counter-productive, as many became more and more fed up with an insistence on the burdens of the past.

There are many possible avenues through which these questions could be approached. In the chapters above, I have chosen selected examples of different forms of historical consciousness, different representations of the past, different public and private articulations of 'collective memory'. Together, these catalogue a series of dissonances which characterize the repeated attempts many Germans made to 'come to terms with' their past in a seemingly never-ending process of soul-searching without any hope of eventual resolution. Even the demand that one should achieve some sort of resolution – the appeal for a *Schlußstrich*, to draw a line under the past and consign it to 'history' – was and is itself deeply contentious. It was these fractures which prevented Germans, in very different ways in East and West, from accepting any one single narrative about their past, but which also prevented them from simply forgetting about it, treating it as irrelevant to an unexamined sense of identity in the present.

Destiny

'Nations' are, however, not constituted only through widely accepted stories about their past, or through myths which, though implicitly agreed to be 'legend' rather than 'history', nevertheless command willing collusion in public rituals of commemoration and renewed commitment to the historically developed national community. 'Nations' depend too on some sense of common identity in the present: they are formed through shared definitions of 'insiders' and 'outsiders', shared experiences, values and patterns of behaviour in everyday life, and (most notably in times of war) common struggles in adversity and a sense of a common destiny in the future. They are, in short, not purely 'imagined communities', but also communities of experience, rooted in institutional contexts and the structured realities of everyday life.

Just as there was no easy, shared view of the intensely problematic German past, so too there were crucial fractures and dissonances in conceptions of German identity in the two new states of the Cold War era. These fractures ran, not only down the Iron Curtain, but also within each state, as official conceptions and popular notions of who belonged to the community of destiny ran at odds with each other, in different ways on both sides of the Wall. These fractures were complex: even as many East Germans, for example, retained a lively sense of common kinship with their West German brethren over the Wall and rejected their regime's attempts to construct a sense of a 'GDR nation', they nevertheless were at the same time growing apart, diverging in attitudes, lifestyles and values from those living in the very different society of the affluent capitalist West.

Thus there were dissonances between official conceptions of the nation – embedded and legally enshrined in crucial areas such as entitlement to citizenship – and the range and variety of popular constructions of the nation. 'Banal nationalism' was, in the end, as important as legal and political frameworks, but it was never simple or running all in one direction. The very different patterns of socioeconomic and political development in the two Germanies had a decisive impact on the nature of society and collective identity in each state. Even though the SED never realized its dream of creating the 'socialist personality', people growing up in the constrained, collectivist and 'double track' society of the GDR developed very different assumptions and behaviour patterns from those growing up in the freer, more affluent and individualistic West. Not so much what they were told, or the content of the ideology which surrounded them, but rather the manner in which myths were propagated and public conformity expected, stamped their mark on the way the majority of East Germans came to live their lives. Meanwhile, in the West a very different direction was taken, towards a cosmopolitan, competitive but at the same time often explicitly moralistic orientation, engaged in constant vigilance against threats to democracy but not always, or in all quarters, aware of whiffs and hangovers from a more tainted past. The two Germanies were truly in a process of (proto-) nation formation which might, if the Wall had stood (as Honecker expected) for another hundred years, have made them as 'self-evidently' different from each other as from fellow German speaking Austrians or Swiss.

Worse, from the point of view of the SED, was the growing dissonance in dreams of destiny. In the early years of the GDR, there was a degree of plausibility to claims, not only to be the 'better' Germany in terms of the overcoming of fascism, but also to hold out the hopes of a fairer, more just society and possibly even a more efficient economy. The caesura of June 1953 indicated just how sharp, however, was the division between those who felt dictatorial means were essential to the realization of one version of the dream, and those who saw other possible avenues or horizons. Some clung on to versions of their hopes and dreams; and even when it was clear that the GDR could never seriously compete with, let alone overtake, the economic miracle of the West, there were nevertheless habituations, compensations, accommodations, stakes in the system for those who had benefited from the social revolution of the first two decades, and repeatedly reawakened hopes for improvements of one sort or another. But when, eventually, even the leadership had to concede that 'actually existing socialism' could not deliver the goods, while pure communism had been indefinitely postponed to some indeterminate utopian future, the self-denying community of common destiny as paradise postponed was a little harder to sustain.

Within the affluent West, the collapse of the GDR disturbed what had been, in fact, a relatively comfortable community of common fate. Unification challenged both the ritualized agonies of collective conversations about the past, and the widespread material certainties of the present. 'Destiny' as western cosmopolitans (emotional roots in a regional *Heimat*, broader sights set on West European integration), was thrown onto new tracks, as the Federal Republic was cast in the new role of mediator between East and West, as bringer of material well-being and democracy to the post-communist East. And the changed international situation meant quite new challenges to inherited practices: it is, for example, all very well to assuage a guilty conscience by having the most liberal asylum laws in Europe if you do not expect many people to take advantage of them; it is quite another when the Iron Curtain has fallen and there are massive population upheavals.

In 1989–90 many people found that their initial joy in the possibility of democratic determination of a common future was
tempered both by fears of a potentially resurgent racist nationalism,
and by amazement at the divergences between easterners and
westerners which had been effected by the divided past. The associated difficulties made many inhabitants of each side wonder how
much they really had left in common. Pre-existing differences were
exacerbated by post-unification social and economic tensions and
strains: what had been the essentially humorous stereotypes of
Wessis and *Ossis* became a somewhat more disagreeable phenomenon when there were real feelings of humiliation, degradation,
and second-class citizenship. Nor was the question of constructing
a common memory of a divided past any more easily solved in the
period after the unification of 1990. Historical controversies
appeared more vitriolic than ever; 'overcoming the past', this time
with respect to a more recent dictatorship, was yet again proving to
be an essentially divisive endeavour, rooted as much in current
politics as in attempts to understand the past 'as it really was'.

What should one conclude from this story? As far as those who
labour under a sense of the burdens of being German are concerned, there are some specific lessons. The repeated quest, in
some quarters, to define some quintessential German national
identity, which would forever place a line beneath the past and
allow Germany to take its place among 'normal nations', is doomed
to fail.

National identity is – always and everywhere – a social, cultural,
and most of all a political construction, and as such is essentially
contested. It should not be reified as a reality floating somehow
above the maelstrom of political debate and struggle, or the clash
of competing moral values. Collective identities are malleable
and constantly changing according to experience and circum-
stance.

If we agree that there is no such thing as an 'essential' national
identity – which, in an older vocabulary, used to be called 'national
character' – then what does the German experience tell us in more
general terms about the conditions for the construction of collective
identities which claim to be 'national'?

The search for one or more *substantive* factors, which will allegedly explain the emergence of a sense of national identity, is
not – or no longer – perhaps the most fruitful theoretical approach.
To construct a list of elements, most or all of which are deemed, in
varying proportions, to be central factors in national identity, is to
do little more than engage in an exercise of redescription. Thus, one

of the central models proposed by Anthony Smith,[2] listing a number of 'fundamental features' – including not only common myths and ethnic core, but also a historic territory or homeland, a common mass public culture, common legal rights and duties, and a common economy – is more a redescription of an ideal unitary nation state than an explanation for the construction of a sense of national identity when some of the specific institutional aspects (common legal system and common economy, for example) are not present. Equally, appeals to 'modernization', to the capitalist system of nation states, and to the emergence of 'print capitalism', made by Gellner, Hobsbawm and Benedict Anderson respectively, are highly suggestive with respect to the widespread emergence of self-confessed 'nations' at a particular stage in European history. However, while they provide key insights, they tell us little in more general terms about the conditions under which particular attempts at nation definition succeed or fail.

In my view, the extraordinary history of Germany since 1945, with the mutually hostile attempts in East and West at radical deconstruction and double reconstruction of an utterly discredited common version of national identity, suggests that we should now turn our attention to questions about the *conditions* and *processes* of collective identity construction. As I have sought to show in the preceding chapters, analysis must focus at several levels: at a wide range of facets of myth, memory and history, in competing attempts to construct a common tale about a collective past; at varying degrees of popular resonance, reception, and transformation of the tales told by those in positions of political power or cultural authority, and at a variety of aspects of the construction of self and other in the present, including not only symbolic constructions and imagery of friend and foe, but also powerful social realities in legal, political, socioeconomic and everyday life. 'Identity' is not only about constructions, but also about experiences, values, relationships, structures; it is a highly complex, kaleidoscopic and ever-changing phenomenon. It is its very complexity, its centrality to the lives of many people and yet its inchoate slipperiness which make it a topic of perennial fascination and irritation.

Residents of the states which occupy the soil of Nazi Germany, and descendents of those who battled both for and against the Nazi vision over half a century ago, should take some comfort from this analysis. It is true that there are cultural traditions which are transmitted over the generations, through processes of socialization,

---

[2] As noted in ch. 1 above, Smith's analyses are somewhat self-contradictory and alternative models are also presented.

education, cultural discourses. There are also behavioural patterns which are both rooted in and reinforced by institutional and legal frameworks. But none of these are immutable, resistant to change. Human beings both inherit and alter the social and political worlds in which they live; they constitute and reconstitute the parameters of an ever-changing world. If collective identity is not seen as – or not seen only as – an inherited legacy, but rather the result of conscious moral and political choices and related values and behaviour, then what is deemed to constitute the 'nation' is open to negotiation and change.

Index